THE JERUSALEM TRILOGY:
Song of the Prophets

THE JERUSALEM TRILOGY:
Song of the Prophets

Samuel L. Lewis

PROPHECY PRESSWORKS
Novato, California

ISBN 0-915424-03-7

SPECIAL THANKS

Editorial Assistance: Masheikh Wali Ali Meyer, Sitara Tessler, Murshid Moineddin
Cover Design: Miriam Mathews, Murad Sayen
Illustrations: Miriam Mathews
Borders & Title Pages: Fatima Jablonski, Miriam Mathews
Technical Advice & Support: Les, Pat & Tim Barlow
Paste-up: Vajda Tyler
Opaquing: Jayanara Herz
Proofreading: Azim Kroll, Paul Rognlie, Kalim Nagle, Mouni Sitton
Design Suggestions: Kathy Keating, Drew Langsner & Lama Foundation
Printing & Binding: Barlow & Sons Printing
Cover Printing: Custom Litho, Sonoma Engravers
Photographs: Mansur Johnson & Sunseed Productions

Thanks also to: Shirin Cave, Parvati Frydman, Sheikh Abdarahman Lomax
    & Rabbi Zalman Schachter

Table of Contents

LIST OF ABBREVIATIONS

A.V.	Authorized (King James) Version
Cor.	Corinthians
Deut.	Deuteronomy
Ex.	Exodus
Ezek.	Ezekiel
Gen.	Genesis
Isa.	Isaiah
Jer.	Jeremiah
K.I.T.	The Kingdom Interlinear Translation of the Greek Scriptures
Lev.	Leviticus
Matt.	Matthew
Mic.	Micah
M.T.	Masoretic Text
Num.	Numbers
Ps.	Psalms
Rev.	Revelation
R.S.V.	Revised Standard Version
S.	Sura
S.L.L.	Samuel L. Lewis

Preface

When one considers the life of Murshid Samuel L. Lewis (Sufi Ahmed Murad Chisti, 1896-1971), the question which naturally arises is, What enabled him to be accepted by so many different religions as a teacher within the tradition of each? For he was accepted by Jews as a teacher of Kabbala, by Christians as an interpreter of the Scriptures, and by Muslims as a Sufi Murshid (Master), as well as by Buddhists and Hindus. These extraordinary facts can be documented. They are living proof of the claim that a fully realized being can function directly as a Divine channel, transcending the differences and distinctions which are accentuated by the various theologies. It is a Sufi teaching that one should be able to accommodate oneself to the points of view of different peoples and show the universality of each. But this art is more easily described theoretically than it is achieved practically — all of which makes Murshid's life and writings truly remarkable.

In the course of these three poems Murshid speaks in the name of many of the Prophets and Masters of the past — such beings as Moses, Jeremiah, Jesus and Mohammed. How can one evaluate such a claim? The only real proof would be if one were to be touched by the beings of these Messengers through the vehicle of the poetry. Sufism teaches that through the link of initiation and attunement one is united with all the illuminated souls, and these illuminated souls of all times together form the embodiment of the one Master, the Spirit of Guidance. These

7

poems can be taken as a demonstration of this teaching. To quote Murshid, "I am being roused and awakened constantly by what we call the Sufis-in-chain, which is a reality, and which you will not read about in books because the book-writers never study Sufism with Sufis, so they know nothing about this reality. . . ."

How accurate is it then to call these works 'poetry'? Might not 'prophecy' be a more descriptive word? There was among the Jewish people the tradition of the Prophet; and the question must be asked, Is there any reason why this was a phenomenon which only happened in the past? Is the spirit of prophethood still alive today? Murshid has written elsewhere about prophecy and its relation to his poetry:

Prophesying doesn't mean predicting, it means just this: When your Heart is open, you receive from God and speak to man. That is prophesying, whether you're predicting or not.

My poetry is not ego poetry. It did not come from me; it came through me. It's a very different thing. You know, in ancient poetry Homer starts, "Sing, goddess, the wrath of Achilles . . . " He lets the goddess sing through him. Ancient poetry was done that way, letting the gods speak through you, not you writing poetry. And my poetry's that way, where I've felt the Divine, not necessarily in the perfect form or level. There's all kinds of levels and quite a few before you come to the Divine level. And the Divine level is pretty rare, but not impossible at all. I have said Christ appeared to me. . . . When you have the mind of Christ, you have to be listening all the time, feeling all the time, and not trying to produce your own particular ideas. And if your ideas are wrong you throw them out immediately. . . . Hazrat Inayat Khan [Murshid's first Sufi teacher] wrote that an artist subscribes his creations to Allah (God). So it is in humility, but not modesty, that one relates here the personal history. Book II of "Saladin" was not an inspiration, but a direct transmission from *Rassul-Lillah* [Mohammed]. In this sense it is questionable how far man is a creator and how far an instrument.

8

The Hebrew Prophets of old addressed the people and the events of the day from the standpoint of a God who involves Himself in the processes of time and thus has a message for man in every stage of history. Murshid's poetic writings, in the same way, invite us to view God not as an abstraction, but as a Presence in our midst who gives specific guidance for the solution of problems in our own time. On occasion, Murshid fulfills the role of the forewarner who shows the shape of things to come if certain trends are not changed; and then he offers the positive alternative. It would be better to hear from him directly on this point:

All my poetry for the last twenty-five years is prophetic and all rejected. . . . The odd is odd and must be rejected, but the fact remains, it is all prophetic and now I am amazed how much is true, but to be correct does not make one popular. . . . More attention is always given to the newspapermen first and the politicians next — whose predictions are seldom true. It was only that during the war the G2 [Army Intelligence] recognized some of my predictions and asked me to shut up. That was not difficult because nobody accepted anything anyhow. . . . A certain person returned my papers after many years, and I found among them my poems written in 1932 on the death of Hitler, the fall of the British Empire, the independence of India, the return of Jews to Palestine, etc. . . .

One does not have to have any 'third-eye' if he is honest, for he sees the operation of karma so deliberately and definitely that it is easy to predict anything. All one has to do is to examine the events and persons dispassionately. Actually, this is the way Sufis teach occultism, without any psychic or *siddhantic* elements [development of powers]. You just have to be impersonal and honest as the scientific researchers are.

Somebody came to me recently, and I had the audacity to tell him that I was much greater than Nostradamus. For two reasons: first, 75% of my predictions, though they are not published, have come true, and not symbolically; second, I have always felt they were under Divine Guidance and with Love and Compassion for humanity, and not with the idea of just looking into tomorrow. St. Paul said, "I die daily," and if you really die daily you can see into the future easier.

The reader is invited to sample one of the short prophetic poems which Murshid refers to above, from his unpublished *Book of Cosmic Prophecy*, entitled "Against Hitlerism, May 9,1932":

The doom of the Ashkenazi.
Say: Ye shall not be doomed,
But insofar as ye turn against the children of the Lord,
Then shall ye be doomed;
Insofar as ye turn unto your self-will,
Then shall ye continue to suffer . . .
The thorn and the briar intended for others has become your goad.
The lash and the whip prepared for others has been hurled against
    your backs,
The servitude for others has been redeemed against yourselves.
Now before you is relief from trepidation,
Or a thousand-fold punishment.
Thus sayeth the Lord, the Holy One;
"On that hour when you hurl the lash against my people,
Yours will be the fate of Sepharad and Lusitania and Sarmatia;
Down shall ye go into barbarism,
Hand will be turned against hand, even brother against brother,
The forest shall conquer the city, and the tares the pleasant fields.
Woe, woe unto you who threaten danger,
For upon you and all your people shall fall the doom."

It would certainly be consistent with Murshid's life and practice not to make extravagant claims as to the nature of the three poems presented in this volume. The internal evidence should be sufficient. Indeed, Murshid often quoted the Sufi Al-Ghazzali who stated that mysticism is based on experience and not on premises. Let us then hear Murshid's own description of a mystical experience which provided the basis for not only his poetry but for much of his spiritual work as well:

10

On June 10, 1925 Samuel L. Lewis of San Francisco left his family home and the city of his birth to go to Kaaba Allah, Fairfax. This was a Sufi retreat in Marin county. He had been in pain for years; there was not an organ in his body properly operating; he had had a complete nervous breakdown and was preparing for death. Too weak to carry books with him he brought only a thin volume of the poetry of Hafiz, a notebook, and a little food.

The first few days in the wilderness he was too tired for anything but meditation and Sufic practices. But he was able to read a little. On the third day he completed the reading of Hafiz as the sun was setting. The rays of the sun fell on the book, and as he finished the last page two doves suddenly appeared, circling his head, cooing. That night as he was doing his spiritual practices he felt a presence and he was sure it was Khwaja Khidr. There are many legends about Khwaja Khidr, the teacher of Moses described in Holy Quran, who, like Elijah, is said to always be present in the world. But while even some western occultists have accepted the reality of the legends, when it comes to actual events that is something different again. If you believe in legends you are 'saved', but if you propose that your belief is based on actual experience that is a sure sign you are a pretender . . .

There was a recurrence of this appearance of Khwaja Khidr on the second night and then on the third. He offered me the gifts of Poetry and Music, and whatever anybody else says, these are now in my keeping. Besides that, he invariably confers longevity. The Poetry came first; and years later the Music came also, and with it the Dance, but these are different stories. After the third night I began writing incessantly. At the end of ten days all the health and vigor were restored, and Sam prepared an initiatory ceremony for noon June 21, the equinoxial hour. In turn Shiva, Buddha, Zoroaster, Moses and Jesus appeared. Then Mohammed appeared, but double, on the left and on the right, and he was on horseback. All the others came singly. Then the Six Messengers of God formed a circle and danced and became one, and as they danced the Prophet Elijah appeared and bestowed on me the Robe.

Pir-O-Murshid Hazrat Inayat Khan said 'yes' to these experiences and initiated me as a 'Sufi'. His mureeds, with the exception of Paul

Reps, said 'no'. It is an unfortunate but common characteristic of those who assay to fame and leadership to reject unwelcome facts, no matter how well substantiated. Inayat Khan died shortly thereafter and his followers split and I never used this term 'Sufi' until it was publically announced by Pir Sufi Barkat Ali of the Chisti Order in 1961 at Salarwala, West Pakistan.

The proof of the validity of the above comes first in the physical and mental vigour of the person blessed by Khwaja Khidr, exactly in accordance with the traditions. And persons who do not accept the personality can not otherwise explain this vitality. In addition to that, there is the poetry, especially great epics which have in the past been snubbed and rejected, and which are now on their way toward publication. The poetry in its finest form is in "Saladin." This attests to *hal* and *makam* better than anything else.

All mystics, and especially those entrusted with responsibilities in the Spiritual Hierarchy, have to undergo certain outer as well as inner crucifixions, so to speak. But the resurrection follows the crucifixion, actually and not symbolically. And this has happened in my own life thanks to the Grace of Allah.

The blessings of Khidr with regard to this poetry are something which the reader can judge for himself. In the last period of Murshid's life, when he functioned as a spiritual teacher to a large family of young Americans, the transmissions in the field of Music and Dance also became evident. Earlier in his life he had been inspired to perform a 'Dance of Universal Peace' at Fatehpur Sikri in India before the tomb of the Saint Selim Chisti. Sometimes he called this 'The Dream of Akbar' (the Moghul emperor of India who convened the first world conference of religions). This became the theme for his *Dances of Universal Peace*, a compendium of sacred Dances which involves repetition of sacred phrases from all the world's religions. These Dances are now being done by thousands of young people throughout the United States and Europe under the auspices of the Sufi Order which is directed by Pir Vilayat Khan (eldest son of Murshid's first Sufi teacher). The center for concentration on these Dances is the San Francisco Bay area where Murshid's Khalif and successor Moin-ed-din Jablonski is in charge. The transmission in the field of Music is manifest today in the work of the Sufi Choir, which was initiated by Murshid and is under the direction of Ala-ud-din Mathieu.

As to Murshid's vitality, the other practical indicator of the Khidr experience which he mentions above, he was a true phenomenon. Picture a man in his seventies teaching numerous classes in mysticism, including tireless Dance instruction, carrying on a world-wide correspondence, writing creatively, handling interviews with disciples with a sense of complete responsibility for their well-being, gardening, running a household, etc., at a pace which his disciples, mostly in their twenties and thirties, found utterly impossible to keep up with — and all this for roughly 18 hours a day. Often at night he was not allowed to sleep, but was kept awake with visions of dances and pageants.

He did everything with an all-pervading sense of service to God and humanity. He said that the greatest Sufis and Vedantists he ever met were the living embodiment of the words of Jesus Christ: "Let he who would be master, be the servant of all the rest." This was certainly Murshid's concentration; and it introduces the subject of the Spiritual Hierarchy, a subject which is one of central importance in understanding Murshid's life and writings. When a man accepts responsibility for all humanity he becomes what is called in Buddhist terminology, a Bodhisattva. It becomes his purpose in life to bring the Divine Blessings into the world for the benefit of all sentient beings. Thus, in specific circumstances different roles may be called for, and one has to be capable of leaving his ego personality entirely behind in order to fulfill the needs of the moment. In the mineral kingdom there is a stone called Bedelium (Hebrew: 'mysterious dividing') which is a change-stone; on occasion Murshid compared his role in life with that stone.

So at different times in Murshid's life we find him fulfilling the most diverse roles. For example, he worked as an assistant in army intelligence (G2) in World War II; when his interests turned to the goal of solving world food problems and reclaiming the deserts of the Middle East, he studied at universities and in the field until he became an expert in the areas of soil science, horticulture and related fields; he lived as a beachcomber and hermit on the shores of both the Atlantic and Pacific Oceans; for 40 years, at the request of Dr. Henry Atkinson of the World Church Peace Union, he made a study of the Scriptures of all the worlds's religions; in Pakistan he became known as a teacher of Islamic philosophy and the inner path (*Tarikat*) of Sufism; in Japan he was initiated as *Fudo*, the fierce Bodhisattva responsible for the protection of the pure-teachings of the Buddha; he spent years primarily as a writer of poetry and esoteric commentaries; and so on, in many roles and guises too numerous to detail here. For he was a practitioner of what Sufis called *Mushahida* and the Buddhists the *Maha Mudra* meditation; this requires the internationalization of the heart and the internalization of all the events of the world into the sphere of one's own heart. Thus one begins to realize and exercise power through the innate capacities in one's own heart for love and peace. Murshid describes this faculty as it operated in his role of Sufi teacher:

Jesus said, "Only God is Perfect." But he also said — and this is not a part of what is called "Christianity" — "Be you perfect as your Father in Heaven is perfect". . . . The relation of a Sufi teacher to his disciple is according to "Love thy neighbor as thyself" — the disciple is not apart from the teacher nor the teacher from the disciple. So the teacher normally and naturally shares with the pupil, and having a much greater operative electromotive force — to use a scientific analogy — he enables the pupil to draw upon it, not by any giving . . . but by attunement-induction, just as what takes place in

14

electromotive operations. Thus the pupil finds he has the same thing in himself as the teacher. . . .

Since this subject of the Spiritual Hierarchy is one of such importance, it would be appropriate here to quote a few statements of Murshid's relating to this point. It should be borne in mind that, as Murshid says, "The standard is our surrender to Allah (God) every moment and in reality."

Even praise or blame do not affect your Murshid, but when the proper questions are asked, then he either is transformed or transforms himself. There is a large sector of your Murshid's history in Cairo which looks as if it came out of something more bizarre than even the Arabian Nights. For behind Sufism and the Sufi Orders there is that Hierarchy which controls the destiny of the world. Only this Hierarchy is not only manifesting through Islam, it manifests above and beyond all religions. You have read this in Book II of "Saladin" which came from *Rassul-lillah* himself [Mohammed], and all wisdoms of the world come through him, and not just what we call 'Islam' alone, separating it from anything. Indeed, your Murshid has had initiations into six great religions, even from the Chinese.

Now, Beloved One of Allah, the Dervish is one, as was said in Cairo, before whom there are no walls. . . . It is time for us to learn, and this is most difficult, that there is no ego personality, that there is a vast Universal Heart which beats in and through all of us, and which is the Nexus of Infinite Mercy, Compassion and Wisdom, and the basis of all religion even before the formation of time.

Pir-O-Murshid Hazrat Inayat Khan has said that the Spiritual Hierarchy is more real than creation itself. This is what he says, and it is published in his books too, but even mureeds do not accept this fact. They are not always very different from the public in wanting a God who is an international banker, or Santa Claus, or sometimes a cosmic policeman. Sufism is divine wisdom and not human sagacity. The imaginary saint, or Sir Galahad, is a picture of human imagination which can be explained by Jungian psychology. It has nothing to do with Hierarchy. . . . Pre-eminence depends neither on silence nor speech, and no saint or hierarch has to act according to rules laid

15

down by the public and non-initiates. . . . Behind 'me' is the Divine Voice which constantly comes from within. To listen to and obey this is Hierarchy. This is reality and this is the way the Sufi works — he does not work by human preconceptions or human desires, and he is not a doll to be admired but never to do anything slightly reprehensible. . . . Big problems are only solved by big effort and behind big effort the Voice of God, which comes from within. Hyprocrisy, according to the greatest Sufis, is the only sin. When we have candor and sincerity our faults will be forgiven; when we are double toward ourselves we are in difficulty. Humility consists in using the ears and bowing the head; it is everything but soft-voiced pride.

God does not leave this world without guidance. And we like to say things like "the people without vision perish," but when somebody comes along who has vision, he perishes. And after a while we find out that God always informs us. The last time I took this matter up, it was with regard to affairs in the Near East. A certain person and I discussed just exactly what was going to happen down to details, but we were not much interested in the politics of it. We want to restore the Holy Land as a *Holy* Land.

Murshid's duties in the Spiritual Hierarchy sometimes made it impossible for him to avoid coming into direct contact with the forces which dominate the world politically and militarily. This work, generally speaking, was most difficult; for as he said, most of the parties lack candor and appreciation of spiritual realities:

It is not a simple matter to out-argue belligerent nationals that 'God alone is great' — *ALLAHO AKBAR* — and that UN's and alliances and weapons have only a finite operative field. Besides, this person is not sure as to whom or who is right or wrong in the political field. He does know that the great powers of this world have not given an iota of consideration to much of the *actual humanity* living in contested areas. This is the rejection in toto of Jesus Christ's "WHATSOEVER YE DO TO THE LEAST OF THESE MY CREATURES YE DO IT UNTO ME."

Murshid was utterly committed to the bringing of peace in the Holy Land, and indeed to the restoration of the Holy Land as a Holy Land. This was one of the most important concentrations of his life. And it was one that in the last year of his life he was able to say he saw "ultimately coming out entirely successful." The three poems in this volume all deal directly with the subject of world peace, the restoration of the Holy Land, and the relationships thereof:

The unity of Israel shall not come by race,
Neither shall it arise from concordance of worship,
But he that sees the Spirit of God shall be known as "Israel,"
And he that follows the Law of God shall be called "Jacob."
    There shall be peace in the world when there is peace in Zion . . .

In a very real sense these poems provide the mystical basis for the accomplishment of this concentration. They contain within them the keys to a lasting peace. They are exactly parallel to the writings of the Hebrew Prophets, such as Isaiah, Ezekiel and Malachi, on the subject of the true rejuvenation of Jerusalem. Murshid said this about the Prophet Malachi:

I am very much disturbed by a complete ignorance among the Jewish people of the Book of Malachi, which was supposed to be the last book they ever received from God in the Old Testament. It's virtually dead today. And the themes are very simple — that if the children of Ishmael (Muslims), the children of Edom (Christians), and the children of Israel (Jews) didn't get together, God would come to the earth and smite it with a curse; and that if man would turn aside from his selfish oppressive actions to God, then God would turn to him. And they seem to prefer the curse. I mean this and not sarcasm. But this is a thing we can all be working for, to receive the blessing; and we receive when the spiritual side of our life is open. And this involves two things: the love side, and the intuitive side, which can spread and become inspiration or even, God-willing, revelation.

It is in Malachi that we find the phrase, "Have we not all one

Father? Hath not one God created us?" The work of bringing peace to the Holy Land really takes this as a foundation stone. Mutual appreciation of the religious teachings of Judaism, Christianity and Islam is one of the real keys to success. Murshid was fond of saying that his peace plan was based on eating, dancing and praying with people. He and his disciples have been successful in bringing together Christians, Muslims, Jews, Israelis, Arabs and others in this spirit of brotherhood. The first such gathering was held at the Chassidic House of Love and Prayer in San Francisco in the fall of 1970. This was so successful that the Muslims and Arabs involved reciprocated with a dinner of their own.

The use of deep religious understanding as a means of bringing peace is a subject Murshid worked on for over fifty years; and in the last year of his life he attended a conference of the world's religions in Geneva sponsored by The Temple of Understanding of Washington, D.C., with the theme of bringing peace through religion. In relation to the problems of the Near East and the various rivalries involved, Murshid was often called upon to function as a strong warner, directly confronting zealots of all camps.

Ever since I was a child I have been moved by the Biblical passage, "My house shall be a house of prayer for all peoples." It seemed to me at an early age that some Jewish people were destined to return to Palestine, but the putting of political concerns ahead of the actual universal Zionism led to the present confusions. . . . Why not restore a temple, even as Nehemiah did, but as a house of prayer for all peoples. The real Jewish tradition, which has been hidden, was that when the Messiah returned the Holy Land would extend even from Jerusalem unto Minsk. All pure Messianism has been repudiated, and in this we have the age-old habit which the Prophets declaimed against for centuries, that every man did according to his own ego. My objection to what is called 'Zionism' is that most of these people don't even pray. I want to see this become a Holy Land, a place of refuge for all worshippers and all the holy places preserved.

Murshid felt that a genuine historical study of the policies of certain rulers of Palestine would give a real basis for contemporary peace efforts, a real basis for the cooperation of the different religions concerned with the area. In particular he felt that the policies of the Khalif Omar, of the Turkish ruler Suleiman the Magnificent and of the historical Sultan Saladin would offer many approaches which would still be valid today. While all of these rulers were Islamic, their policies were quite universal in scope.

The play *Nathan the Wise*, written by the German philosopher Lessing, is a work which also gave great inspiration to Murshid in this sphere. This play was given a great deal of emphasis by Jewish people when they were the subjects of religious persecution, though today we hear very little of it. It features an enlightened Jew who lived at the time of Saladin. The climax of the story comes with 'The Tale of the Three Rings', which occurs originally in the *Decameron* of Boccaccio. Nathan is a rich man, and Saladin is at that time in need of money. So he decides to trap Nathan in a religious debate and thus force him to give him the money he requires. So, calling Nathan before his throne, he asks which religion is the superior one — Judaism, Christianity or Islam. Nathan replies to his question by telling the story of a supremely wise king who had a ring which conferred on the wearer all manner of blessings, that he would be loved by God and man. He decided to pass this on to one of his sons who proved the most deserving. This he did, and things continued in this vein for a number of generations, until there came a time when there was a king who had three sons, who, by all tests, proved equally deserving. The king did not wish to slight two of his sons, so he had two more rings fashioned, each identical in every respect to the first, and passed on all three. The sons were not able to determine which of them had the original ring, though each claimed that his ring was the one. They took their case before a wise magistrate who said that

19

since the rings were identical, no decision was possible. He further counselled that each of them should be careful to make sure that the attribute of the ring, namely that of bringing blessings to the people, remain intact throughout time. That would be the only true test. Upon hearing this story, Saladin fell on his face before Allah and then rose to embrace Nathan as an equal.

This representation of the three religions of Judaism, Christianity and Islam as the three rings inspired Murshid to give this name to his peace efforts in the Holy Land. A group of his disciples are actively continuing his concentration in this field, under the name "Hallelujah! The Three Rings." At the conference of the world's religions in Geneva, Murshid had a great time running around and telling people he was an incarnation of Nathan the Wise. This, he said, could easily be confirmed by his poetry. And it is the three poems here which, like three rings, demonstrate his realization from the standpoint of each of these three world religions.

Murshid's occupation in life was that of a gardener and soil scientist. Consequently, his plan for the solutions to problems in Palestine and the Middle East is very practical. Central to the plan is the reclamation of the desert through salt-water conversion and desalinization, through ascertaining the proper crops for different types of soils, through the use of petroleum waste products and other low-cost materials in the construction of dwellings, and many other similar programs. It is the integrative approach which he champions. Thus he felt that a first necessary step would be to make a complete geographical and economic-geological survey of the entire area.

Murshid was always pointing out that the solutions to these and other related problems already exist, but that the scientists who have the knowledge are not given proper consideration by the news media and the various governments involved. In his life, time and again Murshid had to come face to face with this attitude on the part of the press and the U.S. Government. Valuable reports by himself and others actually on the scene in different countries were simply ignored. And, instead, speculations by newsmen and politicians with the most superficial experience of the lands and cultures were accepted, often with drastic consequences, as in the case of Viet Nam. Murshid's most vitriolic letters are in response to this malefic influence of the fourth estate.

The faculty of integrative thinking, the drawing together and blending of many different factors, is an intrinsic feature of Murshid's thought and life. He had the great advantage of being a mystic, a student of all the world's religions, a historian and a scientist. And he knew how to relate findings of one field to the next. His knowledge was truly encyclopedic. His friend, the well-known late astrologer Gavin Arthur, once used to live in an adjoining apartment; he tells the story that whenever he had a question on any topic he would just knock on the wall and ask Sam; he said he found him faster and more accurate than the *Encyclopedia Britannica.*

One sample of the blending of the religious and the scientific is found in his "Garden of Allah" project:

I submitted two plans for North Africa, the second one being an agricultural program based on the fact that the Date is the sacred plant of Islam; and that Quran itself has a Sura which begins, "By the Fig and By the Olive" . . . And to submit a program calling for large plantings of Figs, Olives, Grapes and Dates in North Africa is the last thing the political and ecclesiastic religieunes consider, even though this area is perfect for such cultivation. . . . What I should like to see is a master idea for the proper soil and water rehabilitation of the whole Arab world.

But this faculty of integrative thinking does not always make Murshid an easy person to read, because he is constantly stretching our consciousness by bringing in new factors and by relating all factors to many levels of experience. So the reader of

21

these poems is warned not to be satisfied with one or even two readings, for there are more and more riches to be found when one begins to get the overall integrative picture of Murshid's vision.

I have refrained in this Preface from commenting specifically on the three individual poems which compose Murshid's trilogy, the work which he considered his most important literary effort. The introductory notes before each of the poems have been written to help the reader enter the poet's perspective. This is also true of the extensive glossaries included for each poem, in lieu of excessive footnotes. These glossaries have been compiled, wherever possible, from Murshid's published and unpublished writings, and are intended to serve the casual reader as well as the scholar. Most the the footnotes in the poems are those of Murshid Samuel L. Lewis and are indicated by symbols (*, †, ‡, etc.); where explanations of specific lines were necessary (indicated in the text by numbers) the editors have written additional footnotes which appear at the end of the poem in a section called "Notes." In addition, three appendices have been included: a) several spiritual practices extracted from the poems; b) Murshid's paper on the reconciliation of Judaism and Islam; and c) the reconciliation of Christianity and Islam.

No doubt, much more could be 'explained', and yet we do not feel this is necessary. The answers to all the questions are contained within the poems themselves, waiting to be found by the reader who takes up the challenge of meeting Murshid face to face.

Masheikh Wali Ali Meyer
San Francisco, California
June, 1975

The Day of the Lord Cometh

Introduction

"The Day of the Lord Cometh" draws its title and substance from the Book of the Prophet Malachi, the last of the Divinely inspired writings of the Old Testament. As the poem says, "the message of the Prophets is for all times, not for the ancients alone, because it abides in eternity." This is what might be called the Eternal Torah, the realization of the teaching that "God's mercy endureth forever and ever." Moreover, the prophecies of the past are not all consummated, but still live today and offer the possibility of fulfillment to those who are attuned to their inner significance.

There is a general point of view with regard to Scripture that Murshid as a mystic and kabbalist regarded as basic. In his words it can be expressed thus: "The Bible is also the story of every soul which has to go through the same training." Or, "The Bible is the unfoldment of your own being." He points out, "The Hebrew Scriptures were originally examined from four distinct levels, called the four *pardes* by the Kabbalists because you were in paradise if you knew life from these four points of view. These four grades are: 'P', the literal scriptures about which everybody scraps; 'R' which are the parallel meanings such as the verbal symbols used in poetry, sea for water, water for sea, and so on; 'D' the deep symbolical interpretations of scripture, as for example how the story of Moses leading the Hebrew people out of Egypt to the promised land symbolically stands for the process of liberation of the human soul from samsara to nirvana; and finally 'S' which means it is your actual experience, an experience that you have gone through — it is the mystical side. These four grades correspond to four states of consciousness: physical, subtle, spiritual, and divine. The mystical experience doesn't deny the symbolic or the parallel or the verbal experiences, but they fit together into something very grand. When we learn that, we learn the Universe."

To call "The Day of the Lord Cometh" or any of the works in this volume poetry, while true, is an unnecessary limitation. It would be like calling the Bible poetry; for while it is poetic, the essential feature is prophecy, which doesn't necessarily mean predicting. The heart of man, by becoming empty of self and universal, becomes the instrument through which God speaks and guides humanity. Not all the writings contained in the Jewish Scriptures are considered as revelation nor even as holy by their own scholars; for it was necessary that an appropriate sign be given, such as "Thus speaks the Lord. . ." And we find a Samuel of today also speaking in this fashion: "The word of the Lord is. . ."

The persona in the poem shifts from Moses to Jeremiah to Malachi, yet all speak in the name of the Most High. The Prophets are not restricted to speaking only of the past, but consider also the historical fabric of the present time, e.g. the subject of Marxism. There is a continuity of the Prophets, like a chain, and it is this which allows Samuel to speak in one voice or in another as determined by inspiration. Rather than confusing one, this change in voice and tense brings one into the timeless world of the prophetic message.

Much of the essence of "The Day of the Lord Cometh" is prefigured within a short poem written by Murshid on May 12, 1932. It is of interest from the standpoint of the predictive and prophetic elements in his writings; therefore we will include the whole poem here. It is found in the unpublished work, "The Book of Cosmic Prophecy."

26

Then the Lord spoke, saying:

"Open thine eyes, Samuel, and relate what thou dost see."

I said, "O Lord, I see a vast desert, a barren desert of sand."

The Lord said, "Thou seest truly, for this is the land of Palestine,

And its barrenness is due to the barrenness in the hearts of men,

To the barrenness of Israel and also to the barrenness of the
    Nazarenes and Muslims."

And He said: "Look thou again."

So I looked and saw naught but a falling rain;

No land, nor sea, nor sky, only falling floods of water.

Then God spoke, declaring:

"This rain is My Mercy, which never doth cease.

But when the hearts of men are hardened, like a rain which stops in
    mid-air,

It touches not the ground, there is no room for it."

Then He said: "Look thou once more."

And behold! I saw a single sprig above the ground,

A single shoot on the bare desert.

Then spake the Lord:

"Blessed be thou, O Israel, the redeemed of humanity, for now
    humanity is saved.

The seeds of righteousness have remained beneath the ground,

From generation unto generation they have remained;

From Baal Shem Tov unto this day hath there been no prophet
    in Israel.

The sprig which thou seest is the fruit of Baal Shem Tov,

That even the life of the Chassidim is not fully dead;

The life from the Gaonim and the Kabbalists has been transmitted
    to this age.

Long have the seeds remained under the ground,

And as to the prophet Elijah the sight of a small cloud meant a
    drenching downpour,

So this single twig in essence contains hosts of forests and fields.

For the children of Israel return to the land of their fathers;

In matter they return to sow the vine and corn in *Eretz Yisroel*,

And in spirit they return to partake of the manna of Heaven.

This day declare a new age and a new doctrine:
O men of Israel, no longer shall ye be a law unto yourselves,
For the synagogue shall be open to all men, or the synagogue shall go,
The *Cheder*[1] shall not be for the *Yahudim*[2] to the exclusion of the
    Goyim,[3]
And *Talmud Torah*[4] shall be naught but the school of Holiness.
As the Scriptures teach — My temple shall be a house of prayer for
    all people,
So only shall that place be sanctified whose doors are open to all,
The saint and sinner, the believer and the heretic, the men of old
    faiths and new faiths,
All shall congregate in the synagogue of righteousness, in the temple
    of peace.

The message of this earlier work is expanded upon in "The Day of the Lord Cometh." The use of the letters of the Hebrew alphabet to represent transcendental realities is quite in keeping with the depths of Jewish mysticism. That the 22 letters of the alphabet are hieroglyphs for states of being is demonstrated, to mention only one source among many, in Fabre D'Olivet's *The Hebraic Tongue Restored*. The ancient *Sepher Yetzirah*, which tradition attributes in part to Abraham, sees all of creation in

---

1. Elementary Hebrew School.
2. The real name of the Hebrews, *Ya-hu-dim*, came from their constant repitition of "*Ya hu!*" One source for such a position is Martin Buber who write in *The Prophetic Faith* (Macmillan Company 1949, New York): "What is the name of the God of this community? We cannot decide from the Bible by which of His names and titles Abraham addressed Him. . . . And we are justified in supposing that at the time when he wished to point to Him, so to say, with his voice, to proclaim Him in an enthusiastic manner, he used that 'tabu word,' that 'god-cry,' that 'stammering,' '*Yah*' or '*Yahu*' or '*Yahuvah*,' that is 'He!' or 'This One!' or 'This is it,' or 'Oh he!' This elemental sound was apparently common to the west Semitic tribes, who hinted by it in a mysterious and enthusiastic way to the deity whose name could not be designated; we find it in this sense still in the mysticism of Islam. It was impossible to call the deity by this sound when they addressed Him directly, because it referred to the third person, but it was possible to use it when proclaiming Him." — ED.
3. Hebrew: literally, stranger; Gentile, non-Jew.
4. Advanced school for the study of the oral and written laws.

terms of the actions and interactions of these twenty-two letters. This is a subject deserving a depth of study and cannot be handled in a summary fashion. "The Day of the Lord Cometh" focuses on the mother letters, *Aleph, Mem* and *Shin*. Only one observation among many which might be made is that *Shema* is composed of these three letters; and *Shem* is described in the poem as the universal Light of God.

"The Day of the Lord Cometh" was written in 1938 at a time in the history of the world when Hitler had just annexed Czechoslovakia. Yet, thanks to the Divine Vision vouchsafed to Murshid Samuel L. Lewis, we are shown the future. This futuresight shows Hitler overcome, but doesn't stop there. The poem proceeds to deal in universal terms with the underlying causes of his ascendancy, and the opportunities available to man for fulfilling the Eternal Torah and thereby attaining a true and abiding peace.

Hitler is seen archetypically as "Madman"; and madman has come before in history: he has even sat on the throne of Israel. Hitler recognized the archetype of Moses and opposed him, but Israel remembered him only in name and not in deed. Madman's ascendancy serves as the catalyst which unites the forces of *Mem* and *Shin* and thus prepares the way for real peace: a peace which allows for freedom in the realm of thought, a peace which is beyond the mere cessation of hostilities in the political arena. In terms of World War II this was a prediction of the ultimate uniting of the United States and the Soviet Union as Allies, and also a warning that a mere physical union in the struggle would be insufficient. (The peace conference which marked the end of the war is anticipated in the next poem, "What Christ? What Peace?")

The union of the forces of *Shin* and *Mem* is not sufficient in itself, yet it leads to the assimilation of *Aleph*, the living law of Moses and the Prophets. Or, in the words of the poet, "Return ye, return ye unto your Lord! Return and rejoice, return and be

29

happy, For happy is the man who walks in the way of the Lord."
And in the midst of political turmoil, Samuel quotes from the
Prophet Malachi: "Then they that feared the Lord spoke one
with another; and the Lord hearkened, and heard, and a Book
of Remembrance was written before Him. . ." In the historical
context, this refers to how the Holy Ones of earth, who might be
called members of the Spiritual Hierarchy, directly influenced
the outcome of the second World War through calling on the
Lord. The promise is received, as in Malachi, of the coming of
the Day of the Lord: "The sun of righteousness arising with
healing in its wings," the descent of *Ruach Hakodesh* (the Holy
Spirit) upon mankind. This is a phenomenon which many are
now witnessing and calling by various names, such as the
Aquarian Age or the New Age. The poem ends on this note with
the universal vision of Jerusalem anew.

The Day of the Lord Cometh

Three are the mother-letters of the sacred tongue,
Three and not two, three and not four:
Aleph and *Mem* and *Shin*.
Thus it is told in the repository of sacred wisdom,
First revealed to the Prophet Abraham in days of old
And recorded in the scroll of Ultimate Foundations,
The *Sepher Yetzirah*, and in the secrets of Israel.

The Lord summoned the Prophet Moses to the Summit of
 the mountain,
And the Eternal One, blessed be He, addressed Himself thus:
"Moses, My servant, stretch thine eyes, extend thy vision, look afar."
Then the Prophet did even as the Lord commanded,
Stretching his eyes, extending his vision, looking afar,
Gazing to the uttermost kingdom, to the ends of the earth.
Then the Eternal One, blessed be He, continued:
"See also those near at hand,
Perceive all, the strange and the well-known,
Holding thy distant glance also,
For all belong to Me, their Creator.
From man another man may be distant,
To man another man may be alien,
But all are kindred in My sight, being of My spirit."

Thereupon Moses did as the Lord commanded,
For the command of the Lord is not a weighty order,
The command of the Lord is not as obeisance required from a slave,
The command of the Lord is as love and light upon the soul.
So Moses set his glance upon the nations near at hand,
Yet extended his vision even unto the furthermost regions,
And there was no country that escaped his apperception.
When he had completed his task he sat in silence;
And after completing his silence, he opened his mouth:
"O Lord, I have done, done even as Thou hast wished,
For a command of the Lord is as a mighty boon,
It is greater than the greatest pleasure to the soul,
It is steeped in sweetness and brings no fatigue,
It bestows blessing upon blessing."

Then the Eternal One, blessed be He, replied:

"Yes, thou hast done well, truly hast thou done well,
For all things in all places have come unto thy vision;
Thou hast seen thy brethren and thy neighbors,
Thou hast also seen the stranger beyond thy borders.
Now then, listen unto the words of the Lord, thy Creator:
Thou hast seen lands rich and prosperous,
Thou hast seen also the abodes of famine,
Thou hast beheld places fruitful with green corn and vines,
And thou hast also perceived where sustenance is meager.
Wherewith is this explanation given:

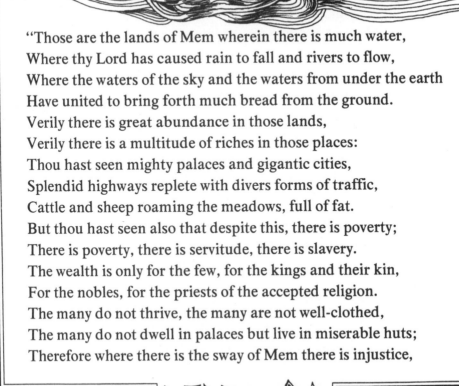

"Those are the lands of Mem wherein there is much water,
Where thy Lord has caused rain to fall and rivers to flow,
Where the waters of the sky and the waters from under the earth
Have united to bring forth much bread from the ground.
Verily there is great abundance in those lands,
Verily there is a multitude of riches in those places:
Thou hast seen mighty palaces and gigantic cities,
Splendid highways replete with divers forms of traffic,
Cattle and sheep roaming the meadows, full of fat.
But thou hast seen also that despite this, there is poverty;
There is poverty, there is servitude, there is slavery.
The wealth is only for the few, for the kings and their kin,
For the nobles, for the priests of the accepted religion.
The many do not thrive, the many are not well-clothed,
The many do not dwell in palaces but live in miserable huts;
Therefore where there is the sway of Mem there is injustice,

In the realms of Mem there is unrighteousness and even unnatural
    sin.
Where Mem reigns there is inequality,
Where Mem is supreme they do not know that I am the Lord,
Where Mem prevails temples are regarded as holy to the gods,
Where Mem holds sway human beings are not of much account.
Therefore the lands of Mem are an abomination to Me,
For they hold the words of man superior to the words of the
    Creator of man,
The blessings whereof pass even as the grass that withers,
And what the Lord has given, that also may He take away.

"Thou hast seen, too, lands where water is scarce,
Where rains fall not in flood, where stream-beds soon dry,
Where the sun is aflame and the ground cries in thirst.
These are the lands of Shin,
Wherein the people worship the moon and the stars,
Regarding the sun as a scourge, not as a sign of favour.
To them the wells and springs of the ground are holy,
They hold water as the source of all blessing,
They evaluate even the smallest drop,
They give thanks for it in every form;
But the people are not regarded as holy works of the Lord,
Passed through the fire to the gods, or left to die in the desert.
In these, the lands of Shin, there is often equality,
None are esteemed too high, few are held too low,
But because there is little prosperity, there is little wealth.
So the people of Shin have become robbers,
They rob the peoples of the lands of Mem,
They even steal, the one from the other, and regard this as right:
Therefore these people are also an abomination unto Me,
Their ways are not the ways of Truth.

35

"Now I, the Lord, the Eternal, say unto you:
Moses, My servant, thy ways shall not be as the ways of the people
    of Mem,
Neither shall thou be like the people of Shin;
Out of Mem, which is to say, *Mitzraim*, have I called thee and
    thy people,
And from Shin, which is to say *Yeshimon*, the desert, shall I
    deliver them;
I shall show them through thee the ways of Aleph,
The ways that stretch neither to the right nor to the left,
The ways that go always forward yet are broad,
The ways of Aleph which are My ways,
And these thou shalt incorporate in the Holy Torah,
And in the declaration of Universality:
I am the Lord, *ANI ADONAI* — My Essence is Aleph."

II.

Then I, the Prophet Jeremiah, did as the Lord commanded,
From an exalted station of the spirit I turned and called:
"Son of man, hearken to the message of your Lord —
One is He by whatever Name you may call Him,
Who is in all things and of Whom all things are,
For Truth is eternal, even as the Holy One, blessed be He, is eternal.
The teachings of the Law abide to this day and forever,
Though man in his unbelief may set them aside,
Though man in his selfishness finds excuses for transgression,
Yet the teachings of the Lord abide.
Torah is from the Eternal and not from man,
The teachings of the Prophets also were inspired by the Eternal,

Verily these are emanations of Aleph,
Verily these are the first and these are also the last.
Son of man, attend to my voice and hearken:
Even to this day is Torah,
Even to this hour is *Ruach Hakodesh*, the source of all inspiration,
Even to this instant is the preeminence of Aleph and Mem and Shin.

"Now these are the ways of Mem:
The ways of Mem indicate the triumph of man over matter,
And the sway of Mem has brought the blessings of heaven
     through water,
And as through water the Divine Blessings infiltrate the ground,
Bringing forth bread and the living products of the vine,
So through the years Mem has learned to draw many riches
     from the ground,
So where there is Mem there is material wealth,
There is abundance of this wealth, there is concentration of wealth.
He who is wealthy is held preeminent,
While he who fails in the quest for wealth is as a sinner;
Whereas the unrighteous is as a sinner before the Lord
So the poor man is as a sinner in the courts of Mem,
For the lands of Mem are the lands of Mammon,
In the lands of Mem the unsuccessful is regarded as a weakling;

Though they preach that the Lord created all,
Though they proclaim the equality of all
(And in truth all are equal in the sight of the Lord),
Yet in the activities of Mem there are inequalities,
In the practices of Mem there are iniquities;
Lips may lead where hearts cannot follow,
And many in Mem-lands give their lip-service
Whose hearts are not affixed upon the Creator,
So steeped are they in their zeal for the created.

"There saith the Lord:
'Even now when the people of the lands of Mem are being awakened,
Even now when they turn to prayer and toward righteousness,
The leaders want God and six percent interest,
The leaders desire God and money, God and debt.
Many may be zealous in sanctifying the seventh day to call it holy,
But the seventh year they regard not holy,
And the seven times seventh year they regard not at all.
The leaders have rejected the Jubilee;
They heed not that when the Jubilee is rejected Torah is rejected;
When Torah is rejected My ways are deserted;
When My ways, which are the paths of peace, are deserted,
There is no room left except for strife, for war, for bloodshed.
Though a million temples be builded in My Name,
Though a million million prayers be offered,
They avail naught, being covered.
For the acceptance of compound interest is inimical to Me,
And the institution of usury is an abomination in My sight;
I proclaimed Jubilee, Mammon-Mem has proclaimed eternal
    interest,
Yea, even after fifty years, even after one hundred and fifty years
    is interest collected.

Man comes, man goes, and new-born babes are shackled with the
      burden of interest;
Their grandfathers reaped and now they must sow,
First the harvest and then the plow,
First the festival and then the planting —
This is the way of Mammon and men under its unholy sway.
The rejection of the Jubilee and the alleviation from bondage
Stand before Me, between Me and these people;
I did not deliver from *Mitzraim* to offer to Mammon,
I did not forswear the idolatry of the temple for the idolatry of
      the mart.'

"Therefore the Word of the Lord is:
'The Land of Promise will be restored when the Covenant is restored,
The Covenant is restored when men alter their hearts,
When increase and usury at the loss of a brother are forsworn;
The glory of Zion will be renewed when men and women trust in
      the Holy writings,
The glory of the world will return when the glory of Zion has
      manifested.

'For the message of the Prophets was for all times,
Even as the Lord has been called *Ancient of Days*.
Why is it that men no longer are inspired to new psalms?
Why is it that there are spiritual famines throughout the world?
Why is it that Holy Prophets appear no more?
They pray and there is no answer — the wars continue;
They beseech and there is no response — destruction prevails;
They cry and cry in vain — death reigns supreme.
The Lord is not a broker, the Lord is not a capitalist,
The Lord is Father of all, Creator of all — THE LORD IS ALL.'

"Who among you, great mathematicians, can predict the course of
   the stars?
Who among you, great mathematicians, can aid in building mighty
   bridges?
Who among you, great mathematicians, can help in perfecting
   ships of the air?
Who among you, great mathematicians, can cooperate in the
   construction of gigantic power plants?
And who among you, O mighty mathematicians of Mammon,
Who among you has solved the mystery of money and debt-bondage?

The course of the stars, the building of bridges,
The perfection of ships, the construction of plants,
These ye can do, even greater can ye do,
But ye cannot turn your faces against the Lord —
In that wherein doth your mathematics avail?
When and how will these colossal bond-debts be unloosed?
Who has given the right to bring forth infants in bondage
Even while proclaiming 'All men are created free and equal'?
Is it freedom when babes are Mammon-shackled?
Is it equality when there is the mark of Cain upon race or class?
Who can reject the Word of the Lord and expect peace?
The Lord hath spoken, aye, He hath spoken many times;

Therefore your prayers are in vain to beseech the Lord against
      the Lord —
Debt leads to war, debt leads to destruction, debt leads to death.'

"Thus saith the Lord:
'Again have I set before thee life and good, debt and evil;
If thou loveth the Lord, thou shalt accept as abomination
What I, thy Creator, have ever called abomination,
For My ways are for the welfare of all, and lead to peace.' "

III.

Then I, the Prophet Jeremiah, did continue:
"Because of the riches of the people of Mem,
Riches coupled with unrighteousness,
Riches coupled with injustice,
Riches not shared, riches withheld from the many,
Verily have the people of Shin protested and rightly protested.
The people of Shin have objected to the ways of Mem,
The people of Shin have forsworn the ways of Mem,
But the people of Shin have not followed in the pathways of their
      Creator.
Verily they have indeed turned from Mammon,
They have rejected many of the institutes of Mammon,
They have delivered themselves from the superstitions of Mammon,
And have also avoided many of the excrescences of Mammon,
But they have even departed from the virtues of the sway of Mem,
Associating Mem with Mammon instead of with the Lord.

"Therefore have the people of Shin not turned to their Creator,
They have not adapted themselves to the teachings of Moses,

41

They have, on their part, established the faction of Marx.
No prophet was this Marx who did not hearken to the Lord,
Who, seeing the evil of the world, blamed the Lord,
Beholding the iniquities in Mammon he turned away from God.
No prophet was this Marx who did not even study the folkways of
     men —
Cooped in a dark library,
Surrounded by a multitude of books,
Books that he accepted or books that he despised —
From his own ego-mind did he conceive patterns,
And from these patterns declared how the world should be operated.
His own life he could not control, but the world he would control;
How it should be governed,
How the multitudes should rule and be ruled.
This he did concerning a world over which he did not travel,
Nor did he mingle freely with the populace thereof,
Nor did he draw inspirations from his fellow-men
Nor did he heed them except to oppose them bitterly —
Apart from all he proclaimed his philosophy,
From his very personal viewpoint he thought and wrote,
From within himself he proclaimed the 'Internationale'.

"Before the Lord the 'Internationale' is not wrong,
Before the Lord the workers will all be unchained;
Verily, the chains of Mammon are the chains of physical bondage
Which return mankind to an Egyptian servitude.
For what profits a man if he gain the whole world
And loses his freedom of thought?
What value is there to be freed from the seen chains of bondage,
To be hampered by unseen shackles which imprison the spirit?
Aye, men of Shin, what is the atomic formula for the 'Materialist
     Conception'?

Of what elements is your *conception* constituted?
Tell us, high-priests of Shin, the formula for a conception.
Show us the materials out of which your thoughts are formed.
Verily, the larger view, the universal view, is akin to divinity,
For the true universal assimilates all other views;
It harmonizes and does not dictate,
It encourages, it inspires, it does not uselessly dispute.
The people of Shin have turned from their Creator,
Accepting instead the teachings of the reformer, Marx.
For this Marx has arraigned against the exploiters of men,
Against the institutions which prevented justice and humanity;
But even more did he attack those who foresaw otherwise,
Who thought or felt differently from what his mind proclaimed,
Though their aims, though their goals may have been identical.

"Therefore saith the Lord:
'The ways of Marx are not My ways;
If the people follow Marx, they do not follow Me,
If the people of Shin accept Marx, they do not accept Me;
Though they are opposed to the ways of Mammon,
Yet they are not in the pathways of peace and truth.
Not only are the *things* of physical earth for man,
But the *thoughts* of the mental heavens are also for man,
The *inspirations* of heart-paradise are also for man.
All things of the Heavens and of earth are Mine,
And to Mine own have I bequeathed them.

"Who is *Mi* and what is *Ma?**
Know this and perceive all things:

* A pun from the Kabbala, for *mi* means 'who?' and *ma* means 'what?' The
interpretation thereof is similar to some forms of Indian thought. [See the Glossary
also — ED.]

43

The ways of the spirit are for man.
Thus the days of the atom were days of inequalities,
But the days of the electron are for equality and justice;
And as the electron reveals the light in things,
So am I the Light in the things of earth and the spirit of man.*
The days of the atom fashioned the thoughts of the atom,
The differences of the atoms upheld the differences among men,
So where these thoughts prevailed, private property was upheld.
The days of the electron fashion the thoughts of the electron,
The identities of electrons suggest collective action,
Bringing new impetus to collectivism.

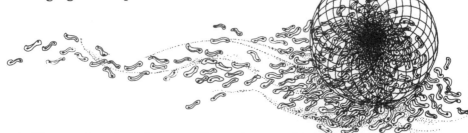

" 'But as chemistry is more than atom or electron,
So My paths leave scope for both the private way and the collective
      way.
If the thoughts of man are to be restricted,
Where is the growth? Where is the advantage?
Who was this Marx to demand one way of thought?
Who was this Hegel to monopolize men's reasonings?
If it be wrong for capitalists to control the wealth of the world,
Is it not worse for the capitalizer to control the thoughts of men?

" 'My hand, yea, My hand shall be against all capitalizers,
My wrath shall be against the mental monopolists,

* In Hebrew this becomes a pun on *adam* and *Adamah*. [man and earth. (See also
Corinthians 15:47, a translation of which appears in Note #1 of "What Christ? What
Peace?") — ED.]

Be they of the paths of Fascism of the right hand
Or the ways of Fascism of the left —
They lead only to dictation, to injustice,
They rob man of the fruits of his inner being;
In Mammon-lands is man robbed of the fruits of labour,
In Marxian-lands is man robbed of the fruits of thought,
In neither nor in both together is salvation found.' "

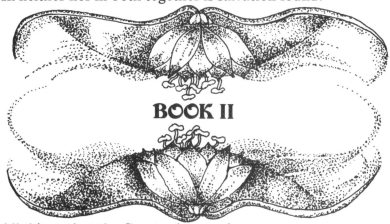

BOOK II

All things that the Creator has made
(And all things that are made come from the Creator)
Are of Aleph or of Mem or of Shin.
From these three come all holy things
Wherefore the Light of Glory is called *Shem.*
The Light of the sky is Shin-Aleph-Mem,
But on earth light is called *or.*
The difference between *Shem* and *or* is this:
That *Shem*, the Light of God, is universal,
Which interpenetrates all things,
From which everything that is has come,
From which Light there is no shadow.
"The sun shall be no more thy light by day,
Neither for brightness shall the moon give light unto thee;
But the Lord shall be unto thee an everlasting Light,

And thy God thy glory.
Thy sun shall no more go down,
Neither shall thy moon withdraw itself;
For the Lord shall be thine everlasting Light,
And the days of thy mourning shall be ended." *

But of *or*, the light of this world, there is shadow,
Or, the light from *rashith*, is of this world,
And the shadow of *or* is *raw*, which is to say, evil.
The Light of *Shem* is in *neshemah*, the soul of man;
The light of *or* is in *ruach*, the spirit of man,
But of *raw* there is not light, it being shadow.
When this shadow is personified it is the Tempter,
And the name of the Tempter may be given as Mephisto.

Now Aleph comes from God and gives rise to Torah and Moses,
And Mem also comes from God though it produces Mammon,
And Shin likewise is of God though its sway be of Marx,
Yet *raw* is not of God but from the evil of man,
Mephisto also arises from the evil mind of man.
Shem may be likened to the sun and *or* to the moon
And *raw* to the darkness of the moon.
When man turns from God he gives sustenance to *raw*.
Or feeds the righteous, but the evil produce *raw*.
There is no shadow in the Eternal, blessed be He,
There is only shadow in man as man turns from the Lord:
When man returns, verily when he returns
He turns and returns to the Light. †
The Eternal, blessed be He, is Light upon Light —

* Isaiah 60:19, 20.
† This is a play upon the Hebraic *shuvo* (Gr. *Metanosis*, Arabic *tauba*, meaning return, repentance, change-about.

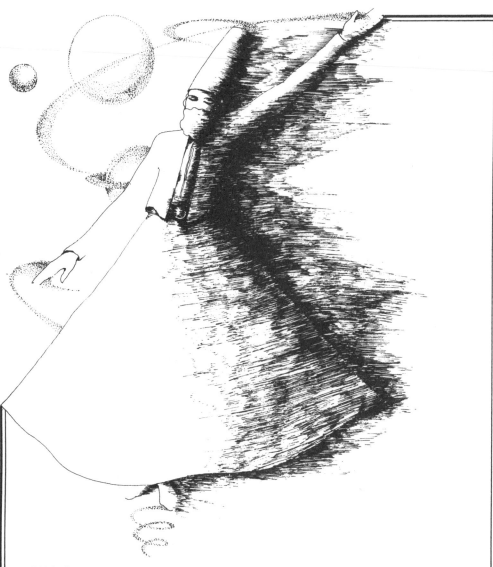

This is the mystery of *Ararat*.
The evil one, the Tempter,
The personification of darkness upon darkness,
Is *tartares*, the opposite of *ararat*, which is Mephisto herein.

Now this Mephisto, seeing the plight of the world,
Whose delight is in plight and not in light,
Beholding the machinations of the men of Shin against the powers
 of Mem,

And the persecutions of the men of Shin by the authorities of Mem,
Concentrated his will upon man, men and weakling,
And in Ashkenazi he found the Nazi,
The weakling lout called *Madman*.
The spirit of Mephisto fed upon this weakling,
And yet Madman's spirit fed upon Mephisto;
Mephisto verily is in all things a vampire,
And his spirit, touching the spirit of the weakling,
Generated in him and in his kind vampirism.
Thus the party of Mephisto was born,
A new party alongside those of Marx and Mammon,
A party which can only stand when that of Moses is not.
Then Madman with his Mephistophelian mania,
Perceiving the struggles between Mem and Shin —
Struggles which arise when the Light of Aleph is dimmed —
Foresaw how to establish the power of Mephisto
And in that, extend his own sway.
For there is a modicum of the Mercy of Moses in Mammon,
And a heritage of the Wisdom of Moses in Marx,
But naught of Moses in Mephisto and Madman.

So Madman addressed the people of Mem:
"People of Mem, my favourites, my loved ones,
The party of Marx are your evil enemies,
Even as they are my most loathsome enemies,
Even as they are enemies of enlightenment and culture.
And the party of Marx is led by the people of Moses;
Let me rid you of the people of Moses,
I shall be freeing the world of the diabolatry of Marx;
The menace of Marx shall be removed
When the people of Moses are no longer in high places.
They plot against the security of the world,

They are enemies of law and equilibrium,
They incite unrest, they produce revolution,
They have caused every great war;
Only uproot them and the world will be in peace;
Ye shall have prosperity evermore."

Furthermore Madman addressed the people of Shin,
He spoke to the people of Shin alternately with the people of Mem:
"People of Shin, the party of Mammon are your vile enemies,
And I, who am your greatest friend, detest the party of Mammon;
They have brought all manner of wretchedness upon the world,
They are the enemies of humanity.
They monopolize wealth and blessings,
They grind the poor down in their poverty —
I, who was born a poor man, know this above all;
I am one of you, I am for you."

Thus did Madman grow and grow and grow,
Thus did Israel wane and wane and wane,
For Madman recognized Moses and opposed him,
But Israel preserved only the name of Moses —
The will to follow him had gone,
*Ruach Hakodesh** had risen from earth;
When, O when would it return?

"Then they that feared the Lord spoke one with another;
And the Lord hearkened, and heard,
And a book of remembrance was written before Him,
For them that feared the Lord, and that thought upon His name.
And they shall be Mine, saith the Lord of hosts,

* Holy Spirit

In the day that I do make, even Mine own treasure,
And I will spare them, as a man spareth
His own son that serveth him.
Then shall ye again discern between the righteous and the wicked,
Between him that serveth God and him that serveth Him not.
For, behold, the day cometh, it burneth as a furnace;
And all the proud, and all that work wickedness, shall be stubble;
And the day that cometh shall set them ablaze, saith the Lord of
    hosts,
That it shall leave them neither root nor branch.
But unto you that fear My name
Shall the sun of righteousness arise with healing in its wings;
And ye shall go forth, and gambol as calves of the stall.
And ye shall tread down the wicked;
For they shall be ashes under the soles of your feet
In the day that I do make, saith the Lord of hosts." *

II.

Then I, Jeremiah the Prophet,
Desiring above all else that *Ruach Hakodesh* descend upon mankind,
Turned and addressed the sons of man, saying:
"The Lord is the Eternal One, blessed be He,
Than Whom is none else,
Whose Mercy and Lovingkindness shall endure forever,
Who is the Redeemer and Who would save."
Today the nations of the world are at war,
Even as it was foretold are they in battle,
And all the lands of earth are being drenched in blood.

* Malachi 3:16-21

50

But fear not, for Mem and Shin have become united,
The ways of the left hand and of the right hand are no more;
Verily this is the first step.
Now unto them should be assimilated Aleph; this is the final step.
To destroy Mammon is not enough:
We must prevent a recurrence,
We must find the ways of peace,
We must return, return, return, O Israel!
The Lord is patient, the Lord awaits;
With the descent of *Ruach Hakodesh* will it come,
With the reincarnation of Talmud Torah in the Holy Land and in
      the world.

"Thus saith the Lord:
'When My Spirit is poured upon all flesh,
When the young really have visions,
When the old actually dream dreams,
When the house of the Oracle is restored,
Then shall come the final day of triumph.
For the Message of the Prophets is for all times,
Not for the ancients alone,
Because it abides in eternity.

" 'Who is this Pharaoh who knows not Joseph?
Not only the Madman of Egypt from whom Moses delivered,
Nor the Madman of Antioch from whom Judas the Hammer
      delivered,
Nor even the Madman of the Ashkenazim —
For I, the Lord, am the Deliverer, the Redeemer,
And in all redemption it is My Spirit, *Ruach Hakodesh* —
When *Ruach* is near there can be no Madman,
When *Ruach* is afar Madman approaches.'

"No peace on earth until there be peace in heaven;
Too often, only too often, has peace been an interval between wars;
Too seldom, only too seldom, has peace been an aim in itself.
What is this peace? Yea, what is this peace?
Is it the period for commercial rivalry,
When great men of wealth hurl their power against one another?
Or is it when capital is aligned against labour
And labour struggles against capital?
Is it peace when the rich rob the poor?
Or is it peace when labour is exploited by its own leaders?
Is it peace when one race is condemned by others,
Only to join its very persecutors in shackling still other peoples?
What is this peace which all would have
But which so many would deny to other men?

"Return ye, return ye unto your Lord!
Return and rejoice, return and be happy
For happy is the man who walks in the way of the Lord. *Selah*.

"What if you destroy Madman and accept the paths of Mammon!
What if you uproot Madman and follow the doctrines of Marx! —
To exclude other doctrines,
To restrict the ways of thought,
To inhibit the free expression of the inner spirit!
If you annihilate this Madman and restore not the teachings
    of Moses,
Pharaoh will come again,
Haman will return,
Antioches Epiphanes will reincarnate,
And Herods will slaughter many babes.
Verily will another Madman come and still another
Till the whole world be doomed.

"Once a Madman sat upon the throne of Israel*
In the very seat of Solomon did this Madman sit,
Who ruled according to wickedness,
Nor did follow in the righteousness of the Lord;
He desecrated the temple,
Even more than the later mad Antioches did he desecrate the temple,
But the wicked priests did not protest —
For unto the priests were powers and privileges granted.
Then did Mephisto reign indeed and Moses was buried,
Moses was deeply buried in the rubbish heap.
Then the Lord, the Holy One, the Eternal, blessed be He,
Seeing the suffering of the holy ones, hearing their cries,
Perceiving the ascent of *Ruach Hakodesh*,
Summoned the King of Babylon, Nebuchadnezzar by name,
And unto the holy city did this Nebuchadnezzar come.
Then what did Israel? What did Israel in time of trouble?
Were many prayers raised to their Lord?
Was there a return to the paths of the Tree of Life?

* See Jeremiah:37-40. This is not the only instance where the kings of Israel fell into this same error. See also Kings I, II — ED.

Verily did the people of Israel accept the madman on the throne,
And hostile were they to the annointed of the Lord.

Then I, Jeremiah the Prophet, spoke in their midst,
And for speaking was I cast into prison,
Into the pit was I thrown.
But the Lord, the Eternal, blessed be He, was with me,
In the darkness His Holy Spirit remained with me.
Then I saw in the days of battle, in the midst of warfare,
The men of Mem oppose the men of Shin,
Even as in latter times the men of Mem opposed the men of Shin.
The men of Mem said:
'Let us turn unto Egypt, the greatest of the powers of Mem,
And the King of Egypt shall deliver us,
And we shall wax prosperous,
Nor fear the King of Babylon, nor any other kings.'
But the men of Shin, being the humbler kind,
Thrown into servitude by the mighty princes of Mem, opposed,
    saying:
'Rather let us turn unto our brethren of Moab;
We were slaves in *Mitzraim*, we are slaves even now —
Workers of Israel, unite, and turn to Moab.'
So fierce was the strife between Moab and *Mitzraim* that Madman
    remained,
Even one Madman after another sat upon the sacred throne of Israel.
And when Madman proved too villainous, to Moses they did not turn;
But the party of the right turned to *Mitzraim*,
And the party of the left looked to Moab,
And I, Jeremiah, was alone as the party of Moses.
Yet the Lord triumphed, verily the Lord did triumph over Madman,
As the Lord will always triumph over Madman.

"Comfort ye, comfort ye, my people,
Return and restore, restore and return,
Assimilate your ways and practices unto God;
Before *Talmud Torah* never can Madman stand,
Though he be of Israel, though he be an Ashkenazi,
Though he be of a nation afar or near.
In the coming day shall many walk to the mountain of the Lord,
And shall journey to the temple of the Mountain,
Those who are near and those who come from afar shall say:
'Come ye, and let us go up to the mountain of the Lord,
To the house of the God of Jacob.' *

"The unity of Israel shall not come by race,
Neither shall it arise from concordance of worship,
But he that sees the Spirit of God shall be known as Israel,
And he that follows the Law of God shall be called Jacob.
There shall be peace in the world when there is peace in Zion,
There shall be peace in Zion when the power of Mammon is no more,
There shall be satisfaction in Zion when the shackles of Marx are
    removed.
Universality is not enough:
Till there is Universality in the mind, in the heart, in the spirit;
For thou shalt love Universality with all thy heart and with all thy
    soul and with all thy might."

"Then I, Jeremiah, beheld a vision,
For the Lord, the Eternal, blessed be He, vouchsafed unto me a
    vision,
Even while I sat in contemplation did this vision come.
There was a vision of Jerusalem anew,

* Isaiah 2:3

55

Not a new Jerusalem of the heavens, but Jerusalem on earth,
Even the self-same Jerusalem that has always been.
In the heart of this Jerusalem was a temple,
And the city of Jerusalem was about this temple,
The streets of Jerusalem led to this temple.
To this temple came all peoples to worship:
The people of Israel on the seventh day,
The people of Ishmael on the sixth day,
The people of Edom on the first day.
'For from the rising of the sun even unto the going down of the same
My name is great among the nations;
And in every place offerings are presented unto My name,
Even pure oblations;
For My name is great among the nations, saith the Lord of hosts.'*
No longer were there fisticuffs in holy places,
No longer did sect strive with sect, cult with cult,
But selected men of Jacob did guard the temple;
No more was there worship except in humility,
Nor were pilgrims robbed,
Nor did innkeepers exploit them,
Nor were pretended relics sold at any price.

"There the exiles of Israel led in humility —
They did not lead in worship,
They did not lead in argument,
They did not lead in ostentation,
In humility alone did they lead, as Moses had before them.
No longer did Ishmael turn upon Israel,
Nor the sons of Edom against one another in holy places,
For the guardian of Israel was the guardian of the temple,

* Malachi 1:11

And the Holy Days of Israel were celebrated in the temple,
And when the temple was not used by the men of Jacob,
The other peoples had access to the holy place,
For the law of the Lord was for Ishmael and Edom.
The teachings of the Lord were for Israel and Jacob.

"Then verily was there brotherhood in the Land of Promise:
They that kept the Sabbath Day in holiness,
Kept also the Sabbath Year in remembrance;
They did not divide the Sabbath of the Lord
From the Sabbath of the Lord, to call it religion,
They did not uphold institutions of usury and debt in sacred places,
And in the seven times seventh year was the land divided anew,
In the fiftieth year was the Jubilee proclaimed. *Selah*!

"Then I, Jeremiah the Prophet, looked again:
This time I looked beyond the Land of Promise,
This time I beheld the nations near and far,
This time my vision encompassed the whole world
And behold! the Law came not merely from Jerusalem unto Minsk,
It came from Jerusalem even over the entire globe,
Over all the earth was the Law broadcast,
For the Law was Aleph
And the Light of the Law is *Shem*
IN WHICH NO SHADOW ABIDES.

"I beheld the cities of refuge restored,
For every sacred city had become a city of refuge,
A city for the disheartened, for the persecuted,
For the downtrodden, for the uprooted
As the ancient Torah proclaimed, as the Eternal Torah holds —
In Edom, in Cush, In Ishmael, in all places,
Cities of Aleph in which Mem did not predominate,
Cities of Aleph in which the restrictions of Shin did not prevail,
And there was peace on earth, verily was there peace on earth.
HALLELUJAH!"

Samuel L. Lewis
ca. 1938

Love and love,

Samuel L. Lewis

58

Glossary

Abraham — (Hebrew) 'Master (or Father) of heart qualities' (*raham*), which include virtue and mercy and love. The great Patriarch and Prophet who brought the message of One God to the people of his time. He was the father of three great world religions. For it is from his descendants, who were called *B'nai Israel*, that came Judaism, Christianity and Islam. In the light of his spiritual realization, God revealed to him the keys to universal life. This revelation was recorded in the *Sepher Yetzirah* which still survives today.

Adam — (Hebrew) 'He-of-blood' or 'he-of-Heart Essence'. Mankind or universal humanity, both male and female, endowed with the Divine Essence, i.e., created in God's image.

adamah — (Hebrew) 'ground' or 'substance'. As the feminine form of *adam*, *adamah* refers to matter as the groundwork of creation. In Genesis it is related that *adam* ('mankind') was formed out of the 'dust of the *adamah*', or 'through the refinement of matter'.

Aleph — (Hebrew) 'A'. The first letter of the Hebrew alphabet. In the *Sepher Yetzirah* Aleph represents one of the three primary principles (mothers) which are the foundation of all things; "from these have proceeded all things that are in the world." As the first and primordial principle, it reconciles and unifies the natural polarity of the other two.

Ancient of Days — Before the creation of the world, God is. He presides over the course of history. This expression first appears in the vision of the Prophet Daniel.

Antioches Epiphanes — King of the Seleucid dynasty which controlled Israel during the second century B.C. In an attempt to force Hellenistic culture on the Jews of his time, he sacked Jerusalem, desecrated the Temple, forcing the Jews to worship

Zeus, and forbade all religious observances ordained by Mosaic law.

Ararat — (Hebrew) 'light upon light'. The 'heights' of *ararat*, usually translated 'Mt. Ararat', are where Noah's 'ark' came to rest after the Flood. Its most ancient translation is 'orbit of luminous effluence', describing an exalted state of consciousness. "All the religions speak of the mountain as representing higher stages of consciousness, and that God attainment may be likened to existence at the summit of the highest mountain." (S.L.L.) [See THEBES in the "Saladin" Glossary for an explanation of the 'ark'.]

Ashkenazi — (Hebrew) 'latent fire'. Germany or a German. The *Ashkenazim* are the descendants of Ashkenaz, great grandson of Noah, who as a people settled in an area later known as Germany. In rabbinic literature of the Middle Ages 'Ashkenaz' is used merely to refer to Germany, whereas 'Sepharad' literally refers to Spain. Since then Jews have been categorized according to their origin into Ashkenazim (from Middle and Northern Europe) and Sephardim (from Southern Europe and the Middle East).

atom — [See ELECTRON]

Cain, mark of — The mark which God placed on Cain when he was sent into exile for slaying his brother Abel. This phrase has come to mean a mark of chastisement or exclusion.

cities of refuge — Six cities assigned by Moses to the Levites or priests of Israel to serve as places of sanctuary. They were governed by a High Priest and granted shelter and fair trial to the manslayer. "For the children of Israel, and for the stranger and for the settler among them, shall these six cities be for refuge." (Num.35:15) More generally, the cities of refuge represent an asylum for the hunted and oppressed, a place where shelter is given and violence prohibited. In the vision of the poet we see cities where one can go and take refuge entirely in surrender to God.

Covenant — (from the Hebrew *berit*, 'cutting', referring to the ancient manner of sealing an agreement by cutting it into the skin of the contracting parties) In the Old Testament, or Book of the Covenant, there are numerous instances of the Covenant between God and man. Its deepest significance can be felt when God tells

60

the Prophet Jeremiah, "I will put My law in their inward parts, and in their heart will I write it." Jer.31:33 M.T.) The Covenant is an act of Grace by which God offers His blessing to man, a blessing which can only be realized when God's will becomes man's will and man's actions reflect God's laws. For "the word . . . came . . . from the Lord, saying, Hear ye the words of this Covenant. . . . Obey My voice, and do them, according to all which I command you: so shall ye be my people, and I will be your God." (Jer.11:1-4 A.V.)

Cush — (Hebrew) 'Black'. Ancient Ethiopa, the territory to the south of Egypt which was settled by the descendants of Cush, grandson of Noah and brother of Mitzraim (ancestor of the Egyptians).

Day of the Lord — This is a metaphor used by the Prophets, particularly Malachi, to refer to the ultimate victory of the Divine Will in human history. The Day of Judgement or Day of Resurrection is seen by them to be enacted on earth as well as in heaven.

Edom — (Hebrew) 'Red'. The ancient country between Israel and Arabia, south of the Dead Sea. It was settled by the descendants of Esau, twin brother of Jacob. The struggle between Jacob and Esau in their mother's womb (Gen.25:22) foreshadowed subsequent relations between their descendants, the Edomites (sons of Esau) and Israelites (sons of Jacob). In time, because of its sympathies with Christian Rome, Edom became synonymous with Christianity.

electron — That part of the atom which orbits the nucleus and by which bonds between atoms are formed. Electrons are lightweight, electrical, flashing, light-forming, bonding together in collectives. They create electricity by mass movement and release light by changing orbit. The view held by Democritus and Dalton that atoms were discrete and indivisible particles was broken by the discovery of the electron. It was discovered that the differences between atoms is purely a numerical one, consisting in the varying numbers of their component parts. Thus the concept of discrete and separate ego selves is shattered to reveal the common underlying identity of all beings. In the poem this change from the point of view of the atom to that of the electron is seen as a psychological change on the part of mankind. It marks the transition from, for example, the idea of the salvation of the individual soul, to the point of view of the mystic who sees his identity with all mankind.

Fascism — A dictatorial government.

Hallelujah! — (Hebrew) 'Praise be to God!'

Haman — Chief minister of Ahasuerus, King of Persia. His plot to destroy all the Jews in the kingdom was foiled by Queen Esther, the Jewish wife of Ahasuerus. He was hanged on the same gallows which he had erected for Esther's uncle. His defeat is celebrated in the Jewish festival of Purim.

Hegel — German philosopher (1770-1831) who presented a dialectical view of history structured in terms of the triad:thesis, antithesis, synthesis. This philosophical system was used by Karl Marx to support his theory of the inevitability of communism as the outcome of political history. Murshid once asked the question, "What is the antithesis to Hegel's theory?"

Herods — Members of a royal dynasty of Israel which originated in Edom after it had been forced to adopt the Jewish religion. They ruled in Israel as vassals of the Roman Empire. By the order of the Edomite, Herod "the Great," all male children up to the age of two were slaughtered in Bethlehem. By this act he hoped to prevent the fulfillment of the prophecy that a child born in Bethlehem would become King of the Jews.

Holy Land — Traditionally, the terrain of Palestine chronicled in the Old Testament. The tradition of mystical Judaism is that the holiness of God is to be found even in the physical land. In the Old Testament, land or a particular place was considered holy when it was consecrated to the worship of God, for "the earth is the Lord's and the fulness thereof." (Ps.24:1) In keeping with its original meanings, therefore, the Holy Land is wherever people live in the Presence of God and fulfill the Divine Covenant.

Internationale — The anthem of the International Socialist Revolution. "Arise, you prisoners of starvation! Arise, you wretched of the earth. For justice thunders condemnation, a better world's in birth. No more tradition's chain shall bind us; Arise, you slaves, no more in thrall. The earth shall rise on new foundations. We have been naught; we shall be all."

Ishmael — (Hebrew) 'God hears'. The son of Abraham by Hagar, his Egyptian maidservant. God promised Abraham that He would make of this, his first-born son "a great nation." (Gen.17:20) His descendants, the Ishmaelites, peopled the north and west of the Arabian peninsula and eventually formed the chief element of the Arab nation and, later, of the Muslim community.

Israel — (Hebrew) 'Ruling with God' or 'God rules'. Jacob received the name Israel when, after wrestling all night with a 'man', he insisted upon being blessed by him before letting him go. "And he said, 'Thy name shall be called no more Jacob, but Israel:for thou hast striven with God and with men, and hast prevailed.' " At this point Jacob realizes the true identity of this being which he feared: " 'for I have seen God face to face, and my life is preserved.' " (Gen.32:29-31 M.T.) Israel is Jacob reborn. The name was given to him after Jacob had faced all sorts of adverse situations and overcame them all by finding God's blessing in each one. Jacob, now Israel, went on to become the third Patriarch of the Hebrew people, who became known collectively as *B'nai Yisrael*, or the 'Children of Israel'. The term Israel is used in the poem both to refer to the Jewish people as descendants of Jacob-Israel and, in a more universal sense, to all people who have had the vision of God and the realization that He is everywhere present.

Jacob — (Hebrew) 'Supplanter'. Twin brother of Esau and father of the nation of Israel. In a subterfuge planned by his mother, Jacob disguised himself as Esau, the first-born of the twin brothers. In this way he obtained the parental blessing and succeeded his father as Patriarch of the Hebrew people. His twelve sons were the progenitors and heads of the Twelve Tribes of Israel.

Jeremiah — (Hebrew) 'Whom God has appointed'. A Hebrew Prophet who appeared before Jerusalem at the time of its downfall and strove to revivify the spiritual life of his people. He repeatedly warned the nation of Israel of the impending fall of Jerusalem and the destruction of the temple, but he was met with enmity and persecution. He lived to see his prophecies fulfilled when Jerusalem fell to the Babylonian king, Nebuchadnezzar. Thus began the long period of Jewish exile in Babylonia. Jeremiah called for peace at a time when nations prepared for war, for inner sincerity when priests were enforcing orthodox codes. He prophesied the coming of a "Day of the Lord" and the establishment thereafter of the Kingdom of God on earth. It is in the voice of Jeremiah that the poet speaks.

Jerusalem anew — The Kingdom of God on earth. The Jerusalem described in the poem after the fulfillment of the prophecies of Isaiah, Jeremiah and Malachi.

Joseph — (Hebrew) 'May God increase'. The elder of the two sons Jacob had by his second wife Rachel. Joseph was known for his beauty and wisdom. He was sold as a slave by his brothers and brought to Egypt, where he ultimately prospered and became the chief administrator of the kingdom and the head of the Egyptian mysteries. During a time of famine in Israel, the Jews came to him in Egypt where they flourished until a new family of Pharaohs "who knew not Joseph" came into power.

Jubilee — (from the Hebrew *yobhel*, 'ram's horn' which was blown in proclamation of the Jubilee) "According to the Mosaic law, not only was the Sabbath day holy, but also the seventh year; and the seven times seventh year was the Jubilee. All debts were forgiven and all land became once again the common property of all. The Jubilee was an integral part of the religion of Moses. It inculcated joy, restoration, release. The whole institution of the Jubilee emphasized the evanescence of the herenow." (S.L.L.)

Judas the Hammer — (a translation of the Hebrew *makabah*, 'hammer' from which the name of his tribe, the Maccabees, is said to have derived) Judas Maccabaeus led a brotherhood of Jews in a revolt against the religious tyranny of Antioches Epiphanes. He succeeded in entering Jerusalem and purifying and restoring the temple which had been desecrated by idol worship and heathen sacrifices. Another derivation of the name Maccabees is that it was formed from the combination of the initial letters of the Hebrew phrase which they used as their slogan:"*Mee Kamocha Ba-Eleem YHVH?*" or 'Who, among the gods, is like unto Thee, oh God ('who is, who was, and who will be')?' The Jewish holiday of *Chanukah*, the festival of lights, celebrates the restitution of the temple to purity.

Land of Promise — The land of Canaan, later known as Israel, which was promised by God to Abraham and his descendants in the Covenant. "He hath remembered His Covenant forever, the word which He commanded to a thousand generations: the Covenant which He made with Abraham, and His oath unto Isaac; and He established it unto Jacob for a statute, to Israel for an everlasting Covenant; saying, 'Unto thee will I give the land of Canaan, the lot of your inheritance." (Ps.1058-11 M.T.) This land, described as "a land flowing with milk and honey," is by extension the purified heart, filled with mercy and compassion.

ma — (Hebrew) 'what'. The substance of creation; in man, the physical body as the accomodation for the spirit or life-force. In Jewish mysticism, this term corresponds to the *Shakti* and *Prakriti* of Hindu philosophy.

Madman of Antioch — [See ANTIOCHES EPIPHANES]

Madman of Egypt — [See PHARAOH]

Madman of the Ashkenazim — Hitler.

Mammon — (Aramaic) 'Riches'. Usually used to denote material wealth when personified as an object of worship; there is, however, as expressed in the poem "a modicum of the mercy of Moses in Mammon," e.g., generosity, charity.

Marx — A German philosopher and political economist (1818-1883) of Jewish parentage. He formulated a system of thought which gives class struggle a primary role in leading society from bourgeois control to a socialist society and ultimately to communism and the victory of the working class. He founded the International Socialist Movement which belittled Christian socialism and other messianic beliefs then current. The "heritage of the wisdom of Moses in Marx," which is referred to in the poem, may be seen in Marxism's remarkably messianic structure. "The materialist didactic that governs historical development corresponds in the Marxist scheme to God, the proletariat to the 'elect', the communist party to the church, the revolution to the Second Coming, and the communist commonwealth to the millenium." (Bertrand Russell)

Materialist — A philosophical idea advocated by Marx which states that physical matter is the only reality and that consciousness arises from the interactions of matter.

Mem — (Hebrew) 'M'. One of the three mother-letters of the Hebrew tongue which represent the sounds by which heaven and earth were made, according to the *Sepher Yetsirah*. In its natural expression, it is the medium of the bounty and mercy of God, "the blessings of heaven through water." [See MOTHER-LETTERS]

Mephisto — (from the Hebrew *mephitz*, 'destroyer', and *tophel*, 'liar')

The personification of evil. It arises from and feeds upon the contractive and isolating tendency in the ego of man.

mi — (Hebrew) 'who'. The life-force of creation; in man, the spirit or life-breath which vitalizes the body. In Jewish mysticism, this term corresponds to the *Shiva* and *Purusha* of Hindu philosophy. "It is the interaction between *Shiva* and *Shakti*, between *Mi* and *Ma*, which accounts for all of life." (S.L.L.)

Minsk — A city in present day U.S.S.R. which was once an important center of Jewish learning. The real Jewish tradition, which has been hidden, is that when the Messiah comes, the Holy Land would extend from Jerusalem even unto Minsk (Minsk representing the furthest city of Jewish dispersion). In the vision which concludes this poem, the Holy Land is seen as extending throughout the entire world.

Mitzraim — (Hebrew) 'Subduing, compressing power'. Ancient Egypt, the territory settled by the descendants of Mitzraim, grandson of Noah and brother of Cush (ancestor of the Ethiopians).

Moab — The ancient country to the southeast of Israel, which was settled by the descendants of Moab, son of Lot (thus blood relations of Israel). Moab's political relations with Israel were strained and marked by frequent border warfare. In the time of Jeremiah, Moab was conquered by Babylon, the empire which struggled against Egypt for supremacy in the East. Israel, which was geographically situated between these two nations, became a focal point of international dispute.

Moses — (from the Hebrew *moshe*, 'water-born') "The most shining Prophet of the Old Testament, he gave to the world the divine law." (Hazrat Inayat Khan) As an infant he was placed in a cradle by Hebrew mother and set in the Nile where he was found and adopted by the Pharaoh's daughter. By this act his mother saved his life from the Pharaoh's edict that all male Hebrew babies be killed. Called upon by God to deliver his people from their bondage in Egypt, he led them on a 40-year trek through the desert and ultimately to Canaan, the land promised by God to Abraham and his seed. It is at this point that we meet him in the poem.

mother-letters — Aleph, Mem and Shin, according to the *Sepher Yetzirah*, are the three mother-letters of the Hebrew alphabet, the sounds by which God created the heavens and the earth. From them proceed Air, Water and Fire respectively, the three primordial elements which underlie all existence. "Water [Mem] is silent, Fire [Shin] is sibilant, and Air [Aleph] derived from the Spirit is as the tongue of a balance standing between these contraries which are in equilibrium, reconciling and mediating between them." (*Sepher Yetzirah*)

Nebuchadnezzar — The Babylonian king by whom Israel was conquered and led into 70 years' captivity. The Prophet Jeremiah warned the people of Israel that unless they returned to God they would be punished through Nebuchadnezzar as the instrument of God's judgment. During his siege of Jerusalem (587 B.C.) the temple of Solomon was destroyed and 50,000 Jews were forced into exile.

neshemah (or *neshamah*) — (Hebrew) 'exalted life essence', sometimes translated as 'breath'. The divine spark in man, the 'breath of life' which God breathed into Adam's nostrils, making him a living soul. (Gen.2:7) "Only in man is what is called in the Bible, *neshamah*, that is, the exaltation of consciousness through the expansive movement of the breath and heart. This has been called 'spirit' and is called *ruh* by the Arabs and Sufis and *ruach* by the Hebrews. This latter may be termed soul, which arises from the individuation of Divine Spirit; but *neshamah* is that expansive movement which leads to Cosmic realization in the Supreme, Exalted Spirit [*Shem*]." (S.L.L.) Therefore in the poem when *ruach* is referred to as the spirit of man, this means the individuation of Divine Spirit which is often termed 'soul'; and when *neshemah* is referred to as the soul of man this means that the non-individuated Supreme, Exalted Spirit, or *Shem*, is the essence of man's soul, and it is in virtue of this that man is said to have been created in God's Image. The Christian teachings, given by St. Paul in First Corinthians, that man has three bodies, the physical, subtle, and spiritual, is an exact parallel of the Hebrew teaching of the three gradations of soul, *nephesh, ruach*, and *neshemah*. [For a parallel discussion of the 'soul' or 'ego' from the standpoint of Sufi metaphysics and its connection with breath, see NAFS in the "Saladin" Glossary. For a distinction of the three-body constitution of man according to St. Paul, see *This is the New Age, in Person* by Samuel L. Lewis (Tucson, Arizona: Omen Press, 1972).]

or — (Hebrew) 'light'. As used in the poem, this light is the light of the created world, as distinct from the eternal Light of *Shem*, which has no beginning and no end.

Oracle, house of — The place where God reveals His Will. During the time of Solomon's temple, the Oracle or Holy of Holies was the innermost sanctuary within the temple; it was considered the physical accomodation or abode of God. The message of the Prophets was that this 'place' is in the heart of man. "The word for a 'female' in Hebrew means a receptive or negative person. This receptiveness was once used in the mysteries of religion where women served as Oracles and Priestesses. Even among the Hebrews one of the first Judges was Deborah. . . . And many Hebrew prayer books to this day have a prayer for the restoration of the Oracle, but nothing is done about it nor can anything be done about it until woman takes her place beside man. Not above him, not partner or superior in masculine pursuits, but in the fulfillment of feminine pursuits." (S.L.L.)

Pharaoh — (Hebrew form of Ancient Egyptian *per-o*, 'the great house') Honorary title of the kings of Ancient Egypt. When the Jews first arrived in Egypt they enjoyed a privileged position under their patriarch Joseph, who had became the Pharaoh's chief administrator. Later, "the Pharaoh who knew not Joseph" became the first in a line of kings who enslaved and persecuted the Israelite people. This period of slavery came to an end when Moses delivered them from their bondage in Egypt. By extension, the term Pharaoh refers to any cruel and unjust ruler.

Prophet — (from the Greek *prophetes*, 'to speak for') One who speaks for God, or one through whom God speaks to man. "When your heart is open, you receive from God and speak to men. . . . And you speak from a spiritual or cosmic point of view rather than from an individual point of view." (S.L.L.) The Hebrew Prophets were the conscience of the people; in the face of powerful priests and erring multitudes they spoke with one purpose:to teach man "to do justly, and to love mercy, and to walk humbly with thy God." (Mic.68) This account of receiving the prophetic initiation is given in Isaiah 6:6: "Then flew unto me one of the seraphim, with a glowing stone in his hand, which he had taken with the tongs from off the altar; and he touched my mouth with it, and said: 'Lo, this hath touched thy lips; and thine iniquity is taken away, and thy sin expiated.' And I heard the voice of the Lord, saying: 'Whom shall I send, and who will go for us?' Then I said: 'Here am I; send me.' And He said: 'Go, and tell this people. . .'"

psalms — Lyrical songs in praise of God, usually sung to the accompaniment of stringed instruments.

rashith — (Hebrew) 'beginning' or 'creation', as used in the poem. The first word in the Old Testament in Hebrew is *Berashith*, usually translated 'In the beginning'. Its figurative meaning, as given by Fabre D'Olivet, is 'At first in principle' or 'not yet in action but in power'. Thus the first chapter in Genesis describes the execution of the plan.

raw — (Hebrew) 'evil'. (According to Fabre D'Olivet this Hebrew word is formed from roots signifying a turning in, establishing a false center of consciousness.)

1. Two are the mirrors before the soul: the mirror of perfection and the mirror of incompleteness or imperfection.

2. Wonderful is the mirror of perfection. It is filled with light. It is filled with love. It pours blessing upon every supplicant. It answers prayers. It returns with added enjoyment. It brings growth and power and inspiration.

3. Wonderful, too, is the mirror of incompleteness, although in a different manner. For he who looks into this mirror has the light behind him. He stands before the mirror and his shadow is cast upon the shining black mirror thereof. Therefore when he gazes into this mirror he beholds the faults of whomsoever his thought entertains. By it he gains the gift of analysis and the faculty of discrimination. By it, too, he sees faults clearly. Yet he is unaware that the perception of faults depends upon the completeness of his own shadow.

from "Salome"
by Murshid Samuel L. Lewis

ruach — [See NESHEMAH]

Ruach Hakodesh — (Hebrew) 'Holy Spirit'. According to the Old Testament, the medium of Divine Sustenance and Blessing. "This is nothing but the Divine Breath, the Holy Spirit which unites and connects all planes of existence. . . . Once the Divine Breath enters the nostrils, it illuminates the atmosphere of a person, and so long as it continues there is no ego-consciousness. However, the moment attention is drawn from God to anything whatever, that hides the light in the consciousness and so makes accommodation for ego. . . . We find in the Hebrew Kabbalah that the Holy Spirit descends whenever the world is in need. It is not the manifestation nor communication from particular spirits or angels, but a whole complete process so that the Will of God can be known to man, especially when man is in need." (S.L.L.) "Behold, Thou desirest truth in the inward parts; make me, therefore, to know wisdom in mine innermost heart. . . . Create me a clean heart, O God; and renew a steadfast spirit within me. Cast me not away from Thy presence; and take not Thy Holy Spirit from me. Restore unto me the joy of Thy salvation; and let a willing spirit uphold me. . . . The sacrifices of God are a broken spirit; a broken and a contrite heart, O God, Thou wilt not despise." (Ps.51:8-19 M.T.)

Sabbath — (from the Hebrew *shabbat*. Usually translated 'day of rest', it has several root meanings: 'seventh', signifying 'fullness', 'completion', 'perfection'; 'to rest', 'to cease from outer activity'; 'the returning', i.e., to Divine Unity) Consistent with its literal meanings, therefore, the Sabbath is a time of rest in which one turns from worldly considerations to the All-in-all. The institution of the Hebrew Sabbath began with God's Commandment to Moses and his people, "to remember the Sabbath day, to keep it holy." The consecration of the seventh day refers back to the second chapter of Genesis, where it is related that "God blessed the seventh day and sanctified it: because that in it He had rested from all His work . . . " The observation of the Hebrew Sabbath was to be an eternal sign of their Covenant with God, "that they might know that I am the Lord that sanctifies them." (Ezek.20:12 M.T.) The early Christians celecrated the Hebrew Sabbath, but the first day of the week, the "Lord's Day" gradually took its place, as the celebration of the day in which Christ was resurrected. Mohammed chose the sixth day as the Muslim holy day of the week, a day in which the community assembles for united prayer.

Sabbath Year — The Sabbath was a keynote to a scale of Sabbatical observances among the Hebrew people — the seventh day, the seventh month, the seventh year, and the year of the Jubilee were all consecrated under Mosaic law. The seventh or Sabbatical Year was one in which all debts were to be cancelled and all farmlands were to rest uncultivated. During this year the spontaneous produce of these lands was free to all, especially the poor. [See JUBILEE]

Selah — (Hebrew) 'Forever'. A musical direction in the Psalms, signifying 'lift up your voices.

Sepher Yetzirah — (Hebrew) 'Book of Formation' or the 'Scroll of Ultimate Foundations'. Ancient Hebrew text, the oldest known of the books which comprise the core of Hebrew mysticism (Kabbalah). It reveals the origin and order of the universe, how heaven and earth were created and are sustained by the power of sound, represented by the letters of the Hebrew alphabet, and how this revelation was granted by God to Abraham. It presents every form of existence as an emanation of God, Who is in everything and everything is in Him.

Shem — (Hebrew) 'Living Light', 'Glory'. "The *Shem* of the Hebrews is hardly described by our limited word 'name'. It means that renown which has come to one because of his absorption of living-light. . . . It indicates the Divine Energy. . . . And it is the coming into consciousness of this living-light which makes for spiritual and holy brotherhood . . . It is the radiating, life-giving, non-self-centered continuous energy endowed with all qualities which operate as if from an infinite source to finite ends."(S.L.L.) *Shem* may also be understood as the Divine Light in man's soul (neSHEMah).

Shin — (Hebrew) 'sh'. One of the three mother-letters of the Hebrew tongue which represent the principles by which heaven and earth were made, according to the *Sepher Yetzirah*. In its natural expression, it is the medium of the strength and temperance of God, the burning away of all impurities.

Solomon — (from the Hebrew *Shelomoh*, 'Peaceful one') The youngest son of David and his chosen successor as King of Israel. He executed the construction of the first temple in Jerusalem which served as the central place of worship for the whole Hebrew nation. He "succeeded in preaching and teaching monotheism to Israel. . . . that the same God was over all, in all and through all." (S.L.L.)

son of man — A common term in the Old Testament, denoting simply a human being. This phrase finds it fullest expression when, in the vision of the Prophet Daniel, it is revealed that "one, like the son of man" can inherit the Kingdom of God. "When the Bible speaks of 'the son of God', and the 'son of man', it means that he is a son of God who has recognized the eternal spirit as his parent and that he is a son of man who has recognized himself as the son of his parents who are as limited as he. We recognize our father and mother as our origin. The parents claim the child as their own and so delude themselves. Its origin is universal spirit; and in this we are all brothers and sisters, without distinction of high or low, of race or caste, of creed or religion." (Hazrat Inayat Khan)

Talmud Torah — (Hebrew) 'Study of the Torah' which, according to Jewish tradition, excels all things.

tartares — (the Greek translation of the Hebrew *sheol*, 'abyss') The place to which the dead go before they are lifted up, a dark netherworld. It is almost the reverse in spelling as well as in meaning of the Hebrew word *ararat*.

temple — It was David who first proposed to replace the moveable tabernacle with a permanent structure, and this was accomplished by his son Solomon with the construction of the first temple in Jerusalem. According to biblical tradition, it was the chosen dwelling place of the *shekinah*, the Divine Presence. This temple was destroyed by Nebuchadnezzar. But the prophetic vision presented in the poem of a temple in Jerusalem to which all peoples come to worship represents the fulfillment of God's will: "For My house shall be called a house of prayer for all peoples (Isa.56:7 M.T.)

Torah, Holy — (*Torah* is Hebrew for 'Teaching', 'Law') The revealed teachings of God through his Prophet Moses, included in the Pentateuch, or Five Books of Moses, the first five books of the Old Testament. In its broader meaning, *Torah* refers to a law or precept directly embodying Divine instruction or revelation.

Tree of Life — According to the *Sepher Yetzirah*, the Tree of Life is the whole universe, the miniature of which is one's own self. It is depicted like a map of creation, showing the paths by which God created the universe; these same paths show man the way of return to the Divine Unity.

Yeshimon — (Hebrew) 'desolate waste'. One of four Hebrew words occurring in the Old Testament which have all been translated into English as 'desert'. This particular word is applied to the wilderness of the Sinai and Negev deserts through which the Israelites traveled in their exodus from Egypt to the Promised Land. Their 40-year period in this area was marked by their joining in the worship of idols at the cult center of Peor; but it culminated in the revelation given to Moses on Mount Sinai.

Zion — (Hebrew) 'Fortress' or 'refuge'. One of the hills on which Jerusalem was built. Originally a Jebusite fortress which David captured, Mount Zion became sacred after he brought the Tabernacle there, containing the Ark of the Covenant and the tablets on which the Ten Commandments were engraved. When Solomon built the temple on the nearby Mount Moriah, he had the Ark transferred, and the name Zion was extended to include the temple and the temple mount. Zion is frequently used to refer to the whole of Jerusalem, the holy city, as well as to the people of Jerusalem as a whole, whose destiny, it is written, is in the hand of God. (Ps.97:8; Isa.1:27, 37:5) In some passages, Zion becomes the equivalent of the heavenly Jerusalem, as in Isaiah 60:14: "And they shall call thee the city of the Lord, the Zion of the Holy One of Israel." Thus in the Bible, Zion is always associated with the in-dwelling Presence of God. Political 'Zionism', however, has concentrated more on geography and race than on God. Thus it cannot be considered Zionism in the Biblical sense.

What Christ? What Peace?

Introduction

"What Christ? What Peace?", like its predecessor, "The Day of the Lord Cometh", was written during the Second World War. Once again, we are given a perspective on the world struggle which far transcends the events of that time. For in 1942, during one of the darkest times of the war, Murshid, speaking throughout in the voice of Christ, addresses himself to the problems facing the people of the world after the war has been won. Similarly, the theme of the spiritual hierarchy returns as in the previous poem. We hear Christ telling us,

> "And now the world must face its Armageddon.
> But he who holds the standard which I raised,
> Even though he be a minority of one,
> Finding another one who is like himself,
> Can save the world — they and Me together;
> For even a few so gathered in My name,
> Can bring about the greatest of miracles,
> That is, if I be really Lord of Heaven,
> That is, if I am an example to the world."

The tone of this poem, which asks the nations of the world the question, "What Christ? What Peace?" is challenging to the very core. It takes as its basis not a verbal Christ but the example of Christ himself. And if one faces the issues confronting the world from the standpoint of the actual teachings of Christ, one is forced to ask some uncomfortable questions. These questions are raised with great depth and power in the course of the poem: *Is* the earth the Lord's and the fullness thereof? *Is* it more blessed to give than to receive? *Will* you forgive the debts of those who owe you, as mentioned in the Lord's Prayer? *Will* you love your neighbors as yourselves?

In his unpublished book *The Bestowal of Blessing*, Murshid puts it this way:

The words of Jesus Christ have not always been understood by the discriminating mind of the generality. The words are simple yet in their depths most profound. The Christian Scriptures themselves say, "Put ye on the mind of Jesus," which is to say, 'get into the *buddhi*'. *By the mind of Jesus only can the words of Jesus be fully comprehended.*

And what was and is that spirit which was in Christ Jesus? What is this mind of Jesus? It is to seek perfection, to seek God, to rise above limitation unto the unlimited. Even all morals, all principles, all doctrines, all distinctions shall go and only *baraka* [blessing] remain.

As Christ says, "I am the vine and ye are the branches thereof." Thus we are all parts of each other. And it is not enough to believe in a hypothetical brotherhood of man. So Christ, speaking in this poem, tells his would-be worshippers such things as, "Look not to Me upon the cross, Look to the Hospitals filled with the lame. . ." He denies the claims to authority of any that would use Him to speak for a vested interest. To quote from a lecture of Murshid's that he gave on First Corinthians, "My poem that Christ gave to me, He made it very clear. He was not of the left nor the right nor the center, and He was not against any of them . . . because they belong to Him, not He to them. They are wrong when they claim He is on their side; He is on all sides, and all sides are on Him. God made all mankind in His image, All. And while ethically there may be a right and a wrong, spiritually this has nothing to do with it. As long as we have breath and as long as we have blood, we give evidence of the spirit which is in us, no matter what ideas we may have or what our behavior may be. 'Though our sins be red as scarlet, they can be made white as snow.' This is the difference between ethics and philosophy on the one hand, and spirituality on the other. As long as we are *alive* we have spirituality in us."

This theme of God making mankind in His image is developed in "What Christ? What Peace?" as a profound system of Yoga. Saint Paul has said, "Know ye not that your body is the temple of the Holy Spirit which is in you which you have of God, and you are not your own?" This yoga system is based on the spirit, or breath, and on the circulation of the blood with every heartbeat. As Murshid says, "I have told in my poem, Christ is the purified blood in our body and Adam is the unpurified blood in our body. By one we live and by one we die with every breath, every pulsation in our whole life. The outward pulse, Adam, the inward, Christ — every heartbeat — Adam, Christ, Adam, Christ, pollution, purification, going on perpetually." This yoga takes into account the actual teachings of both Hebrew and Christian mysticism — that the Holy Spirit is in truth the Divine Breath. So, when Christ says in the Beatitudes, "Blessed are the poor in spirit," he is actually giving an instruction to those who have ears to hear: to make the breath gentle and refined.

This practice of looking deeply into the Holy Scriptures is one which characterizes Murshid's life and work. He often complained, however, about mistranslations of the Bible which came about as a result of the translators not having had the experiences which were being described in the text. This is a subject into which he goes in great detail in his lectures on First Corinthians, where he points out many ambivalent and even contradictory translations of terms. In the case of the quotes from the Beatitudes which appear within the text and the quotation from Frist Corinthians which appears in the footnote,

Murshid's own translations are used. The First Corinthians translation is taken directly from the Greek text, which has been mistranslated in *The New Kingdom Interlinear Translation of the Greek Scriptures*. The quotation from the Epistle of John which appears in the text is from this latter source. Murshid describes his point of view on the Bible when he says, "The whole teaching I was given is this: the Bible is the unfoldment of your own being. It is. It isn't what you believe; it's what you become. Jesus didn't get up and say, 'I believe'; he said, 'You shall be transformed.' 'You shall be born anew.' " And this is possible with every breath.

Murshid understood Christ's words, "A new commandment I give unto you, That ye love one another, as I have loved you," to involve taking the suffering of humanity as one's own. The words of the risen Christ, "Feed my lambs, feed my sheep" prompted him to undertake the solution of world food problems. And he said that it was the manifestation of Christ which brought to him the original message and plan for peace in the Holy Land. He relates that when he presented this plan to Gunnar Jarring many years ago, Jarring's response was that it was the best plan he'd ever heard. Murshid said he didn't dare tell him that it came directly from Jesus Christ. While this plan was never given any consideration by the competing factions in Palestine, he took to heart the phrase, "Every valley shall be exalted and every hill laid low." And thus the machinations of power politics could not in the long run interfere with the ultimate vision of peace.

Returning specifically to the poem before us, one notes the interesting prediction concerning the controversy over the prayer which would be said at the meeting of all the victorious nations at the conclusion of the war. It points out how the seeds of Hitlerism would remain, predominantly in their own inability to agree to anything transcending their own limited national aims. An irony of history was that this meeting and this argument over the prayer actually took place a number of years later in Murshid's home town of San Francisco at the Organizational Meeting of the United Nations.

In this poem one meets a Christ who has not been emasculated by the various divisive groups purporting to act in His name, a Christ who is not interested in the abrogation of His teachings in the name of something called Christianity.

In *The Bestowal of Blessing* we find the following description of this problem:

Jesus has been made the authority for the way of passivism, quietism, asceticism and all manner of incomplete living, as if avoiding sin were the purpose of life. According to the mysteries, ancient and modern, purgation is one part of life; it is needed in the beginning. When purgation becomes the goal, the way of affirmation becomes impossible and the way of affirmation is the way of the abundance of life. . . .

People who practice non-resistance may be good people, but they do not increase life or livingness, they do not see God, the Ever-Living. The initiate makes God the center of his universe and of his being and does not eschew any portion of *life*, as all come from God. The evils that he avoids may be those of wasteful living, of needless dissipation of vital energy, of misuse of the love and power and magnetism that God has given him — these things he always guards against. For the rest he has the spiritual freedom, so he treads as far as possible the path of affirmation, and removes himself from the path of negation except when in the silence.

It is on the note of the Beatitudes that the poem culminates. For the Beatitudes are invocations not only of blessings, but of joy. And blessed and joyful above all are the makers of peace.

The version of "What Christ? What Peace?" printed here was slightly edited for style by Murshid in 1952, but no changes of any substantive nature were made at that time.

What Christ? What Peace?

THE LORD SPEAKS:

Why does mankind ascribe divinity to Me,
Address Me in exalted terms, then leave to Me,
To carry the burdens of the race?
O man that worships Me, and man that doubts,
Listen to My voice, hearken to My plea!

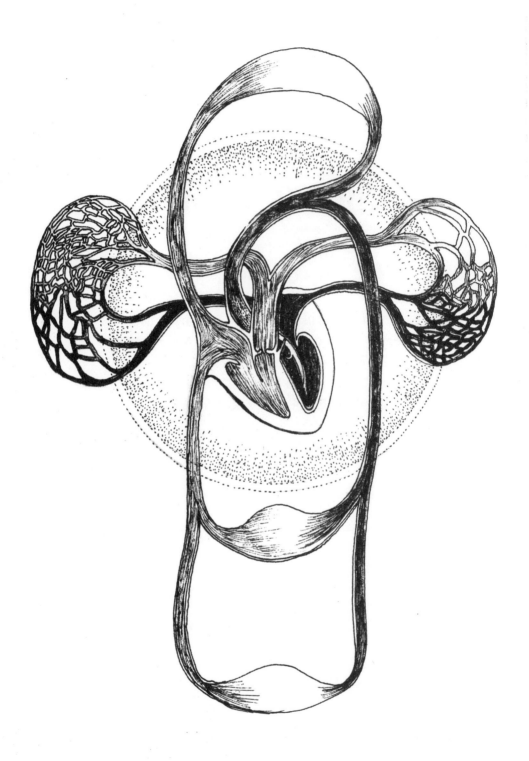

Were I to visit earth where would I go?
Were I to visit earth how would I pray?
These have become subjects for deliberation —
For argument, dispute and general debate —
Whence clashing of minds that foment disturbance,
And every disturbance filled with seeds of war.

God is love, from love the world became,
And back to love does everything return;
Love binds the different atoms into forms,
Love holds the cells of bodies as a unity,
Makes possible the marvels of growing life,
Turns man into a miniature universe,
And congregates all people in brotherhood;
From love, the complete panorama of life —
Its absence leads to death, to war, to fratricide.
This is no mystery to the awakened heart;
Peace on earth to men of universal will,
Who rise above their selfish limitations
And see the world as God would have them see.

Yesterday, today, tomorrow, it is ever the same —
Each mind presumes its own supremacy,
Each mind fails to appreciate another
Unless there is a mutual communion,
Yet minds are changing from one hour to the next.

Tell Me, how can these imperfect mechanisms
Become the instruments of that perfection
Which can bring to man the desired goal of peace?

Do Baptist, Catholic and Unitarian worship together?
Each calls on Me, acclaims Me in his way;
How can I be bound by them if I am divine?
How can any man or church or institution
Proclaim its mastery over the universe,
Without some proof of such pretensions;
Without the binding of the course of things;
So if war comes, are they not to blame
For failure to uphold their grandiose claims?
Forgive them, Father, for their deep shortcomings,
Bring them closer to Me, that they might learn.

Learn, O man, the mystery of heart-blood,
That Adam in Hebrew means 'he-of-the-red-blood',
The blood which circulates life within the body,
The blood which evidences love within the body.
The original blood connotes the sinner Adam;
It leaves the heart and works throughout the flesh,
It partakes of worldly things, becoming defiled,
By the flesh it is defiled, by lust and appetite.
This is the *psychic* blood mentioned in the Scriptures [1].
For every spurt of the blood brings psychic power
Used by the body and mind in every action,
Stirring the material life with every spurt,
Sustaining the intellect and thought of man.

Though sins be red as scarlet they can be made white,
For the blood is purified after defilement;

The blood so tinged with earth returns to heaven,
It goes into the lung-mesh to be cleansed there,
Cleansed by the Divine Spirit in every breath,
For the breath is from the Lord and is the Lord —
This is proclaimed by the Scriptures and can be proven,
For every experience testifies of its truth.
Water and breath and blood embody great mysteries,
Water and breath and blood testify unto Christ.

Let Me repeat the Law of the Living Blood,
Let Me repeat the Message of Infinite Love:
With every outward pulse is psychic force aroused,
With every inward beat is it purified.
This shows the principle of Adam within the body,
This gives the evidence of the Living Christ:
Outward Adam, inward Christ, pulse beating pulse,
Not in the past, not in the future, eternally now
Am I the resurrection and the life.

Let Me repeat the Law of the Living Blood:
The outward pulse enhances the psychic life
And builds around the self an accomodation
So that man says 'I' and thinks much of himself;
The inward pulse enhances the spiritual urge
And brings man ever closer to My place,
So perceiving Me in love, his heart says 'Thou',
The former sway gives scope to reciprocity,
And as man sows, thus also will he reap;
The latter leads straightway to renunciation,
The latter leads to the ever living Christ,
For I am ever the resurrection and the life.

Thus every beat of heart may be a communion,
The outward psychic functions revealing Adam,
The inner spiritual functions evidencing Christ,
The resurrected Adam through purification.
Whenever man attains this blessed communion,
He never will grow old, though long in the flesh;
He will attain to the proclaimed kingdom of Heaven,
Becoming perfect, even as God is perfect.

Were I to visit earth? Why not reverse
And invite the earth to come to Me,
Follow Me to My heavenly habitation,
Take of the cup and table spread before Me?
Then, verily, could I minister unto the world,
Then could I teach the mysteries of the heart,
Then could I spread the blessings of that peace
Which hearts and minds and bodies are now seeking.
Mankind must rise above binding mentality,
Learn more about the nature of true love,
That bodies are the temples of the Holy Spirit,
And in your flesh you surely may see God
Who is your very being and your life.

As with the flow of blood within the body,
So is the course of love throughout the world.
The psychic blood is purified by breath,
And as such is the overtonal nature of the blood
That it also can be healed by the Divine Breath,
By the Holy Spirit which permeates the world,
Which is the common breath for all mankind,
The nexus of the union of God and man,
Obtained through Christ, the Universal Savior.

II.

What is the way in which to govern the earth?
The laws which govern the flesh of your very bodies
Apply not only to things below on earth,
But reveal the way by which God operates
Through all the various branches of the cosmos.

In ancient times the Christians held love-feasts,
Not feasts in the name of love but love in the name of feasts —
And this was love and not the thought-of-love,
A callous and a brutal substitution.
Milleniums have passed with only a memory,
Milleniums have gone with only a tradition;
And now catastrophes embroil the world,
When blood, unpurified by the Holy Spirit,
Pours into the earth in countless streams
As if the globe itself were crucified,
Yet by some magic expected a resurrection.

Aye, this resurrection shall surely come
When the flesh of Christ is shared in the spirit of love,
When the blood of Christ is drunk in holy communion.
From imperfection to divine perfection,
From veniality to joy and peace —
This is the course of love when we awaken.

What does it profit a man to gain the world,
Without the faculty of psychic control,
Who cannot transmute his life-force into love,
Who cannot transcend his limited ego,
Who has not merged with Christ in holy marriage?

Greater than church is life, greater than sect is love;
The very idea of heresy precludes peace,
The very idea of strangeness foments war;
God would unite, man would divide —
Come unto Me ye heavy laden and I will give you rest:

I do not ask a bitter price,
I do not want a special creed,
I seek, rather, the open heart,
I greatly prize the noble deed.

I offer to you all My love,
Again present My healing power,
And I would save the world once more
From its great peril at this hour.

When man in his great effort fails,
When earth is swallowed in holocaust,
Come to Me, children, for I am near,
And in God's Light nothing can be lost.

The Gospel offers all the truth,
Teachings can not be bound by time,
Eternal salvation for the world,
God's love is infinite and sublime.

I am not of the party of those who claim authority,
I am not of the band of those who would revolt;
They really are of Me, not I of them.
When I am sought to plea for some special group,
This is not peace, this scorns divinity.
When it is assumed I hold to some narrow way,
This is not peace, this mocks divinity.

God is not of a faction nor Christ of a selfish cause:
When the hearts of men open themselves to Me,
When the hearts of men are open to each other,
Then, at last, shall true peace be forthcoming,
And then shall you sit with Me at the table of Christ.
Abraham offered his son to his Beloved,
God offered His Son to His beloved;
But the selfishness in man has dominated,
And now the world must face its Armageddon.

But he who holds the standard which I raised,
Even though he be a minority of one,
Finding another one who is like himself,
Can save the world — they and Me together;
For even a few so gathered in My Name
Can bring about the greatest of miracles,
That is, if I be really Lord of Heaven,
That is, if I am an example to the world.

(Let Me explain the mystery of *Name*,
The usual translation of the Hebrew *Shem*;
Interpreted thus My prayer will read:
"Our Father Who art in all realms of *Shem*,
Most holy is Thy *Shem*,"
Which is to say, God is eternal Light;
That Light includes His many attributes,
His Beauty and Beneficence and Love,
His Glory and His Mercy and His Life
Which extend from everlasting to everlasting;
So when we pray our prayer becomes a ladder
To take us to the presence of our Father,
To share in all the blessings which He offers,

From earth below to the highest of heavens.
How pitiable are they called 'anti-Semites',
Yet most appropriate is that term for them,
Meaning 'those who stand against the Holy Light',
Those who antagonize *Shem* and the scions of *Shem*.
They are not just anti-Jews or anti-Hebrews,
But enemies of all the children of the Light,
Who set themselves forthwith against My Gospel.
Let the name of 'anti-Semite' remain with them,
Who prepare their places in the outer darkness;
Let them be cast thence forthwith and turn to Me,
Gather in My *Shem*, beloved ones,
And share with Me the blessings of the Father.)

When Moses brought the Sabbath hour,
   He brought the Sabbath day,
He also brought the Sabbath year
   And taught the Jubilee.
When Christ held forth communion cup,
   It was not for one short minute,
For the cup held the gift of holy love
   For him quaffing all within it.
Who would partake of bitter pain,
Who would withstand life's woes,
Who would willingly suffer on the cross,
Follow Christ wherever He goes,
Who would search for God's salvation,
Let his heart be filled with light;
Such a one would dwell eternally
In a realm that knows no night.
   And that is the real Sabbath day,
   That is the real Sabbath year,

That is the final Jubilee
Where I welcome every one, for to Me you all are dear.

HE THAT BELIEVETH IN ME, THE THINGS THAT I DO,
SHALL HE ALSO DO.

Has it ever been? Can it ever Be?
And if man cannot follow Me,
How can the nations rest at peace,
How can they gain security?
Will factious fighting ever cease?
Or must man go and judge his brother,
Forget My 'Love ye one another',
Create a thought and call it 'God',
Condemn whole races at a nod,
And think I shall accept his soul
For whom Hell-fire becomes the goal?
For Hell is nothing but the end
For all who hate and scoff and rend
Any of God's beloved ones,
Any of His blessed daughters and sons.

I did not offer you a selfish peace;
I came to bring a challenging sword,
To drive the evil from your selfish minds,
To close the evil from your selfish tongues,
To bring you joy and life and peace —
The same with men, the same with nations of men.

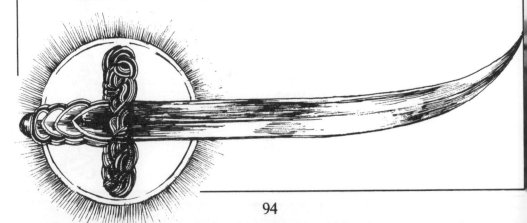

94

III.

How many times have legates met?
How many parliaments convened?
Their sessions opened by a prayer
And God invoked to give His aid,
Until the first speech has been made.
Then ranters rise to plead their cause,
To cast all vileness on the enemy,
As if the strong were righteous men,
Or goodness came by just defying evil.
If what has been is still to be,
The parliament will exclude Me,
And though they gather in My name;
They only add to their own shame.

Many sheep have I which are not of your fold,
Call yourself Christian or Muslim or Jew;
You are mad if you consider Me divine,
Then limit Me to your own point of view.
If I be God, all men are Mine,
All hearts are Mine, if I be divine;
And those who exclude from the fold
Are the very ones I can not hold
If I be God, if I be divine.

Beloved ones, will you now yield to Me
And heed the Message that I must repeat:
That love alone can point the path to peace,
That love alone can save the universe.
So when your mighty rise to state their aims,
Forgetting the teachings that I gave of yore,

They cast themselves from Me and can't partake
Of My communion at the unseen Table,
Which My disciples share with Me in heaven,
To which all men on earth have been invited.

Let the parliament of the world forthwith assemble;
Let them begin their sessions with a prayer.
But who will pray? What prayer will all accept?
If the sway of man is roused at the beginning,
Where is your God, and where shall your Christ enter?
For the believers of many folds shall be collecting,
And with them, too, many who do not believe;
And when you force your own creed upon another,
Already is there strife, the door of peace is closed.

IV.

"See what lovingkindness the Father has given, so that we should be
     called children of God,
On account of this the world knows us not, because it knew not
     Him."*

The moment a person speaks without divine authority,
That moment the cause of peace is straightway lost,
Lost has it been, lost shall it be because of this.
Then one shall rise and state his nation's aims,
And another arise and state his country's cause,
And another evoke complete attention,
And another arouse lengthy applause,
And on the beaten enemy shall be thrown the blame —

* First Epistle of John, 3:1.

Emotions dominate the scene, and the thoughts of men
Overshadow the efforts of inner love,
For even between the victors will be no union,
Because between themselves is no holy communion.

When will man listen to the stirring in his heart?
When will he look to Christ within his breast?
There is no race that I shall represent,
There is no cause for which I bring a plea,
For peace is mightier than the best of causes
And brotherhood grander than the tinge of race.

Look not to Me upon the cross —
     Look to the hospitals filled with the lamed,
     The broken in spirit, the totally maimed,
     The silent old houses whose youth have all left,
     The widows and orphans and many bereft,
     The millions of valiant returned to the dust,
     While powerful editors lead on in lust
     To stir up more madness, cast some new spell
     To egg on the remnants to a still madder Hell,
     That their private portions may be unaffected
     And all who oppose them remain unprotected,
     Permitted in churches to bend their vile knees,
     Using My name in their devilish pleas,
     Producing more trouble and bringing damnation
To those who would uphold their proud civilization.

Look not to Me upon the cross —
     I died in vain, I died in vain indeed
     If for selfish gain, if for lust and greed.
     I lived and died to help the human race,

And in God's heaven have prepared a place
For all of you — Christian, Hindu,
Muslim, Parsi, Buddhist or Jew —
For the Heavenly Father loves each one of you.

And yet the cause of peace is not assured,
For though all Hitlers be removed from earth,
Yet Hitlerism has so smeared many souls
That their very words are hollow mockeries,
And though the devil die and tyrants flee,
The tyrannous disease stays on to crucify Me;
For by every selfish thought am I crucified,
By every selfish word am I crucified,
By every selfish deed am I crucified.

V.

IS THE EARTH THE LORD'S AND THE FULLNESS THEREOF?

This question must be faced upon the morrow,
For if evaded shall only rise again.
'Praise Thee, Lord Christ, but this is economics;
Praise Thee, Lord Christ, but this is politics;
Praise Thee, Lord Christ, but this, of course, is business;
Praise Thee, Lord Christ, but this is philosophy.'
If I be God, wherefore your economics?
If I be God, what avail your politics?
If I be God, why such stress on business?
Mercury was the ancient god of business —
Why don't you go and build some temples for him,
For I shall not consign to Hell-fire

The one who worships Mercury in full faith.
But I am not Mercury; and if you use My name
As the supreme businessman, you speak in vain,
And by yourself are you confined to Hell,
Not in the afterworld, but *here* and *now* —
YOUR MANY WARS ATTEST, THIS ONE ABOVE ALL.

O economist, look upon the dying;
O politician, look upon the dead;
O business-pleader, look upon the impoverished
And tell Me, is this the goal of life?
I came to bring Life, you take it away;
That ephemeral fortune lasts but a day,
Is borrowed from Nature and must be returned,
This was the Gospel, but you have not learned
That to gain great riches and lose your soul
Makes Hell-fire the only possible goal:
YOUR MANY WARS ATTEST, THIS ONE ABOVE ALL.

And if philosophy becomes your aim,
Why not open temples to Pallas Athene,
Remembering also, if you are so minded,
She was not only goddess of the intellect,
She was also goddess of war and worshipped so;
For thought encountering thought results in war.
You who worship logic, whereupon do you agree
Other than in your adherence to this logic?
When thought lashes thought, what hope for peace?

MARX AND MAMMON AND MINERVA WILL CONTRADICT,
MARX AND MAMMON AND MINERVA WILL THEN CONFLICT,
IN THE NAME OF PEACE WILL IT BE WHEN HITLER IS GONE;
WHAT PRICE GLORY?   WHAT PRICE PEACE?

Is the earth the Lord's and the fullness thereof?
Do you accept this or prefer the Hell-fire,
Not in the future, but here, before your eyes;
For the Horsemen of the Apocalypse are riding forth,
With a greater power than a few years back,
And the next scourge will be worse, far worse —
When will you return to Me, beloved ones?

VI.

IS IT MORE BLESSED TO GIVE THAN TO RECEIVE?

After the holy prayer is offered before them,
What nations will exemplify these principles?
They will look askance at the fallen enemy,
And men in hate will excoriate the villains,
Themselves the victims of the very disease,
As if an epidemic can be cured
By merely ending the lives of its sorry victims
Without removing the death-germ of the disease.
When Hitler is gone, yet Hitlerism will remain
Not because of Hindu or Buddhist or Muslim
But the very Christians gathering at the conference,
Adhering more to economics than to Me,
Striving to be steadfast in their politics,
Become successors of those erstwhile devils
Who sowed disunion and trampled on the just.
For if injustice is followed by injustice,
If you cast out Satan to follow Beelzebub,
What hope have I, have you and has the world?
Will you receive My love or gain the world,

Losing your psychic power and inner light?

Better build temples instead to lame old Vulcan
Who was the god of all mechanical arts,
With warped mind and body as is your world
With all its mighty monuments of power,
Yet wherein recently no Gothic temple
Or such as David built has been erected,
Because the heart is lost within the meshes
Of materialism, folly and decay.
And if you worship Vulcan you shall not be lost,
For those who worship, though of a different faith,
Can still attain admission to their God.

But if you use My name and Vulcan's deeds,
Or call upon Me, holding Mercury's aims,
Or bow before Me, wrapped in Minerva's thoughts,
Go, cast yourselves into the outer darkness,
You are the Tojos of the future world;
Not those who call Me Lord are thereby saved,
If they do not do the Will of My Father in Heaven.

The same with man, the same with nations of men:
The Pharaohs, hard of heart, are turned from God,
Though they may whisper or shout a Holy Name.
When nations starve, are you willing that they starve?
When ships go down, will you succor the survivors?
When life is at stake, how important is your money?
Is it really more blessed to give than to receive?

I hear the call of altruistic reformers
Who feel that Christ can somehow save the world,

That I am not limited by man's religions,
That perhaps, in all things man can follow Me.
If that be so, God's blessing will abound.

I do not say: 'Do it this particular way',
I am not come to plead a special cause;
When the spirit of man awakens, him shall I trust,
For the earth is the Lord's and the fullness thereof,
And all things has He placed before man's feet.

The day of lovely words shall turn to night
If the deeds of lovely words come not to day.
The loveliness of thought is sanctified
When the deeds of lovely thoughts are exemplified.

VII.

WILL YOU FORGIVE THE DEBTS OF THOSE WHO OWE YOU?

Or repeat a million times My sacred prayer,
Holding fast to the words, neglecting the spirit
And sending a curse again across the world?
You cannot follow both Satan and Me,
Nor worship Mammon and Me in the same edifice.

Shall I come? I come with your every prayer,
With the communion cup and the wafer;
I shared the communion cup, the loaves and fishes,
The food of the ground, the food withdrawn from water.
I gave to all and ever invite all to Me.

But when you demand *just* payments of your debts,
Meaning by 'justice' that your aims are requited
Regardless of involving circumstances,
My words become religious mockery.
What use is there to dethrone physical Hitlers,
Excoriate their names and damn their deeds
Nor set a path more worthy of My name,
While summoning Me to claim Me for your cause?
I am not troubled over the impious devils
Whose very darkness casts a curse upon them.
But those who claim to battle in My name,
Who repeat My prayers and doubly swear allegiance,
They are followers of that unworthy son
Who said to his father, "I will," but did not go.
Christ or the banker? Christ or the worldly rich?
How can you serve God and Mammon? Christ and Mercury?

I came not to destroy but to fullfill;
Yet in the many centuries since My coming,
The ancient laws of Moses have been removed,
Any property rights stand first in your societies,
And excuse upon excuse has been presented
To lay aside the teachings which I upheld.
I do not blame humanity for this;
I only say again, Go, and sin no more;
I further add, Come, and sin no more.

For once the Divine Light shines within your bosoms,
Then is your love for Me made manifest,
Your living silence shall speak more than your prayers,
Your shining light shall plead more than your voice,
You will become, in truth, my fellow-workers,

And nothing more is asked of any man.

Whatever the past has been, let the past be;
Come, children of men, and hearken now to Me:
The conqueror, who keeps His word to the end,
Him shall I give authority over the nations,
I shall make him a pillar in the temple of God,
And him shall I clothe in white and holy garments,
And him shall I give to sit down on My throne.

WILL YOU LOVE THE LORD YOUR GOD WITH ALL YOUR
    HEART,
WITH ALL YOUR SOUL, WITH ALL YOUR MIGHT,
AND LOVE YOUR NEIGHBORS AS YOURSELVES?

If so, it will be well with all the world;
If so, already you are acting in My name;
If so, you need not offer further prayer;
For you have become your very highest prayers,
Which God the Father in Heaven will receive;
If so, even churches may be dispossessed;
If so, you have become true channels of holiness;
If so, you are already co-workers in My cause;
If so, the kingdom of Heaven is open within you;
If so, that kingdom will manifest without.

If not, what care I for further protestations?
If not, what use are vain supplications?
If I condemned the Pharisees for their manners,
Should I not condemn my followers even more
Who hold that Christ stood far above the Pharisees,
Yet act as if the Pharisees were better than they.
For by your words and your hearts shall you be judged.

By your works and by your hearts produce Heaven or Hell
And determine your future status through the ages —
Thus for men, thus for the collectivity, for the nations.

If you have mighty weapons and do not love,
Build magnificent structures and marvelous cities,
Have all earthly comforts and material ease,
And find some satisfaction for every passion,
What is the whole of life? What is its aim?
But if you have love, though only in a cottage,
And by loving find your happiness,
You are the vessels of the living God,
And you shall be My brethren at the Table.
For you shall I break bread and offer wine,
For you shall I appear in heavenly glory,
And prepare fine mansions in My Father's house.

I would gather you as the mother-hen gathers her chicks,
I would give you My blessing and ask only a pittance;
But it is not your kneeling and calling Me 'Lord',
It is not your many praises that I need —
You gain by your praise and benefit thereby.
I am willing to carry your burdens and share your lot,
If you knock at My door, I shall straightway open it,
By subjugating your agitating egos
And opening the heart of love within you,
You shall be fulfilling the purpose of your life.

When the essence of words means more than the words,
When the essence of thought means more than the thought,
When action is proven by the action alone,
When brotherhood sets the path for society,

Love will appear and religion be affirmed,
  Then Christ shall be truly king.

When prayers are uplifted, with no selfishness
Fixed on the heart of the pious at worship,
When claims are not made with an eye to publicity,
When the lowly and meek are properly treated,
When the mountains of pride are laid at My feet
And the valley of humility raised high aloft,
  Then indeed will Christ be king.

When you go to worship for the worship alone,
Nor heed if your neighbor's creed be different,
When all churches are recognized as sacred,
And My words have become the basis for actions,
  Then am I crowned King of the world.

When there is no hatred, then is there love,
When there is no gossip or back-biting talk,
When people strive to help one another,
When the light within is opened to man
That the Father in Heaven can see his good works,
  Then is your Christ crowned King of all.

When the life is understood as being within,
When the Kingdom of Heaven is sought from within,
When men look deeper down into themselves
To find that God Who is every soul's seeking,
And men follow Me truly in all that they do,
Rest assured, you are blessed and I sit on My throne.
When I sit on My throne I shall radiate peace,
Peace to the world, joy and thanksgiving,
For the Lord then is come, the Lord then is come.

Blessed and happy are they who serve the Lord,
Blessed and happy are they who are humble of spirit,
Blessed and happy who mourn over others,
Blessed and happy the meek and self-denying,
Blessed and happy who yearn after righteousness,
Blessed and happy those who purify their hearts;

But blessed and happy above all the makers of peace,
Who extend the sway of blessing on their earth,
And by their becoming channels of blessing,
They serve both Me and God the Father.
Such are the very lights of manifestation —
Will they become the leaders of the nations,
Or continue to be persecuted in My name?

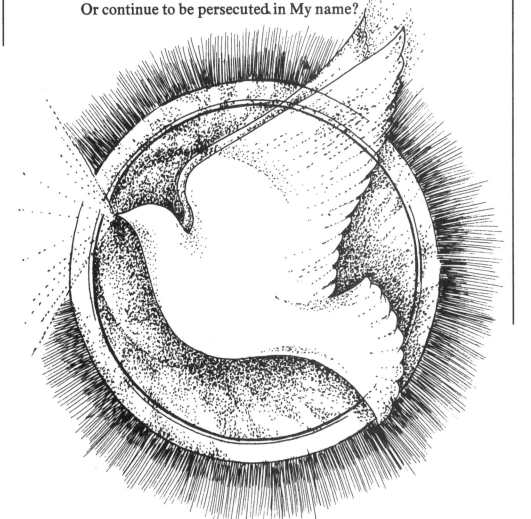

This is the question that stands before humanity.
This is the question that stands before humanity:
Christ, or the verbal worship of His memory?
Christ, or an institution condemning others?
Christ, or conflicting opinions as to His nature?
Christ, while ignoring even His simplest teachings?
Christ, that thereby all become children of God.

THIS IS THE PROBLEM THAT NOW STANDS BEFORE
    THE NATIONS;
THIS IS THE QUESTION FACING EVERY SOUL.

Now may the peace that passeth understanding,
By the awakening of your inner self,
Show its light and wisdom straight before you
And make My vision be a reality.
O God, O God, enlighten the hearts of mankind;
Awake, thou that sleepest, arise from the dead!
           I COME! I BRING THEE LIGHT!

Love & blessings
Murshid.

Samuel L. Lewis
1942

Notes

1. "But now Christ has been raised from the Dead, a first fruit of those having fallen asleep. For since through a man, there is death, through a man, also, there is a resurrection of the dead. For, as by Adam all die, so by the Annointed also, will all be restored to life. . . . And thus is the resurrection of the dead. It is sown in corruption, it is raised in incorruption. It is sown in dishonor, it is raised in glory. It is sown in weakness, it is raised in power. It is sown a psychic body, it is raised a spiritual body. And so it has been written, 'The first Adam became a living Soul [*psyche*].' The last Adam, a life-giving Spirit (breath). The spiritual, however, was not the first, but the psychic; afterwards the spiritual. The first Man was from the Ground, earthy [the first *Adam* from the *Adamah*]; the second Man is from Heaven." (I Cor.15:20-22, 42-47) The above is Murshid Samuel Lewis' translation of these passages; these subjects are taken up in depth in his ten lectures on First Corinthians published under the title, *This is the New Age, In Person.*

Glossary

Adam — (Hebrew) 'He-of-blood' or 'He-of-Heart-Essence'. The first man, created in God's image. Universal mankind, composite of all humanity. So long as he dwelt in *Eden* (or 'Bliss'), his state was heavenly. But he was attracted to the knowledge of duality and, having tasted of it, became covered by the impressions of good and evil. This led to his temporary separation from his true nature, the original pure sense of unity.

Apocalypse, Horsemen of the: In the revelation granted to St. John, four riders on horseback who bring God's judgment upon the persecutors of men. (Rev.6:1-8) They represent calamities which have appeared again and again in history: war or conquest, international or civil strife, famine, and pestilence and death.

Armageddon — (Hebrew) 'Hill of Megiddo'. Historically, the city of Megiddo was a famous battlefield in Israel's history and the scene of violent conflicts between Israel and her enemies. It has come to symbolize the battleground where the conflict between the forces of good and evil is decided. In the Book of Revelation it is described as the place where terrible retribution is wrought upon the wrongdoer.

Beelzebub — (probably a Hebrew pun on the name of the Phillistine idol, *Baalzebul*, 'Lord of the Flies'. In its punned sense it may mean 'lord of dung' or 'prince of false gods'. His name appears in the Gospels where he is identified with Satan or the prince of demons.

blessing — (*berachah* in Hebrew, *baraka* in Arabic) That living vibration which comes from God and can flow through man when he is immersed in Perfection. It causes an increase of exaltation, bliss, love and peace in the hearts of those who receive it. This

111

magnetism can also be felt in the atmosphere of certain physical objects as, for example, healing springs of water.

blood — Heart Essence. "It is the homogeneous substance common to all. . . . The life that touches one heart touches all hearts." (S.L.L.) The blood, through the action of the heart, brings food and air to every cell in the body; in man this fluid may, through effort and Grace, accommodate the etheric element and thus carry the Divine Qualities, which work both through and beyond simple physical sustenance: "for the heart contains its own medicine." (S.L.L.)

breath — The Latin *spiritus*, Hebrew *ruach* and Greek *pneuma* all have in common that their original meaning is breath; but, in most cases, they are incompletely translated as 'spirit'. "Man, in his ignorance, has created a difference between spirit and breath, between life and breath, and between God and breath. When we bring these all together . . . it means the beginning of the awakening or reawakening of life's currents in us, and the transformation which transforms and is not a mere mental operation culminates in the spiritual rebirth of every devotee. . . . Christ is born when God's breath enters man's nostrils, and he is crucified when man's thought enters his mind. . . . It is breath which invigorates each and all men and breath or spirit which unites men. . . . Not only do we all breathe the same atmosphere, but we all receive from the same Spirit, or take communion with God, when we breathe." (S.L.L.) In accordance with original meanings, therefore, "spiritual realization" may then mean that one has realized the identity of his being with the Divine Breath. Thus the Brotherhood of Man in the Holy Spirit.

brotherhood — Brotherhood is experienced whenever people are gathered in the Parenthood of God, or Love. "It cannot be sustained on earth or in heaven without this feeling of integrated oneness." (S.L.L.) In First Corinthians the brotherhood of the members of the church is compared to the relationship of the different parts to the single body, which mystically speaking is the body of Christ.

Buddhist — One who walks in the footsteps of the enlightened sage of India, Gautama Shakyamuni; especially one who follows his exhortation to "Seek out thy salvation with diligence."

channels — As the channel of a river is the place of the greatest and deepest flow of the river's course, so a human being becomes a channel when he or she surrenders to God and allows the stream of blessing to flow through.

Christ — (from the Greek, meaning 'Annointed One', recalling the ancient Hebrew custom of anointing a person in recognition of his having been endowed with the qualification for exalted office) "Jesus, of the *Beni Israel*, tried to restore and purify the teachings that had been given to His people, and also to add one more lesson for which the world was being prepared: this was the brotherhood of humanity. Christ added the doctrine of universal brotherhood to that of the Unity of God which had been given out by Moses. He also taught the supreme value of love and explained its preeminence over morality and mentality. . . . Moses had given the people God as a Creator and God of Law, which He is; the next step was to proclaim Him as God of Love, which He is. After that it would be possible to teach that God was within man and that we were within Him — the esoteric teaching of the early followers of Christ." (S.L.L.) "There are some who cannot conceive the idea of Christs' divinity. The truth is that the soul of man is divine, and that divine spark deserves to be called really divine when with the unfoldment of the soul it reaches the point of culmination." (Hazrat Inayat Khan)

Christ, blood of — The Wine of the Sacrament, signifying the *Presence* of God; the love element, the intoxication of which is a bliss. The two elements of the Sacrament, bread and wine, are symbolic of Christ's flesh and blood and represent the soul's sustenance and ecstasy. Christ's injunction to His followers to eat of His flesh and drink of His blood may be said to mean: "The being in which I am living is God's being; take this as the food to nourish your finer being; drink this to stimulate your spiritual being." (Hazrat Inayat Khan)

Christ, flesh of — The Wafer or Bread of the Sacrament. The Communion, or Sacrament itself, is realized when man dies in God and God lives in man.

Christian — One who practices the Beatitudes, really.

communion — (from the Latin *comunis*, 'union'("In all men I see myself." (Walt Whitman) The Christian ritual, which is the central feature of the Mass, was inaugurated by Christ when he shared the Last Supper with his disciples. In the words of St.

113

Paul, the communion celebrates the fact that "we, being many, are one bread and one body: for we are all partakers of that one bread." (I Cor.10:17 A.V.)

crucifixion — "This is a double act of surrender, surrender to a process which symbolizes the giving up of self in the highest sense." (S.L.L.)

David — The Psalmist-King of Israel whose story is related in First Samuel in the Old Testament. "God gave David the plan for the temple, as he had previously given Moses the plan for the tabernacle. This plan David communicated to his son, Solomon, directing him to erect the building." (S.L.L.)

disciples — The most immediate pupils and companions of Christ; those to whom the secrets of the kingdom of Heaven were openly revealed. A disciple of Christ may be said to be anyone who accepts Christ's teachings fully.

Divine Light — The actual All-Pervading-Light which comes to man through the kindling of his heart. When reflected in our beings, it causes us to awaken to spiritual liberty. This Light is symbolized in Christian art by the halo.

Divine Spirit — Divine Spirit, Holy Spirit, Holy Ghost and Divine Breath are synonomous. The Divine Spirit might be called the Soul of God which is everywhere Present succoring mankind and offering Guidance to all.

Father — Father and Heavenly Father are one and the same. Father is He Whose bosom contains the Universe in boundless Love. Father is Peace.

Glory — (from the Hebrew *Kevod*, 'weight', the everywhere-present splendor of God) The Divine Light which shines forth through Masters, Saints and Prophets and is inseparable from constant and selfless praise to God. Glory may also be an effect of direct identification with God.

Heaven — The Illuminated Heart. The abode of the Divine Qualities.

Heaven, kingdom of — This reality is deeply rooted in the teachings of the Old Testament and constitutes a central theme in the teaching of Christ: "Seek ye first the kingdom of Heaven, and all else shall be added unto you." (Matt.6:33) "Behold, the kingdom of Heaven is within you." (Luke 17:21) Its meaning is similar to the Sanskrit words *alaya* and *akasha* and to the English words "ether" and "space." There is an infinite accommodation in the universe, an emptiness capable of creatively containing all, which manifests in and through the Illuminated Heart. "The world stands out on every side, no wider than the heart is Wide." (Edna St. Vincent Millay)

Hebrews — (from the Semitic root *habar*, 'beyond'; the Hebraic derivative is *habri*, a 'Hebrew' and the Arabic derivative is *harbi*, an 'Arab') An early name for the Jews; first applied to Abraham by the Canaanites because he had crossed the Euphrates.

Hell-fire — However distant one is from one's Inner Peace, so deeply is one in Hell-Fire, and the pain of this separation is like burning.

Hindu — A practitioner of the Dharma (religion) as presented by the Avatars, Rishis, Saints and Sages of India.

Hitler — (1889-1945) Dictator of Germany and founder of the Nazi Party. His "new order" for Europe called for the discriminate extermination of whole peoples; the Jews of Europe were the most numerous among his victims. He was ultimately defeated, but the poem suggests that his ideas have contaminated the minds of others in the form of extreme selfishness and apathy, if not outright cruelty.

Holy Name — Any phrase which is intended to directly convey the being of God to the one who recites it. According to the traditions of the esoteric schools, a sacred phrase is given by the Teacher to a disciple for him to repeat until such time as he has the experience of awakening into God-realization. In Sanskrit such phrases are called *mantra*, in Arabic they are called *zikar* or *wazifa*. However, when words are repeated without a sense of Divinity and devotion this practice can degenerate into what Jesus called "vain repetitions." Thus he gave his followers the Lord's Prayer to repeat.

Holy Spirit — [See DIVINE SPIRIT]

house — The greater Kingdom of Heaven in which God has prepared many special abodes, or 'mansions', to accomodate the evolving soul in her journey.

Jews — (from the Hebrew *Yahudim* originally signifying those who repeated *Ya Hu*, 'O, He', calling on God in His transcendence.) A branch of the descendents of the Patriarch Abraham who founded the religion of monotheism, the realization of the unity of God. Historically, a central feature of Judaism was the tradition of the Prophets who spoke to mankind in God's name.

Jubilee — One of the laws of Moses, honored by Jesus. It is explained in depth in "The Day of the Lord Cometh" glossary.

love — This word and the word "Heaven" appear most often in the poem. To define it is to lose it. To say it is the purpose for which we are born is too little, and too much. Without demonstration it has no meaning whatever.

love-feasts — A gathering of friends presumably to eat together, but actually to commune with one another in the spirit of Christ who said: "I am the Vine and ye are the branches thereof."

Mammon — (Aramaic) 'Riches'. Wealth, personified as a god.

mansions — The older meaning of this word is simply 'abode' or 'dwelling place'. [See HOUSE]

Marx — (1818-1883) A political economist who formulated a system of thought that gives class struggle a primary role in leading society from bourgeois control to a socialist society and ultimately to communism.

Mercury — (from the Latin *merx*, 'wares') The god of merchandise and business worshipped by the ancient Romans. Even the planet seems to have a role associated with 'busy-ness'.

Minerva — (from the Latin *mens*, 'mind') In Roman mythology, the goddess of intellect and warfare. She was associated with warlike prowess and skill in the arts of life.

Moses — (from the Hebrew *mosheh*, 'water-born') One of the greatest of the Old Testament Prophets. To him is attributed the Pentateuch, first five books of the Bible, which contains a definite code for a religious society as well as for human behavior in general. His face was said to be illuminated with the Light of God so much so that men could not face him at times.

Muslim — (Arabic) 'One who surrenders to Allah (God)'. Muslims are associated with the religion of Islam which the Prophet Mohammed founded; but, consistent with the definition above, all the messengers of God from Adam on are referred to as Muslims in the Quran.

Pallas Athene — The Greek counterpart to the Roman goddess Minerva. [See MINERVA]

Parsi — A follower of the Zoroastrian religion, descended from Persian refugees who settled in India. Zoroastrianism, founded by the Divine Messenger Zarathustra, celebrates the victory of light over darkness. The *magi*, whom tradition refers to as the

116

'wise men' who visited the infant Jesus, were the holy men of this faith.

Pharaohs — Honorary title of the kings of ancient Egypt. Pharaoh, as used in the poem, refers to any ruler who substitutes his will for the Divine Will, stemming from the Pharaoh who stood against Moses.

Pharisees — (from the Hebrew *parash*, 'separate') Members of a religious sect among the Jews who, at the time of Christ, exercised great political authority; and, because of their exaggerated zeal for the law and its accurate observance, held themselves separate from those they considered unclean. They were denounced by Jesus as hypocrites ("for they say, and do not"), for making differences and distinctions among men. Their whole tendency was toward analysis, and their conformity with the "letter" of the Law and not the Spirit marked them as directly opposed to the real mission of Jesus.

psychic — Man has three bodies, as taught in Christianity (I Corinthians) and all the world religions: the physical, psychic (also called astral or subtle) and the spiritual (also called causal). The psychic body corresponds to the world of *jinns* (from which our word 'genius' comes) and fairies; it is a world of emotions, powers and faculties of mind. The spiritual body corresponds to the world of angels; it refers more to faculties of the heart and Divine Breath.

resurrection — Rebirth. This refers to the rising of Christ from death to eternal life and the example he held forth to the world of the possibility of this victory of life over death to all men and in all times. "The acme of self-effacement in Jesus comes in the resurrection. . . . The spiritual rebirth or resurrection comes after the self-effacement or Crucifixion." (S.L.L.)

Sabbath Hour — The Sabbath, which comes from the root word in Hebrew signifying 'completion' or 'perfection', refers to that period of time when one turns away from worldly preoccupations and, in an attitude of self-surrender, contemplates Perfection. "It is our work to restore this sanctity in ourselves and in our fellow man. . . . It is our attunement to and our union with God which enables us to experience life on all planes and not be pulled down by a troublesome world." (S.L.L.) The use of the term "Sabbath

117

Hour" in the poem indicates that man need not limit his observance of the Sabbath to one day of the week.

Satan — (Hebrew) 'Adversary'. Although we use the term "Devil" to refer to Satan, he is perhaps better understood as the false ego which causes all the agitation that prevents mankind from appreciating love, joy and peace.

Shem — (Hebrew) 'Light'. The all-pervading clear light of the Absolute which is replete with all qualities and is everlasting. The scions of Shem are the real Shemites or Semites, i.e., the descendants of Noah's eldest son, *Shem*, "meaning the pure, the holy, the upright, the heavenly." (S.L.L.)

Table, unseen — The place of communion; even on earth this occurs where "heart speaks to heart, and soul to soul." (Hazrat Inayat Khan)

Tojo — Tojo Kideki (1884-1948), the Japanese general who served as minister of war and premier at the time of the attack on Pearl Harbor. He was tried by the International Military Tribunal of the Far East and executed for war crimes in 1948.

transmute — Refine, transform into a more subtle state.

universal will — "In unison with the Will of God we will to have peace." (Hazrat Inayat Khan)

Vulcan — In Roman mythology, the god of the mechanical arts and fire, particularly in its destructive aspects, such as volcanoes and conflagrations.

wafer — The disk of unleavened bread used in the Mass to represent the body of Christ, which is ingested by the communicant during the Communion. It symbolizes the consecration of the bread and wine used by Christ at the Last Supper. [See CHRIST, FLESH OF]

water — The symbol of "spirit". "As water gives life to the earth, so the nature of the spirit is to give life to the body. Without water the earth is dead; so is the body without the soul." (S.L.L.) It is one of the three mysteries mentioned in the poem: water, breath and blood. The Christian Bible teaches that these are "three witnesses on earth . . . and these three are as one." Water as a witness to Divinity, as a medium of purification and blessing is common to the rituals of Christianity, Judaism and Islam: in Judaism and Islam through the ritual baths and ablutions, in Christianity through the rite of baptism.

118

wine — "The juice of the grape . . . symbolical of the life of non-ego . . . of the unrestricted life of soul. . . . Ego of grapes disappears in the production of wine." (S.L.L.) The Blood of Christ, Ecstasy. The Divine Presence.

Saladin

Introduction

"Saladin," written ca. 1960, is the culmination of Murshid's trilogy: it completes and perfects the vision of the two preceding poems. It was considered by Murshid to be his magnum opus, and he often compared it to Dante's *Divine Comedy*. He offers it as an example of the state of mystical absorption in the *Rassul*-consciousness, i.e., that of the Messenger of God.

Murshid's experience of the Prophet Mohammed, described in part in the Preface, coincides exactly with the poem of Hali quoted by Murshid's first Sufi teacher, Pir-O-Murshid Hazrat Inayat Khan. This is quite different from the stereotype of the Messenger usually presented in Europe and America:

> He who was truly a merciful teacher,
> Who helped the feeble to fulfill their lives,
> Who was an ever-present help in sorrow,
> Who grieved with his own people and in the trouble of others,
> He was my beloved Mohammed.

> He who forgave the faults of wrongdoers,
> Who cleansed the hearts of the timorous and despairing from
>   their fear,
> Who vanquished evil with power and might,
> Who reconciled families long at war and embittered against
>   each other,
> He was my beloved Mohammed.

The fact that Murshid was so moved by the being and

teachings of the Prophet Mohammed does not mean he agreed with so-called 'Muslims' who ignore these teachings for their own personal ends. In a letter of March 1963, Murshid says:

You may understand now why I do not call myself a Muslim, but an *inshallah*-ist.[1] While originally a Muslim meant one who surrendered to Allah, it later came to mean mostly those who accepted *Shari'a*,[2] and finally those who followed openly or blindly an *Ijma*;[3] the source of which is not only unclear but often has nothing whatsoever to do with revelation. . . .

Rahm is common to both *er-Rahman* and *er-Rahim*. Offhand I call them "the compassionator" and "the compassionating," without holding too fast to these words. To explain further, I call Mohammed the example of *er-Rahman* and *Isa* [Jesus] the example of *er-Rahim*. This comes out in their prayers, that Mohammed begins with praise toward God and the concern is with Allah, while Isa is concerned with mankind and says, "Give us this day our daily bread and forgive us our debts." Or, in the practical life, I am called upon to bring man to a greater spiritual realization following Mohammed; and also trying to increase the world's food supplies following Isa. There is no contradiction here, but this takes *er-Rahman* and *er-Rahim* out of the realm of the abstract into the concrete and practical. . . .

Now Mohammed has said in Hadith that Holy Quran was given in

1. *Inshallah* is Arabic for 'if Allah wills' or 'God willing'. It is a recognition of the supremacy of the Divine Will and the necessity for surrendering the human will to that universal force. Of course, Murshid's remark here is in his wry style. Saladin's realization in the poem comes in answer to his prayer to be "a Muslim," but by this he meant a Muslim in the original sense of the word. [See "Saladin" Glossary entry for 'Muslim'.]

2. In a general sense, *Shari'a* refers to "the clear path to be followed, the path which the believer has to tread, the religion of Islam. As a technical term, the canon law of Islam. . . . The *Shari'a* regulates only the external relations of the subject to Allah and his fellow-men. . . . It is only concerned with the fulfillment of the prescribed outer forms. . . . Among the Sufis the law may be a starting point on the path which is fulfilled by *Hakikat*, or 'direct vision of the Divine' " (*The Encyclopedia of Islam* [London: Lusac and Co., 1934]).

3. Consensus, i.e., the general usage of the community which has been established by agreement in the larger circles of believers independent of the written, traditional or inferred law.

seven dialects and each of these dialects has an inner and outer meaning. . . . The basis of Holy Quran was revealed on "The Grand Night," and in the Grand Night experience Mohammed travelled the universe and saw the seven facets of this universe. And then he gave Quran, knowing he would have to offer it in the Arabic language and to most ignorant people. For a revelation cannot be complete unless it is given to and understood by the most ignorant.

Murshid lived and travelled extensively in Egypt, Pakistan and India and was accepted as one fully qualified from the standpoint of inner realization to teach Islamic philosophy and Sufism, which is sometimes identified with the mystical essence of Islam. He was initiated into eight different Sufi brotherhoods (Chisti, Naqshbandi, Kadiri, Sohrawardi, Shadili, Rafai, Bedawi and Kalandari), in addition to the Sufi Order founded in the West by Pir-O-Murshid Hazrat Inayat Khan. And in the Chisti-Sabri Order he was confirmed as a Murshid upon producing two illuminated disciples. His accounts of meetings with living masters and his encounters with the spirits of saints in a state of communion at their tombs may be published in some future work. In relation to the poetic transmission [see the description of the *Khidr* experience in the Preface], Murshid tells this story:

In front of the tomb of Amir Khusrau, the saint appeared and presented me with a robe, saying, "You are the successor of the late Mohammed Iqbal in the succession of Maulana Roum [Jelal-ud-din Rumi, the great Sufi poet who wrote the *Mathnavi* and founded the order of 'whirling dervishes', the Mevlevi — ED.] And this robe, which was bestowed in open vision, was being made at that time, to be presented to me, in Pakistan while the body was in India. . . .

This is also mentioned because the writer is copying his poem "Saladin," which is a vast epic and which, *inshallah*, will be famous after my death. Book II has to do with the living experiences of *Miraj* in which the Seal of the Prophets (Mohammed) played a dual role, acting as Virgil in Dante's poetry and also in full capacity as

Insaan-e-Kemal ('the perfect man'). This is the confirmation of the poetry of Maulana Roum.

"Saladin" is sub-divided into four books. The first book introduces Saladin (Salah-ud-din Ayyub), whose name means 'Sword of the Faith'. The theme of the sword is carried throughout the whole poem. The first book presents the songs of the various Swords: the Sword of Metal, the Sword of Wood, the Sword of Water, the Sword of Fire and the Sword of Wind. These Swords represent realizations of different faculties and states of consciousness; for example, mastery of the Sword of Wind would entail the realization and manifestation of the Divine Breath.

In the poem, Saladin tells us that the Sword is more powerful than the Pen. The Sword, seen as the spiritual practice which brings about these different realizations, can cut directly through to the Truth, rather than reading or thinking *about* it. In the history of the world, theologies and verbalisms have been repeatedly used to turn man against man. But the 'Sword' of Saladin cuts through all this and presents the picture of man fulfilling his role as the vicegerent (representative) of God on earth. Thus, when he truly functions, man is able to master the attributes of strength as well as those of beauty.

This poem shows us how a ruler of nations, who has a genuine love for God and humanity and follows the precepts of the religious law, can find ways of truly bringing peace.

Book I introduces the theme of the reconciliation of Judaism, Christianity and Islam, which is developed throughout the whole poem. At times Saladin speaks directly to the reader of the poem, and at other times (and these are identified by quotation marks) he lectures to a group of captured so-called 'crusaders'.

There is a depth in these teachings which patient study will reveal to the reader. This is especially true for those who are interested in seeing the continuity of the Divine Message through the different religious forms. Saladin is a practicing Muslim; but he practices the universal Islam taught in the Holy Quran, which is based on the eternal truth of the Unity of God. It will be interesting to Western readers to see such a sympathetic treatment of the Islamic religion.

The vision of Allah (God) as all-Compassionate and all-Merciful is one which thoroughly permeates the whole fabric of this poem. No sectarian legalisms are allowed to displace this overriding Compassion from the central place which it deserves in the Islamic teachings, even as each Sura of the Quran opens with the phrase, *Bismillah er-Rahman er-Rahim* ('In the Name of Allah, Most Compassionate, Most Merciful').

In the course of the poem, Saladin, who has penetrated the outer forms of religion and found the inner blessing, interprets this realization as an ongoing message for men of all times. By Divine Grace he is granted the Miraj experience of the Prophet Mohammed, ascending through all the heavenly planes to the Throne of God. This vision is given in its entirety in Book II. It was this Book which Murshid said was dictated to him "directly by *Rassul-Lillah* [Mohammed]."

The journey begins with Saladin in the company of his *sheikh*, or spiritual guide. He travels with his teacher in this stage called *fana-fi-Sheikh* through the 'everlasting gate', called by the Hebrews *shuvo* and in our times 'repentance' — the gate of turning from the thought of ego-self to the experience of Divine Light. And we are taken through the heavens of Jacob, Isaac, Abraham and Ishmael, to the abode of the Voice of the Turtle, to the Sword-ark of Noah.

Then, when one feels there is nothing left to be experienced, we find that the stage of *fana-fi-Sheikh* has been completed, and we are ready to face the reality of the statement *In God we live and move and have our being*. Here, standing at the pinnacle of everything that is nameable, Saladin perceives before him the Grand Sword of the universe, across from which stands the

127

Empyrean. And God's Messengers, Moses and Jesus, come to him to guide his footsteps over that narrow blade, to give to him words of wisdom and blessing, conducting him to the *Arsh*-Throne (the God-realized human heart), where everyone is every other thing/being. And here he meets face to face the Prophet Mohammed who greets him with the words, "I am the Seal of all the Prophets whose testimony is my testimony and I their testimony, who are all Muslims, accommodations of Divine Will, empty egos filled with the Eternal Spirit. . . . "

Mohammed continues to present to him the message of an eternal Islam, as all-embracing as the Being of Allah Himself. And with this Divine vision, that the best of all religions is *the* Religion, the best of all messages is the one Message, the best of all guides is the Guidance itself, Mohammed presents to Saladin the greatness and wisdom of other Divine Messengers. And thus we meet Ram and Sita, Shiva — the dancer who performs the universe, Narayana-Krishna, Buddha, and the procession of all the Messengers and Prophets of all times passing and re-passing on the cosmic stage, light upon light! This vision culminates in the effacement (*fana*) in Allah Himself. This is the conclusion of Book II.

In Book III Saladin returns to deliver his yearly lecture to the captured crusaders, bringing with him the grandeur of his Divine experience. Now we see how the experiences described in the previous section are brought down to earth and applied directly to life in the world.

We are shown the picture of the gradual transformation of these crusaders who had been told they were fighting in the name of Jesus Christ, but who were utterly unaware of His love and forgiveness. It is Saladin's tactic to avoid trying to convert them to Islam; rather, he presents to them the depths of a Christianity which their priests, blinded by theological dogmas, could never provide them. Many deep religious questions are discussed in this section, sometimes from the perspective of the practices of Islam, sometimes from the words of Christ, or from the teachings of the Hebrew Prophets. And it is more than mere theological questions that are discussed, for the whole gamut of man's life and history is brought to the crucible. Yet throughout we always have the sense of an overriding unity, which is the result of the mystical penetration of the being of the poet, speaking in the name of Saladin.

The subject of peace in the Holy Land is taken up in depth in this Book, not only from the ideal point of view, but from the standpoint of actual historical precedents in the lives of such rulers as the Khalif Omar ("The Great") and Saladin.

Book IV, the final Book of the poem, is the shortest, and, at the same time, the most prophetic. The time is more explicitly in the present; and yet, as in all the poems in this trilogy, we have the wonderful integration of past, present and future. By looking through the eyes of Murshid we see the prophecies of Messengers of God in the past still living today, still holding forth the possibility of fulfillment. The poet directly faces our own historical moment and offers solutions to the particular problems of our own time.

In Book IV the predictions of the Prophet Isaiah concerning the Arabian peninsula and Sinai are accepted as if there is something we can do about it right now: the desert will bloom because it has been SEEN to bloom. And we feel in our being the need to fulfill the request of Isaiah: to "Make straight in Arabia a highway for our God," on every level, including the most literal. Thus Murshid treats us to the vision of a way of pilgrimage between the holy cities of Jerusalem and Mecca.

There is the vision of Egypt resurrecting as the phoenix from its ancient ashes, bringing anew the message of Divine Light. And there is the recognition of the inescapable need to fulfill the words of Christ, "Comfort ye, all my people." One must resist being drawn into arid political partisanship, which demands justice for wrongs committed against one while ignoring wrongs committed against another.

The poem ends on the note, struck again and again throughout the whole trilogy, that the Glory of Allah (God) will truly return to the earth depending only upon man's sincere desire for right Guidance.

Saladin

BOOK I, in which Saladin
relates the Song of the Swords,
begins his talks to the captured crusaders
and meets his Sheikh.

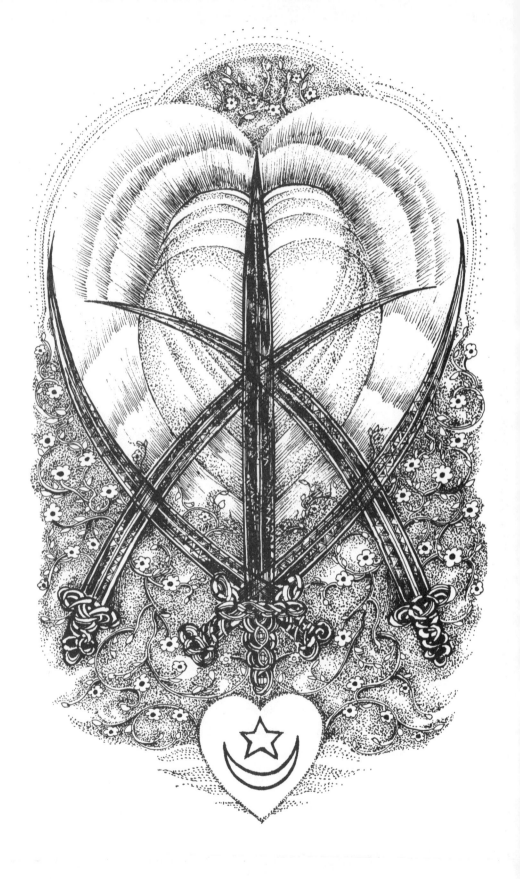

In the name of Allah, the Compassionate, the Beneficent.

Sing, Ya Allah, and let Your song be one of triumph for the world!
Sing, O man, and let your song be one of rejoicing in your God!
Sing, O heart, and let your ebullient harp-strings resound!
Sing, O breath, and let your flute-notes penetrate the air!
For in this time of trepidation and uncertainty,
In this time when man fears even his own endeavours,
When the fear toward God is but a shadow of that fear,
Hearts and minds and inner beings have lost their anchors
And the Word of Allah by which heavens and earth were made
Has been turned into a complicated mystery
Which the ego-mind of man does not comprehend.
Let the soul now sing that it become utterly triumphant,
Let the soul now sing that it become totally free,
That murmurs and forebodings be dispersed,
And the universal Light become known to all.

This is the book of Saladin, sultan and conqueror,
This is also the book of universal brotherhood,
For wherever two or three gather in devotion
There is the spirit of Divinity —
Thus the origination of the mosque,
Thus the fundamentals of the spirit of Islam,
Thus to demonstrate that humanity was made in the Divine Image,
Man in the totality — all, all, all mankind.
What is the true Islam? What is the false Islam?
There is no falsehood in Islam, only imperfection,
Even as the child is the imperfect man,
Even as the seeker is the imperfect sage;
So Islam has its grades of attainment,

From surrender to traditions bearing the name of 'Islam'
To utter surrender to Allah, Nearest and Dearest of all.
What is the true *jihad*? What is the false?
He who fights against the evil in himself,
He has become the true disciple of his Lord,
He alone performs the great jihad.

The Sword is mightier than the Pen, says Saladin:
Verily by the Sword was Saladin renowned as monarch of chivalry,
The conveyor of loving-kindness to friend and foe,
The establisher of equilibrium in the Holy Land.
What was the Sword of the Prophet but his keenness and character?
What is the true Sword of the Faithful, practicing Muslims?
Count me among the Muslims, Ya Allah, and I shall be satisfied.
I came not to bring peace but a Sword, did Jesus preach,
But conniving ones have discarded the Sword and taken the Pen,
So the scribes are seated in the places of authority
And dissimulation has been substituted for insight.

Verily Jesus, upon whom be peace, was a Muslim,
Verily all the Prophets of God have been true Muslims —
May I also be counted among the true, Ya Allah,
For by the Sword and not by the Pen did I bring peace.
Go, even unto China in search of wisdom, said the Prophet.
So I have sought for wisdom even to the ends of the earth.
I have not been caught in the webs of verbalists,
I have not been intrigued by the stirrings of rhetoricians
Nor limited myself to interpretations of the *kadis*,
But have striven to follow the Prophet in many things.
So although my footsteps did not reach as far as China,
The wisdom of China and of many lands came to my doors.
Praise be to Allah Who has graced me with this wisdom,

With the triumphant knowledge of five invaluable Swords,
With the wisdom which has been preserved through the ages.

This is the song of the Sword-of-metal,
The Sword which cuts its way directly to the Truth —
Do not fear those who would kill the body,
But rather those who torture the soul with hell-fire,
A lesson man can learn from Messiah Jesus,
A lesson which greatly impressed the consciousness of Saladin.
My Sword-of-metal is a needle,
To draw fibers into threads and threads into cloth;
My Sword-of-metal is a needle
To make garments and tapestries from such cloths.
This I have used to draw people together,
To integrate, to synthesize, to coalesce,
To bring those of many faiths into one society.
Pens are propagandists,
Directed by conniving minds to the undoing of righteousness;
Wars may come and go, but hatreds linger on
And the Scribes, among the few accursed by Jesus,
Have gloated over their ability to influence men
To battle, to hatreds, to endless exploitation.
Saladin waged endless wars upon all kinds of plotters,
Holding the unity-principle before all men:
The unity of God, the brotherhood of man, the universal harmony.
Brothers-in-arms are blessed who never hate,
Who fight the good fight of faith, daily;
Who fight the better fight of love, eternally.

Now I, Saladin, shall sing of the Sword-of-wood.
How can wood ever produce an effective, piercing sword?
A tiny sprig, gathering dust, can split a precipice;

A tiny sprig, gathering soil, can force a mountain slope;
Verily, by God's Grace the roots accomplish wonders;
Verily, the plant has what the dormant stone has not.
If the tiny root, the tender sprig can so accomplish,
How much more the sanctified Sword-of-wood?
Tannhauser was among the mobs that battled Saladin —
Brought before his eminence, the sultan forgave,
Bestowed upon the pilgrim a Sword-of-wood
And in the end, by Grace, was Tannhauser saved.
The Sword-of-wood bears the brunt of many battles,
Building tender floors to comfort your feet,
Producing effective beams to support your houses,
But even more it was used for the holy rood,
For the cross of Jesus was this Sword-of-wood
Upon which the ritual of crucifixion was held,
But the spirit of Messiah was not harmed,
The body of the Messenger was saved by Grace. [1.]
(Muslims and Christians differ, but Allah knows the Truth.)

The Sword-of-water brings the spirit of joy,
The Sword-of-water delights most in dancing.
Can you not see its birth among the glacial stones?
Singing, dancing over rock and boulders,
Cutting its pathway through the forest singing, dancing;
Winding through the meadows, singing, dancing;
Out to the broad plains no longer singing, still dancing;
Into the great reservoirs and tanks no longer dancing, still singing;
Brought to grain mills, turning wheels, singing, dancing;
Led to factories to move machinery, singing, dancing;
Finally wending its way to the ocean, singing, dancing.

The Sword-of-water knows neither fear nor hatred,
Has no enmity, no snobbishness, no hauteur;
The Sword-of-water is happy in its place, singing, dancing.
Among the people of Tao is the Sword-of-water most revered,
But also among the people of Allah:
Verily by the Sword-of-water did Abraham discover *Zem-Zem*,
From which well has come the plenitude of *baraka*;
Verily by the Sword-of-water did Moses strike the rock,
Verily also by it did John the Lustrator pass blessings on,
For wherever the Sword-of-water are blessing, *baraka*.

The Sword-of-fire is as something new under the sun —
It penetrates even into darkest corners,
It pierces through the most hidden of secret places,
Like the *jinn*, passing through walls and windows,
Finding its way to the uttermost parts of the world,
And this, without destroying a single thing.
Many vibrations spring from this Sword-of-fire,
Many inventions have come from its activities:
The telephone, the radio, the television,
The secret recorder, the sky watcher and others.
Verily with Saladin was this Sword-of-the-heart,
For love also penetrates anywhere, everywhere.
Verily under the sun are all men brothers,
Verily under the sun there is no deep cause for strife,
Verily with the Sword-of-fire are all united,
Verily this may, *inshallah*, bring everlasting peace.

Now to tell of the Sword-of-wind, ah! the Sword-of-wind!
Cutting its way — through itself,
Mending its way — through itself,
Utilizing itself to become other than itself,
Creating a laughter that is the wonder of the universe,
Producing that wit which is the partner even of wisdom.
It may penetrate your body and cause no harm,
It may travel through a wide space and do no harm.
How the gases in the atmosphere adjust to each others' ways!
How wonderfully do their molecules synchronize
Manifesting the possibilities of the subversion of ego,
Manifesting the possibilities of an immediate wisdom.
By the breath are many things made known,
By the conquest of breath all doors are opened,
By the Sword-of-wind is the Divine Will made known.

There is a welding of Swords and a crossing of Swords,
Thereby molding them into the perfect Scimitar,
Shaped like the moon, empty like the crescent;
The Sword, emblematic of the expression of sacred will,
The symbol of power of the righteous Khalifs.
Utilized for selfish ends, it long seemed lost,
Even when the supposed cause of Islam triumphed was it lost;
After the tragedy of Kerbela it seemed far away,
But it returned by Grace into the hands of Saladin.
By means of the Sword was victory vouchsafed,
By means of the Sword was the Holy Land delivered,
Delivered to be open to men of every faith,
Delivered for all the world and not for a mere portion.
No longer can the men-of-the-Pen incite its use,
No longer may there be a limited war,
No longer is there a place to hide —
We must unite or die in wholesale destruction.
A new war, and then men-of-the-Pen shall also die,
A new war, and the wielders of propaganda shall be its victims;
The rays of destruction cannot be circumvented by ego,
The rays of destruction already bring fear to anti-theists.
The public shall learn in a righteous way
The existence and presence of Allah — praise be to Him.

There is a welding as well as a crossing of Swords,
There is a welding into an indestructible shield,
The shield of utter submission to the All-being,
Which shield shall save the world.
When the Pen fails, when war fails, when even prayers prove
     nothing,
Allah the Merciful does not fail;
When terror reaches the uttermost, when there is nothing left,

Allah the Merciful does not fail;
When there is no course left, when there is dismay,
When push-buttons threaten the very universe,
Allah the Merciful does not fail;
When religion stops at the door of places of worship,
Allah the Merciful does not fail;
When armies of peasants were thrown at the feet of the conqueror,
Allah the Merciful did not fail —
So says Saladin, the Muslim, the Sword-of-the-Faith.
What has been said before can only be repeated:
That places blessed by Allah belong to no man,
That sanctuaries of *baraka* because of the Prophets of God,
That sanctuaries of *baraka* because of the miracles of Allah
Were not, can never remain the sole possessions of a group.
Verily did ancient Hellas prosper when people listened to oracles,
Verily did ancient Hellas disappear when politicians interfered.
For the paths of God are utterly free and cannot be contaminated;
No men-of-the-Pen, no conniving partisans
Can predetermine revelations of God to man.
When holy places become causes of wide-spread dispute,
When ownership is limited to certain communities,
The way of blessing is impeded and all humanity may suffer.
I, Saladin, sought this deliverance for humanity in my time,
I seek it again in another age for the sake of the whole wide world.

II.

I was a king, glorious in battle, excellent in administration,
I was the paragon of practical virtue,
I was the beau ideal of chivalry,
I diligently studied Quran and *Hadith* and *Sunna*,

I tried to fulfill the precepts of Islamic teaching,
Imagining myself an exemplary follower of the Prophet,
Near to perfection in many, many things,
Commiting a single sin.
I followed the example of the Prophet toward my companions,
I did not enrich myself when others were poor,
I did not neglect even my most humble subjects,
Respecting *Taurat* and *Injil* along with Holy Quran,
Consulting imams and *kadis* and sages,
Demanding the uttermost justice for all petitioners,
Vowing allegiance to the living Khalif at Bagdad,
A practice long abandoned by selfish rulers in Islam
Who confused the realm of ego with the realm of truth:
Islam is the perfect religion and should be practiced to perfection.

I do not consider him a Muslim who contradicts his brethren
Nor do I consider him a *Mumin* who pays verbal respect
But whose heart and behaviour are far from the righteous Way;
In all ages the wicked substitute orthodoxy for repentance,
But I would speak in the Name of Allah, the Compassionate,
    the Beneficent,
And consider it incumbent to examine the heart daily.
Many are the verbalists who insist on exactness of text,
Who depart from the spirit of Islam
Producing nothing but stigma for their religion,
Whose companionship brings no satisfaction.

I was a king even to my many enemies,
I was a ruler who accepted responsibility,
Who realized the all-pervading Mercy of Allah,
Nor did prejudge the private opinions of men,
Permitting the broad tolerance enjoined by the Prophet,

Continuing the policies of the noble Khalif Omar,
So there were no forced attempts at proselytizing.
I exacted only honourable excises and taxes;
Then war and a horrible horde of ravaging men-beasts,
Calling themselves "Christians," performing unspeakable deeds,
Such as one would expect from hyena or jackal
And that, in the name of what they called "religion."
Allah, the ever-Victorious, the Just, was with me,
Who vouchsafes victory for whom He will,
Nor did His victory diminish my humility,
Nor cause me to depart from the sacred precepts.
I considered forgiveness as part of regal behaviour,
And never lost sight of that deep, inner jihad
To battle against the weaknesses within the self —
Committing a single sin.

When the battles were finally crowned with victory,
When I could no longer rely upon broken promises,
I sought neither revenge nor called for reparation
But spoke in kindly words to those who surrendered:

"Men of Frankistan —
I call you *men* though you seem not to know its meaning,
O sorrowful ones for the terrific damage you have wrought,
O fortunate ones to have become captives of merciful Islam,
Who have been blinded to believing you have fought for Jesus,
Who do not know that I feel I have been fighting for Jesus,
Who is regarded as among the Divine Messengers by Muslims.
You think you have fought to redeem your holy sanctuaries,
You desire most of all the right to your pilgrimage,
I also seek to sanctify those holy places,

I also desire free and untrammeled pilgrimages,
Pilgrimages for those who worship Allah in many fashions,
Pilgrimages for devotees of every faith.

"Have you studied your Scriptures that you should be so assured?
Have you studied your Bible enough to comprehend religion?
Have you ever heard of the revelation of Quran?
Jesus of Nazareth was in every way a Muslim,
Jesus, son of Mary, constantly sought guidance from God;
Even I, Saladin, the victorious sultan
Strive to be a Muslim, seeking guidance from my God.
Jesus forgave all men, excepting the Scribes, the men-of-the Pen
Who opposed and tormented him and offered martyrdom.
Your Scriptures advise that soldiers be content with their wages,
But your men-of-the-Pen have incited you to carnage;
They rouse, they exhort, they propagandize
And they reap huge rewards if you happen to be victorious
While you alone suffer when doomed to defeat.

"If Allah had granted you victory, these lands would go to
    your inciters;
When Allah brings defeat, the men-of-the-Pen do not suffer,
Still occupying lands and homes, safe, far, far away;
While you shed blood and suffer from your wounds,
They are safe with their possessions, at home, far away;
When you have learned to distrust these men-of-the-Pen
As Jesus, the blessed, distrusted the Scribes of his time,
Verily you have taken the first step toward Islam.
In those long forgotten times they so conspired:
'The religion of Jesus is surely most effective
Only it makes no claims against the Caesars of Rome,
Let us establish superclaims against the Caesars,

Let us call Jesus 'King', 'King of Kings', 'Lord', 'Lord of Lords';
Whereas the Caesars claim to partake of Divinity,
Let us identify Messiah with ultimate Divinity' —
Surely a blasphemy for Allah begets not, nor is begotten.
Whereas Jesus offered blessings for all without distinction,
The men-of-the-Pen have established a special church;
Where Jesus would not refuse even the women of Samaria,
The men-of-the-Pen have demarcated heresy:
Whosoever does not agree is regarded as doomed —
Thus into nescience the wisdom-teachings of Jesus,
Thus to oblivion the beauty of his holy words,
Thus the whole world sank into darkness until Mohammed
    appeared
To proclaim anew the revelations of Divinity.

"Now I have assembled monks from *Jebel Musa*,
Men versed in Scriptures, excelling in the Book,
Who shall testify whether I speak truly or falsely,
Whether I quote directly from your Scriptures
Or am concocting fables of my own imagining.
Therefore I read the words: 'Ye are the light of the world.'
Monks, is it true that this comes from Divine revelation?
Monks, are not these the words of Holy Jesus himself?
O you poor people, astrayed by men-of-the-Pen,
O you poor people, misled by false propaganda,
Thinking you needed to conquer to have your pilgrimages!
Who has ever prevented you from the holy shrines?
Ye are the light of the world — there are no others;
Ye are the ones created in the image of Divinity,
Ye are the chosen of the Compassionate, the Beneficent.
O poor *Feringhis*, who know so little of the Book,
Who know so little of the love and forgiveness of Jesus;

When did he ever anathematize anyone as a heretic?
Where did he divide into the orthodox and schismatics?
When even a harlot was brought to him, did he not say:
'Neither do I condemn you, go and sin no more.'
Therefore I, Saladin, the sultan, the seeker of Islam,
In the spirit of Islam proclaim, 'Sin no more.'

"There are lands and flocks before you, such as you have never
        enjoyed;
There are suitable homes for you, such as you have never enjoyed,
There are opportunities awaiting you, such as you have never
        enjoyed,
Even as Jesus declared: 'In my Father's house are many stations,'
So I in turn offer a place for each of you,
And in the spirit even of your New Testament say:
'There are no high nor low nor Jew nor Greek in Messiah,'
Neither are there high nor low nor black nor white
Nor Arab nor *Ajami* in the brotherhood of Islam,
In the ubiquitous Presence of Allah, the Ever-Living.
I shall not judge you according to Quran or Sunna
But rather let your own Book determine your fate
For, by divination of your Holy Scriptures your lot is set:
That you remain in this land for the coming seven years.

"Your prayer has ever been: 'O Lord, have mercy.'
While Islam always proclaims: 'Allah *is* Mercy.'
That Mercy which you thought far away is now at hand,
That Mercy which you regard as a Grace of God
We consider as an essential attribute of Allah —
O people of the Book, Israelians and Christians,
There is nothing in your Scriptures which Mohammed did not
        respect,

There is nothing in the words of Jesus he did not accept —
And most of all, that Sermon on the Mount
Which is regarded by many as the norm of highest morality.
Why is it no more of tabernacles or *shechina*?
No more holy dances around altars, no more sacrifices?
Why permission of usury and the abrogation of the Jubilee?
So much rejected, what is left to be considered valid?
The battlegrounds have been drawn in all the worlds:
Not on earth alone but in the heavens are crusades wrought,
Nor on earth alone but on all planes the jihad;
Through trust in Allah have I conquered, to Whom all praise;
The cosmos itself has assented to your fitting recompense."

III.

I then truced with mutual satisfaction,
With more than verbal discontinuance of war,
With positive establishment of friendship and honour;
But as the Christians were concerned with the souls of men,
I also considered their spiritual future on these terms:

"O you poor rabble, peasant captives from lands far away,
Where now the leaders who have so allured you?
Who the stalwarts who have urged you hence?
You call your leaders 'lords' despite the Scriptures
Which demand obeisance to the One alone.
Not for me to determine your spiritual future,
Yet Jesus has declared: 'Ye are the salt of the earth,'
Who even in your palaces, at your meals, are divided by salt; [2.]
So man is separated from man by other than Grace.
What religion is this? In Islam such can never be;

146

In Islam even the most degraded are considered;
In Islam blessings are shared in common, by custom,
For this was the way of the Prophet and the Righteous Khalifs,
This was the habit of Omar, the splendid Commander.

"Omar was the selected Commander of the Faithful,
And Amru ibn Aas commander for the Commander of the Faithful
Who, by the Sword and Grace of the Ever-Victorious,
Became the most successful conqueror of Egypt;
He invaded an Egypt tyrannized by Greeks
Who insisted that they were the most devoted Christians,
While the Egyptians also proclaimed themselves as such,
But between them strife and calumny and vilification,
And in the name of Jesus anathemas were hurled
While the masses lived in most extreme subjection:
Kept in a state worse than chattel slavery — in the name of Christ;
Not even permitted to practice religion — in the name of Christ;
Deprived of human privileges — in the name of Christ.
So Amru easily conquered the whole country,
Not with the usual course of rapine and plunder and murder,
Indeed with a minimum of battling and bloodshed,
And so delivered the Egyptians from their captivity,
Taking only possessions of Greeks as fitting spoils.
All else did he conquer but not himself,
Forgetting the greater jihad in pursuit of the lesser,
Departing from the customs of the Prophet,
Taking booty and appropriating a castle —
Whereon the Khalif addressed him an epistle:

" 'Commander for the Commander of the Faithful,
In whose name war? In whose name this victory?
If in the name of Allah, then to Him the glory and bounty —

ALLAH MANSUR!   SUBHAN ALLAH!

If in the name of the sword for the sake of the sword,
You have unleashed your own, not the Sword of Islam;
You have invaded to battle for justice,
To free the people materially and spiritually,
To re-enfranchise the ancient **Land of Two Truths**.
To whom is this earth? to the powerful? or to Allah?
If the earth be to the powerful of what am I Khalif?
If the earth be to Allah, then all must enjoy it;
If instead of following Sunna we adopt the ways of the Greeks,
As the Greeks have long been doing and also the *Ajamis*,
Then we surrender to the faiths of Greeks and *Ajamis*
And you are guilty of *shirk*. *
Must I refer to wars between the Greeks and *Ajamis*?
Shall I repeat the prophecies of God's Messenger?
What is Islam? Where is Compassion? Beneficence?
Bounty has there been and spoils and shares,
And who among the Companions is entitled to more than I?
Who among the Faithful has accepted less than the Khalif?
Verily though I am the Commander of the Faithful,
It is as one *of* the Faithful and not as one *over* the Faithful.
Whose position is foremost in the mosque?
What is the bowing of heads simultaneously?
What is the meaning of touching the ground?
If simple things are not yet understood,
How can you continue to function as *Amir*?
Have you not read the instructions of the Messenger?
Are you not acquainted with his commands and requests?
In whose name do you war, O Amru ibn Aas?

" 'The course is clear to me if not to you:

* Infidelity.

148

Either to imitate unfaithful Greeks and blind *Ajamis*,
Exploiters of the down-trodden everywhere,
Or continue in the footsteps of the Prophet.
What are the Hadith? Which is the way of Sunna?
Consider the multitude of sands of the desert
Which stand side by side, row by row, in their simplicity,
Which are as equal before the sun, the wind, the elements—
So also is mankind before Allah, so all things before Allah.
Sand in the desert, devotees at their prayers,
Gratitude and Glory and Majesty to the One.
Here I live in humility without servants,
Staying in a tent like Jacob, cooking my meals,
While endless piles of trophies arrive from afar,
Through the victories of Khalid and Mothanna and yourself,
Bequeathing the riches of the world to the *Mumin*,
Distributed in equitable division to the faithful.
When shall this accumulation terminate?
When is the instance man says to his lusts, 'be still',
To his anger 'be calm,' to his greed, 'enough'?

" 'The jihad against political enemies is easy,
The jihad against the unfaithful is simple enough,
But the following in the footsteps of the Messenger
Is a difficult task, most worthy of all.
Remember how the gracious one spoke at Mecca
To the fallen who had been most bitter enemies:

" ' "Men of Mecca, people of the Kureish,
I greet you in the name of Allah, the Compassionate, the Beneficent,
I come not to impose upon you my religion,
But to present to you the majesty of Oneness,
Not an empty unity, but one endowed with qualities,

149

Preeminent among which are Compassion and Beneficence;
Therefore in bringing tidings of Islam to you people
I also present Compassion and Beneficence.
First know there is Allah, the One, the All, the Only;
This now I hope to show by demonstrations,
By treating you as children of that One,
By acting toward you as an elder brother;
Whether you accept His Eminence or not,
Whether you submit to His Guidance or otherwise,
You have submitted to me, your elder brother.
Not to Mohammed the conqueror, the despoiler,
Not to Mohammed the self-enriched, the despotic ruler,
But to Mohammed, the Messenger of Allah.
The work of the spiritual Sheikh is to enlighten disciples,
Not to become leader or exploiter or intermediary
Which are the by-ways of the charlatan,
And though you have not known Allah, He knows you all
And all abide in Him. *Subhan Allah*!

" ' "The *Beni Israel* were custodians of the Message
To whom Allah sent many Prophets in ages past,
Although He also sent Messengers to the Arabs
And the names of these Prophets have been preserved in honour,
Though the teachings of Prophets have been superseded
By folkways; the wisdom trampled in the dust.
Now it is presented to the world once more,
To be shared with all, to be known by all.

" ' "The Nazarenes declare God is the son of Mary—
Have they, in invocation, been able to alter the universe?
Have they, through prayer, succeeded in times of trouble?
Daily they repeat: *Kyrie Eleïson*, 'Lord, have mercy,'

But to Muslims Allah is Mercy indeed.
Sects have appeared with curses for one another,
Heresies have arisen with mutual persecution,
Arguments set forth with spite and malice and rancour —
Is this submission to the revelation of God?

" ' "No priests do I bring to act as intercessors,
No prayer do I commend that will produce divisions,
No complicated theology do I impose,
Nor a faith that is not easily comprehended:
Quran and the Five Pillars should be enough,
Provided one illustrates teachings in his daily life.

" ' "I come, then, to restore the Message of all Prophets
And you must not regard me with honourifics —
Honour my person and Allah will be far away,
Worship Allah and you will honour me no end:
Peace upon you all.
The teaching of Noah and Abraham I give again,
The lessons of Moses and Jesus would I restore,
Synthesizing all revelations into a whole,
Presenting you this summation in Quran,
Thereby to prove the rectitude of my mission,
Thereby to demonstrate I truly am the Seal.

" ' "Do not worship the Seal and neglect his proferred warnings,
Nor cast any shadow between yourselves and Allah,
Nor regard Mohammed as a kingly intercessor
Whose upraised prayer will save your souls from Hell.
It is for me to demonstrate the attributes,
The attributes of Beauty, of Majesty, of Perfection,
And exemplify the goal of *akhlak Allah*.

151

For Allah is closer than the veins of your neck,
And His Mercy has been from the founding of the world.

" ' "Go! your homes are yours, your wives and your possessions,
Even the things that formerly belonged to the house of Abbas —
These are but miniscules in this world of sensual enjoyment,
Yet even if they were not, I have no need for them,
For Allah grants each day as He sees my needs —
Al-hamdu Lillah!

" ' "Two blessings are also vouchsafed,
Testimonials of the Mercy of your Lord:
The *baraka* of Zem-Zem, spring of fortunate delight,
Spring whence manifest Grace and blessing
To be shared by friend and wayfarer alike,
To illustrate the Beneficence of Divinity;
When the Friend of Allah was in direst need,
When the Friend cried out in uttermost distress:
'I need Thee, I depend upon Thee, grant, I thirst!'
The inner eye of Abraham was opened
And then before him was Zem-Zem manifested,
To become the source of tremendous gladness for mankind.
Verily does its *baraka* partake of divers aspects:
The *baraka* of vibrations in its holiness,
The *baraka* of atoms in its healing salts,
For thus is man healed both internally and externally,
That body and soul receive their blessing together.

Then also is the wonder of the Kaaba,
Formed of solid materials from the outer space,
A testimonial as if from heaven to earth,
Manifesting the Omnipresence of Allah;

Cherish it:
You can build temples and avow that they are holy,
You can erect shrines and insist that they are holy,
You can establish institutions and declare them holy,
But this is something that Allah has brought you —
They who bow in prayer together shall become harmonious;
Concordance in prayer and devotion leads to brotherhood,
And Kaaba is the *Kibla* for this earth." ' "

"Thereupon did Omar, the Khalif, continue:
'Before me the examples of the Prophet, my director and friend;
Why should I, his earnest companion, otherwise?
If one possess Guidance and Blessing and Grace,
What need for further properties and material glory?
Before you, O Amru ibn Aas, is this selection:
Shall they of Islam gather acquisitions for themselves
Or live as if in imitation of the Prophet,
Praying, as they do, to follow the proper Path?

" 'We have not come to demonstrate another religion,
We have come as disciples of the true Islam,
The religion of all Prophets, upon whom peace,
The religion of submission in everything man does,
The religion which can truly be called *din*, the faith.
Wealth or righteousness — the Greeks have chosen wealth;
Honour or submission to Allah — the Greeks have chosen honour;
Self-security or unstinted mercy — the Greeks desire security;
We have not come to Egypt to make it a land of slaves,
We have not come to Egypt to enrich our personal selves,
We have come to demonstrate the Glory of Allah,
That the Glory of Allah be set before the people and the land.' "

"Therefore I, Saladin, set the Glory of Allah before you
Following, I trust, in the ways of the Righteous Khalifs,
Following, I hope, in the pathways of the Messenger of God.
If you do not follow the sultan in this,
It will be well if you retain your ancient faith;
Better to submit yourselves to Allah —
Peace to you all."

IV.

Then I, Saladin, sent for the leader of the *Beni Israel*,
A very wise man, known in later ages as Nathan,
Saying, "Nathan, thou art reputed to be a noble sage;
No intention have I to contend with you save in a friendly manner,
For that is the way in which the Prophet advised,
But answer me: Did Allah create Israel only in His image
Or did He fashion Adam so, who is the father of us all?"
Then answered Nathan: "There is no dispute between thee and me."

Yet I have not been able to understand these people
Who seem to have substituted Ezra for their Prophet Moses,
Even declaring intermarriage a heinous sin,
A sin much greater than the breaking of commandments
Although Moses himself married outside the Tribes.
Yes, I do not understand this very strange people
Who have a special holiday for one Queen Esther,
Born of the *Beni Israel*, yet married outside;
And also they have a book for Ruth, not of their blood,
Though later she accepted their God and their religion.
But I have summoned the leaders of the synagogue
Addressing them, according to my standards:

"O children of our common father, Abraham,
In your books it is said that all shall come to know God;
Even though you have not been prone to proselytize,
This teaching appears among your holy writings
Which also declare His House should be built for all,
Not only for descendants of Jacob and the Tribes,
Not only for them that have retained selected rites —
Ceremonies not performed by the Prophet Moses
And different from the rites ascribed to Abraham.
It has been said the righteous shall come from thy brethren,
Not necessarily from the *Beni Israel*,
For one of your Prophets extolled the scions of Edom, [3.]
And some of your rulers were descended from Jacob's brother.

"We also, scions of Arabia, are monotheists —
How can you call us *goyim* who accept the Torah and the Prophets?
Why do you insist we are not monotheists?
Did not the *Arabim* feed your own Elijah? [4.]
Was not Jonah an Arab? and Job? and Habakkuk?
Welcome, very welcome are you in this Holy Land,
Even as in your teaching shall it be 'Holiness unto the Lord',
Not holiness to any because of ancestry,
Not holiness because of theology,
But holiness because of submission to the One God.

"Be therefore informed, O scions of the *Beni Israel*,
That in my kingdom are others of the Tribes
Who do not accept traditions that you have adopted,
Who place the Book above commentaries and folk-customs,
Who are known to the world of the time as '*Karaim*' —
In my empire shall all groups dwell in tranquility,
In my empire all must dwell in amity,

155

In my empire a universal tolerance —
Surely it must be so within the empires of the heavens,
Surely it shall be so within this sacred land —
Therefore listen to one who has submitted to God alone,
Although some of you have enmity toward us Muslims
And minimized examples of cooperation,
Let it be known to you, I so proclaim:
Regardless of what happened within the *Hedjaz*,
I shall retain the policies of Khalif Omar
To make this the abode of all believers
So the peoples of the Book may continue their rites,
Have full access to all their holy places,
To be welcomed by the people of Quran,
For whatever the past many now worship One God,
And we pray that this truth be recognised through the ages —
Peace between thee and me, peace between me and thee,
Peace between Jacob and Esau, Isaac and Ishmael. Amin."

Then I, Saladin, Commander for the Commander of the Faithful,
Assembled the nobles of Frankistan, my captives,
Loosened their shackles and addressed them thus:

"Seniors and noble gentlemen of Frankistan:
You who have been ransomed and you as yet unransomed,
All who feel that their mission is to return,
Nothing is asked save that you listen to the sultan —
You have accepted a religion in the name of revelation,
You have accepted blindly without access to records,
Although people of the Book, yet ignorant of the Book,
Who follow your scribes and priests so blindly;
How can you blindly comprehend the Felicity of the One?
How can the ignorant of God submit to His acclaimed Will?

"I, who am sultan and a ruler among the Muslims,
Which means that I am only a directing tax-gatherer,
Feel myself rather as a steward of stewards;
You have been given teachings the source of which is unclear,
You have been told that the Trinity is fundamental,
You have accepted theologies foreign to your Book,
You do not regard the nobility of Jesus,
Remaining ignorant of the bases of your faith.

"Now Allah, the Beneficent, has sent a Book in Arabic,
A revelation which we regard as final,
Not to be mauled into conflicting expositions,
To be used in inane debates by philosophers,
But rather as the guide in our daily life.
You, who claim a Book and revelation,
Continue to follow the common laws of the Caesars,
Your property rights the legacy of the Caesars,
Your human rights, or lack of them, accordingly,
Your womenfolk debased, your commoners enslaved,
So you really follow the Caesars more than Christ.

"Verily I say: 'This earth is of Allah and all therein,'
And if a single sentence I have spoken
Is contrary to the spirit of your Scriptures,
The monks from Jebel Musa may interrupt —
The teachings of your Testament are in their hands;
And as Jesus said: 'I have not come to destroy the law
But to fulfill,' so would I fulfill,
For Mohammed completed the missions of Moses and Jesus,
Mohammed perfected the work of Moses and Jesus
And all the Prophets. Go in peace. Amen."

Then another meeting with the captives,
All necessary arrangements were properly made,
Ransoms received and many permitted to depart
With mutual satisfaction in final treaties,
With pilgrimages vouchsafed, with peace restored.
The status of all persons being settled,
I gave my final talk to those that remained:

"O my presumable captives, men from Frankistan,
I treat you not as my captives but as those of Allah,
Freed potentially from superstition
And, accordingly as laid down in your Scriptures,
You shall remain in this land for seven years
When, if not ransomed, a choice shall remain to you
To continue in the faith in which you were raised
Or accept the teachings of Islam as presented.
Every year you must therefore be congregated
To listen to the *khutbah*, hear your sultan speak
And you shall judge, each according to conscience,
For with us there is no compulsion in religion,
Only endless opportunity for every soul
To learn about the inner and outer ways
Which lead to the realization of the Supreme.

"We hope you will learn that this captivity
Does not present a heavy burden; you will be more free
Than in your lands where you had so few rights.
I do not wish to overweigh emotions
Nor force any to perform against his will;
Heaven will rejoice when there is repentance
Which springs from the open and happy heart —
The rest is false and only leads to hyprocrisy.

It shall not be among your punishments
To listen to endless sermons by any of us —
You will learn the ways of Islam as you work,
In your daily life in all its manifold aspects,
But now you are tired and anxious for some rest,
Even if it be the sleep of a lowly slave;
You shall not starve; you shall be garmented and housed
And cared for as if juveniles.

"I wish upon you God's Love and Beneficence and Blessing,
For Saladin, the sultan, bears no one ill-will
As he has demonstrated to King Richard and many others —
This is my final word for the immediate season,
Returning to my palace also for rest,
To rule the empire, once again, in peace. Amin."

V.

I slept; I slept, for peace had come,
Peace to my people surfeited with long fighting,
Peace to the satisfaction of all concerned,
To the warring Crusaders and Feringhis
Gone to return to mutual jealousies.
I slept, free from the stringencies of war,
From the bloodshed, the awfulness of battle,
The cruelty enforced upon a warrior;
I slept, loosed from the strident cares which beset a ruler,
From the stern responsibilities of empire;
My enemies, my allies and all others submitting,
Now even in sleep was I submitting.

O modern people who know so little of sleep,
Who have forsaken prayer for the cocktail hour,
How can you enjoy the sanctity of that deep
Blessing which blots out all care
To share
In Beneficence God has given all.
This is a wonder which alcohol
Can never bestow,
So you do not know
Beauty and joy and rejuvenation.
Prayer for the Muslim, drink for civilization,
Presenting elements of another crusade,
Fighting for what man has made,
Placing his erudition
Above Allah and holy submission.

I slept.
This is a Mercy of Allah from Whom we come, to Whom we return;
There is a daily life with consciousness on and off,
There is an aeonic life with consciousness on and off,
The smaller reflects the greater, the greater focuses the smaller.
People demand proofs, blind to those closest at hand,
Repeating 'Allah' as 'twere a word among a multitude,
Thinking of 'God' as one in an endless array of thoughts,
They fight for these words, die for these thoughts,
Considering this nobility and saintly martyrdom,
So man becomes the measure of his universe,
And God, the All-Being, seems hidden.

I slept, and earth was removed from my vision,
And with the loss of selfness perturbations ceased,
Sensual faculties no longer beclouded the mind,

The Light of the universe became more evident,
And Saladin was caught in a by-play of lights and shadows,
With a curtain drop of augmenting twilights and rays,
The lights and darknesses commingling
Until I became aware of another type of existence,
As if lying upon my bed like a patient in illness,
Where ministering spirits attended to my needs
And one among them more assiduous than the rest;
Food and drink and sweet perfumes were at my command
And such lofty incense permeated the atmosphere
That sometimes I felt as if in heaven;
My slightest wish was immediately fulfilled,
Till vision and mentality became much brighter
And the garments of pain and decay were cast aside.

Then my eyes beheld the most attentive of all,
That Sohrawardi Maktul whom I had persecuted,
That Sohrawardi Maktul whom I had martyred,
This the single sin of a rather virtuous life,
This the single sin for which I became ashamed;
And there he was, kneeling by my side,
Reproaching himself over and over again:

"O King, Sultan, O Commander of the Faithful, forgive!
Greatly did I sin before you when alive,
Sin before my Prophet and my God. Forgive!
What vanity that *Iblis* must have aroused, forgive!
Enthusiasm is blind, infatuation worse than sin,
And in presuming surrender the ego became so puffed
That my intoxication overcame my insight; please forgive."
The sobbing melted into the surrounding brightness,
Our hearts began to reverberate in harmony,

Drawn by some force toward a unification,
Even as if he were now to become my Sheikh.

There is the *Tarikat* in Islam
Wherein one imbibes the wisdom of the universe,
Preserved through the ages through chains of Prophets
And spiritual teachers, these last mostly unknown.
The wisdom persists, for otherwise Allah
Would be existing without His epithets,
And name-calling would replace realization.
It is not necessary for all to come this way,
For without the consent of Allah, no one comes to Him,
Nor is this in thought or idea, but experience.
Many have there been who have had this experience,
Many in all ages, without worldly fanfare,
And perhaps it will be so forever.

But I, Saladin, relate my own experience,
That it be recorded and left emblazoned in history,
Hoping that others will follow where I have gone,
In the daily life, in the historical career,
And in the most supreme, the search for Allah.
Thus I cease my personal tale, to be concerned with Allah,
Who in truth am naught save what Allah has desired,
I being the patient instrument of that accomplishment.
As-salaam aleikhum. Peace be with you.

Book II

THE JOURNEY THROUGH THE HEAVENS

In the Name of Allah, the Compassionate, the Beneficent.

Arise and come quickly, my love;
Arise and come swiftly,
For the soul of the universe beckons to the soul of man;
There is the sphere of time and the sphere beyond time,
There is the arena of ego-activity and that beyond
Where the Supreme reigns supreme, but man can get a glimpse;
So come and follow, and give no thought to the morrow
Nor to the self, nor to the troubles or delights or duties,
For the greatest duty and greatest opportunity are before thee.
So arise, come quickly, come swiftly, come in good-will,
The answer will be in the reward and the reward in the answer.

Now over the *barzakh* of the kingdoms of limited outlook,
Up on the phoenix-wings of the spirit of the universe,
Riding on the Cosmic Dove which is ever at man's service,
And over the construct-heavens of followers of many sects
Where the self-esteemed provide their own Elysian Fields,
The self-deluded homestead in higher dimensions
Exclusive for each of its kind, with marked complacency
And total unawareness of those who differ.
All, even these, dwell within the confines of Divine Mercy
Which is beyond limitation, boundless,
For Allah permits child-souls to erect building-block heavens

As narrow as the outlook of their intellects,
As broad as the sympathies of their hearts.

There is no absolute Hell in the boundless universe,
But there are fires of healing and purification,
Fires of punishment and restitution of propriety,
Fires to restore the consciousness to equilibrium,
To permit the energies of passion to fulfill compulsion
And allow the lusts of men to pass from experience to reaction.
Laws of morality and physical being are not different —
There is an entropy which operates with love,
Which enables the treasure-gatherers to administer
To those less capable in vital capacities,
Yet contrives to give to each full measure of freedom;
So Allah has decreed an infinitude of conditions
Masked within the personalities He has created.

In truth the soul of man is completely unshackled,
Free as the air one breathes on the heavy earth,
And even freer to breathe when life erupts from these bodies,
Limited by a circus-parade of personal shortcomings,
Harassed by the interference of selfish motives,
Caught in the web of consequences to acts and schemes
But not, as many have presumed, punished by a Loving God

I did not survey these confines of happy captivity,
These lotus-eating worlds of presumable satisfaction,
Some restricted by themselves to a hundred and forty-four thousand,*
Some restricted by themselves to those of equal inclinations,
Some restricted by themselves to similar narrow outlooks,
Some restricted to themselves because they love restrictions,

*Some fundamentalist Christian sects restrict the number of the elect to 144,000—ED.

166

All yet veiled, unawake to the vastness of the cosmos,
To never-ending Love and Compassion and Forgiveness.
Such is the operation of Infinite Wisdom
That these souls are permitted to heavenly corrals
Until the agitating forces within their beings,
Reacting to the deeper forces latent in their hearts,
Pushes them up or down to further resume their quest
Toward the complete expression of these deeper urges,
To find a further fulfillment on earth, or in a higher heaven.
Theologians will dissert on what they do not know
With feigned humility and lack of childlikeness,
Confounding through mistranslations and surmisings,
Ignoring differences of times and climes and habits,
And by-passing fundamental principles.

ALLAH IS — *ALLAHU*
With Him your *sameness* and *difference* have no meaning,
For this finite mind, self-limited,
Is not qualified to garner the vast expanse
Nor to attribute that beyond attribution,
Nonsense breeding endless confusion,
Bringing ignominy to religion and the spiritual search.

The Greeks had reached a stage of settled culture,
Yet were bound by the Olympic faith of finite gods,
Themselves subjected to the whims of Nemesis,
So their worshippers sought through philosophy
For a broader, more hopeful outlook.

Moses was blessed with the mission of prophethood
And sealed within a Book in the ancient Hebrew
The mysteries and doctrines of his age

In such a manner that these became obscure,
Lost through mistranslations and disuse,
Pushed into idioms and thoughts which satisfy
Ecclesiasts given to worldly existences.
Thus humanity has followed an elephant-trap trail
Into a zoological mental maze
Which it confuses with the very universe.
People devoid of Love and Compassion and Kindness,
Those unconscious of the unlimited Mercy of Allah,
Are led into their special construct-heavens,
Deluded as regards their presumed salvation,
Sinning against man, atoning before a nominal "God",
Returning to sin further against man, quite unaware
That they are ever subjected to moral laws.

The world has become aware of Grecian limitations
But not of personal shortcomings which are endless —
It is of little avail to describe these phantasies
Which do not represent the more noble heavens,
But nonetheless bear witness of Allah's Compassion,
Keeping the child-souls in their infancy
Until they are ready to grow, and learn.

Let us turn from them in devotion to the One;
Let us turn from them and leave them as they are,
Concerning ourselves with beauty and majesty,
Pursuing our path to its final destination.

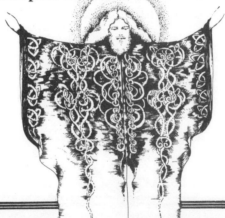

II.

Thus we arrived at the threshold of the **Heaven of Joseph**,
The entrance to that grand portion of the pluriverse
Which manifests to those awakened in heart
As to the fullness of the **GLORY OF THE LORD**,
That so-called many-coloured-land of the ancient **Celts**,
Symbolized by the coat mentioned in the **Bible**,
Where light flashes and reflashes, scintillates and shines,
For there, **Joseph**, the archetype, rules in splendour,
Garbed in radiant purity which emanates from his soul.

We were first required to pass the gate of *tauba*,
Which is also known as the 'Everlasting Gate',
Called by the Hebrews *shuvo*, and in our times 'repentance',
The gate of heart-turning, the gate of awareness *from* self,
The gate of the birth of the tremendous inner life.
If the heart be as dead, if the heart be burdened,
The experience of heaven remains incomplete
Though the Grace of Allah is ubiquitous and eternal,
Which Grace must be collected to be realized,
Whose Glory is secluded in the atoms and dynams of space,
Separated from the labyrinth of self-scheming,
Where the totality of All remains uncognized.

There is no lowly grovelling in the dust,
No cacophonous wailing over imaginary sins,
Neither judgment upon the self-of-self or another;
Ego-aggravation holds one outside the door —
We sin against man and then ask God for pardon,
We sin against man — this is the course of history,
We sin against ourselves and ask God for pardon,
We sin against our consciousness and harden our being,
But we do not sin because we transgress theology,
We do not sin because of any orthodoxy;
The Pen has ever interfered with universal justice,
Though men-of-the-Pen acclaim devotion to justice,
But the Merciful always inclines to the side of Mercy.

There is no judgment-hall in the heavenly portions;
There is only redemption from our own shortcomings,
Though by limiting redemption one is left outside.
Left where he may express himself to success or his undoing,
Where he remains outside the kingdoms of the heavens
And so is unaware of the abodes of blessing.

I sing: "O turn, turn then to the palace of the heart;"
I sing: "O turn, turn, turn to the heart of palaces;"
Singing and turning I entered the Heaven of Joseph,
The ruler of the land of the Light-of-Egypt.

There was that ancient Egypt, long divided
Into *Khebt*, region of the light of divinity,
And *Kham*, region of the darkness of ego
Where Pharaoh, the ruling tyrant, had full sway,
And in the teachings of the secret mysteries
These archetypes were used as illustrations

Of forces that permeate the consciousness.
For Joseph is the example of manly beauty
And loftiness of character, both in legends
And in the traditions of holy writings —
Ruler of a land of many running rivers
With groves and gardens and fruiting plants,
Where *houris*, embodiments of heavenly light, are dwelling
And ecstasy becomes the common experience
In that *Gan Eden* or *Jinnat*, which is our aspiration.

Tell me, O Sheikh, why so many dwell in that region?
Why among them those not Muslims when on earth?
Why synagogues and strange places of worship?
These my questions who did not yet understand the Mercy,
Nor completely realize the depths of surrender.
"Were *you* there when *they* crucified *my* Lord?"
Presumes the Supreme to be a politician
Rejecting foes and accepting friends,
Regardless of principles involved.
So blame has dwelt in the hearts of ignorant men,
Which attitude dissolves when Love in uncovered
And the black spot of deterioration is removed.
Each comes to his place by a kind of gravity,
According to his sense of atonement and compassion,
Finding an unlimited vista in the grandeur,
Freed from the dominance of rulers, nobles and landlords,
From the machinations of usurers and creditors,
From the tyranny of others and greater tyranny of self,
Freed from the subtle allurements of desire,
Entering into that Paradise which brings release.

First repentance and then the reception of blessings,

First redemption and then the reception of mercy
To uncover the latent genius within,
To achieve what seemed impossible upon earth,
To find compensation for earlier inhibitions,
No more inane frustrations or vicious domination,
No more blockages preventing free expression.
In the heavens such evils cannot be.
Where the last becomes as the first, and high and low
Do not persist as they appear on earth.
The clergy and the scribes demand,
Who do not have the vision of liberation,
For there is no sin as great as tension,
No evil save the centration of ego.
Nor can one describe in earthly terms
What is not earthly; nor, save in symbolic language,
Convey what seems more evanescent than our dreams,
Where fluidity and fixity are not exclusive.

The mathematicians come nearest of all in understanding,
Who do not force the terminology of some science
Upon another branch where it would not fit,
And so have arrived at toleration,
For nothing else can fit their various departments.
Nor can the psychologists, with all their efforts,
Describe the processes of endless integration
Which go on in the recesses of the universe,
High above the fixations of this sphere.

There is a play of light from some supernal realm
Which light itself is healing, and as one breathes
He assimilates the blessing of the atmosphere,
Attaining freedom and bliss unknown on earth

Or in the darker realms referred to in traditions;
For while one is clothed in darkness,
He remains unaware of the nature of the atmosphere,
For there is more in breath than a mechanism,
There is more in life than its description.

We did not tarry long in the Heaven of Joseph
Which also can become a Lotus-land —
This for the multitudes who seek no higher goal,
This is the Pure Land for those unwilling to proceed,
This the natural outcome of many hopes
Where the beauty conceived on earth comes to full bloom.
Each seeks that Paradise which best befits him:
The heavy will drop, the light rise higher
To find a place in the universal harmony
Where all things and forces tend to equilibrium.

God does not punish:
We reach that destination in accord with our actions,
We determine our pathway on this earth and beyond,
And every activity that affects the nervous systems,
Brings pleasure or pain, hope or desolation,
So the wayfarers of the dust do not become the wayfarers of
    the skies.

III.

However deep our sins, however great our transgressions,
These are nothing before the Mercy of the Lord;
However much we are entangled with self-pride,
However sincere presumable repentance,

173

These are nothing before the Infinitude of Grace
For all the creation is nothing outside of Allah.

I, Saladin, the sultan, was permitted to enter this Grace
Garnered in a certain sense in the heaven ascribed to Jacob,
The father of tribes known as *Beni Israel*,
Not in the limited sense of the people of the Book,
But in the supernal sense of every devotee.
Here I falter. The pen is unavailing
And words, at best, are but shadows of the grander life,
Taken in whatever sense is thus conveyed.
So I would sing, but even if the music were recorded,
It would reach only a level of understanding,
So I tell, knowing the ineptitude of expression,
But write according to my surrender to Allah,
Trusting to Him that the message be conveyed.

Man has devised a heaven to be the reward for all;
However much we plan, prepare, explore,
The avenues for progress are quite limitless,
Even as the sciences of one particular day
Extend far beyond the imaginings of the previous;
So many the types of heavens, many the modes of freedom —
Thus the twelve-fold division of the *Beni Israel*
Where each, according to his type and inclination
Finds a maximum of potential satisfaction.

The Prophet Moses gave the spiritual law
Combining in it the wisdom of the ancients,
A formidable Law to provide for all men's wants,
A transcendental Law veiling the mysteries;
And though its protectors might not know its essence,
Though its guardians would lose even its outer meaning,

The words remain, both as covers and revealers.
Who, among nations, has dared to practice the polity of Moses?
Who among all groups that proclaim allegiance,
Who derive their faith from carefully selected passages,
Really accept all the teachings of the Book?

When Jesus, the Messiah, came to restore,
He failed in his historical efforts to the world,
And in the repudiation of the Law by his successors,
So that man may pray, but does not willingly *forgive*,
And prayer becomes an almost meaningless jumble.

There is a significance to the heavens of Jacob
Wherein and wherefrom extends that ladder-of-light,
That spiritual path that takes one through the spheres,
Which has no gates nor doors nor hindrances —
Open up ye gates, open ye everlasting doors
That Allah, the Eternally Merciful be perceived!

What is this persistent, perennial Islam?
What is this religion of all Prophets for all peoples?
Not a phrase, not a theme, not even in a sense, a teaching:
The Torah of Moses was in its time a perfect code,
Offering to mankind forgiveness and the Jubilee,
But man has chosen instead the slavery of indebtedness,
Crying aloud to God but keeping his *shekels*.

I beheld and saw and wept,
Wept even in the heavens of felicity.

I, Saladin, have prayed to be counted among the Muslims;
I, Saladin, in company with Sheikh Sohrawardi Maktul,

Entering this portion of the universe,
Rejoicing that because of Mohammed and Quran
All doors to all portions of the cosmos stood ajar.

They are the true *Beni Israel* whose hearts are alive,
Who respond to mercy, compassion and love,
Who know how to dance and laugh and have no complaint,
Which things come neither by blood nor inheritance.
Who cares, in the Heaven of Jacob, what others believe?
Who dares, in the Heaven of Jacob, to judge and condemn?
To lift himself regardless of heavenly Grace
Or circumvent Truth with conditions and definitions
Or dividing formulae which exclude even the least?
Where *shalom aleichem* and *salaam aleikhum* are united.

What is the Holy Land which makes it holy?
What is the blessing if there is no spirit in it?
What is humility within the restricted heart?

The twelve doors open when the gate of *tauba* is passed,
The twelve doors open because the translucent Love-Grace
Permeates the world which Allah has created
And, when the shadows of materiality are removed,
The state of idealization becomes the norm.
One reaches places of seemingly boundless delight,
Be it in lights that scintillate as if jewels
Or in forms of beauty purified from dross;
Be it in dreams or visions or manifest creative desire —
This is the nature of the heaven ascribed to Jacob
Whose vibrations permeate the lesser worlds
So that the Kingdom of Heaven is really close at hand,
Not a kingdom in any restricted sense

With a man ruling over men, with some commanding others,
But rather a world where man may be ruler of himself
And the latent genius within his nature be unfolded,
Where the propensities and potentialities of us all
Shine like rays of a boundless sunlight.

What was the *manna* mentioned in the Bible?
The *Beni Israel*, released from the servitude of Egypt,
Were led by a Messenger toward the Land of Promise
And fed by the bounty that was closest at hand,
So whatever they desired, it was their own,
This being the nature of the food of heaven;
Earthborn philosophers would inscribe the universe
Verbalize as 'reality' what they circumscribe
And intoxicate themselves with phantasmagoria,
Sneer at the sincere seekers of the Path.

We passed through the doors with praises,
We passed through the doors with blessing,
We passed through the doors with exultation
To awaken in the Kingdom of Joy.

IV.

There is an inscription in the upper heavens:
Abandon all tension ye who enter here
For tension is the preventative of bliss,
The mark of Cain upon the nervous system,
The force of centration giving rise to *nafs*,
The spirit of agitation and of craving
Which seeks its satisfaction through acquisition,

Feigning achievement by power and possession and rank.
In more symbolic form it is known as Iblis,
Too often regarded as an external devil
Armed with allurements which drive man to the brink;
But man is lured because of egoicity,
And the tendencies toward rage, envy and hatred
Are the forces which compel hell-fire purification,
While those who are competent to overcome these evils
Are fitting themselves thereby for the heavens.

From the beginning God has His Khalif on earth,
The spirit of prophecy coming with the soul of Adam,
And through the ages the Guidance has always been near.
The law of compensation is active everywhere
And when man assumes authority over this world,
Regardless of the moral principles involved,
He must undergo the results of every action,
For good and evil alike produce a tension,
And until every sort of tension be released,
The full experience of bliss can not be his.

Happiness comes when tensions are released —
Then the Voice of the Dove is heard throughout the land,
Then the psalmist rhapsodies his heart-songs,
Then bliss becomes the natural state,
And this within the Heaven of Isaac.

There is a world of only smiling faces,
Faces with smiling foreheads and smiling hearts,
Where great lights radiate from the personality,
Where the atmosphere of each is like an aura
From a brilliantly furbished lamp,

Where the soft glow emanates incessantly,
And charm is a natural function of the character,
Each seeking to please the other for the sake of pleasing,
And little consideration is given to the self.

The Heaven of Isaac is the abode of joy,
Of youth and agelessness, of everlasting morning,
A timeless springtide with all its offerings,
The apple-garden of Hesperides.
Tension is gone and desirelessness so widespread
That one will never hear it mentioned,
Nor are there any of those dualisms
Which bring perplexities and problems —
All, all disappear from this Elysium.
The inhabitants are ever singing and dancing,
Not as they do upon earth for purposed reasons,
But there is incessant urging to joy,
The joy which is the natural efflux of soul,
The joy which permeates the atmosphere,
The joy inherent in the very molecules,
And though we call the denizens 'angels' or '*devas*'
Or do not consider naming significant,
They partake in the portioning of the creation.

Who has really heard the song-of-joy in Allah?
Who has danced to the music-of-joy in Allah?
Modernists have turned against the dervishes
Instead of against the evils in themselves
And so hindered reception of this music.

The small space is of Allah and the great space also;
The small event is of Allah and the great event also;

Terrific tragedies of history and tears of tiny infants;
The sobbing of the poor, the wailing of the wealthy,
The delight of children and ecstasy of lovers
Must be considered, and put in proper perspective.
When the *Beni Israel* first entered the Land of Promise
They made a coffer for the spirit of the Eternal,
Nor did they move without this guiding spirit,
And because of it were brought to victory.
Can it be that Allah fits in a small space?
Must it be that this is the kingly throne?
The last shall be the first and the first the last,
Written not only in Scriptures but in truth.
Who wants to the last even if it bring bliss?
Let the seekers of crowns and thrones and honours seek,
But those who seek Allah shall find their reward,
And their blindness and suffering disappear forever.

Do not look homeward, sweet angel, for God is everywhere;
Look earthward and see where there are distinctions,
Distinctions lurking in the shadows, dissolved by the light.
Distinctions made by man because of ancestry,
Because the skin is dark, the nationality different —
Laugh, Iblis, at the followers of religion,
For who has ever been excommunicated therefor?

In the house of Allah are many palaces,
In the worlds of light one's light shines forth,
But only in the worlds of shadows these distinctions
Producing *sins* for which there is no retribution.

Laugh, O Islam, at your enemies,
Laugh at those who make artificial demarcations,

Who overpride themselves for ancestry;
Cry, O Islam, for the damned peoples of the Book
Who travesty their faiths and look without
For compensation for absence of inner zeal.

Times have not changed, only the calendars,
And the battles of Saladin continue on in Africa
And in the rural sections of America,
Whose ignorant do not realize
That only excluders are excluded from God's bliss.
The frowning forehead is the visa of exclusion,
The frowning forehead is the sign of criminality,
Successful on earth, creating its hells even in the heavens,
Unable to partake in the communion of endless joy.

The dance of the spirit is the natural function of self,
The dance of the spirit reveals acceptance of Allah;
Movements of *Nimaz* and movements of *Zikar*
Belong to the lower and higher orders of Islam,
Enabling the devotees to appreciate the Closeness,
Persuading the devotee to true humility.

Turn to the positive expressions of awakening,
Cast out dualistic reflections of false security
Or hypocrisy which blinds one with illusions —
Therefore a further and final revelation
Was needed to bring salvation for all mankind,
Was needed to bring the teachings to all peoples,
WHEREFORE IS QURAN THE BOOK PAR EXCELLENCE.

Read Quran in joy, chant Quran in joy, pray Quran in joy,
Joy is the most wonderful aspect of Islam,

Foreordained for believers first and then for all,
To the ending of circumscription in outlook,
To the ending of imperfection and suffering,
To bring that state of ecstasial jubilescence
When the soul of the soul emancipates in entirety all;
Then light from a ceaseless sun invigorates the being,
Breath from a hidden source arouses energies,
That all cells and atoms of being may take refuge in Allah,
That all cells and atoms of being take joy in Allah,
That all cells and atoms of being sustain themselves in praise —
Great, exceedingly great this joy. Amin.

V.

Praise be to Allah who has made it possible
For His servant to undertake a supernal journey,
Following the Prophet through the higher heavens,
Ending all doubts through his experience,
To reinvigorate believers on the earth.

So to the sphere in hyperspace attributed to Abraham and Ishmael
Where one comes to the totality of thingness,
Learns all names and forms, acquires that knowledge
Which is the supreme undertaking of the mind,
Imbibes pure wisdom and attains to moral maturity.
The spatial consciousness with which man has imposed limits,
The almost inability to perceive beyond,
The conceptual dogmatism of authorities
Insisting upon the impossibility of divers outlooks,
Stand as bulwarks against comprehension
Of superspaces and the constantly shifting areas

Which are not transfixed in hardness as on this earth —
The solid, liquid and gaseous states of matter
Are but partially explored, and then, by extension,
Man forces theories upon his colleagues,
Throws dampers on the grander examination of the universe
Where senses are not limited to measurable vibrations,
Where other vibrations find response in consciousness,
Where the questionable logical faculty
Can not impair full functioning of insight.

Suns of superspheres are replete with qualities,
And shining light gives impetus to grand activity,
While in the transcendent sphere of heart
The light in which one functions proves to be love,
Where there is no activating distinction
Between the functions and the heavens themselves.

God has periodically sent out Messengers
That man receive instructions and thus progress,
For all this seeming creation is only a cover
Under which Allah functions from sub-electron to archangel,
Exploring His own creation under these guises
Without in the least being affected thereby.

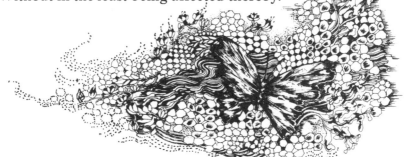

The absolute play of light in the ultimate stage
Is so vast, so immeasurable, so much a pleroma

That the human mind becomes lost in speculation
Unless, of course, it is totally stunned in wonder,
Failing which it should turn to meditation,
To concentration and awe-inspiring contemplation,
To discover the immensity of that which is.

Total light is mentally unfathomable.
Total light is completely coalesced with love,
Total light can become a realization,
Fulfilling and completing the life we know,
Wherein the disciple, trained in self-effacement,
Removes from himself all evidence of shadow.

The impact of the mission of the Patriarch Abraham
And the equal impact of this transcendent heaven
Can be assimilated by those on the path to God
By methods known today as metalingual,
By processes which are super-logical.
The hieroglyphical language of the ancients
Was esoteric, and the uninitiated,
Whose consciousness is focused on the immediate,
Have not yet the capacity for its understanding.

Abraham was the Friend-of-God, coming from the region of light,
Bringing light with him into the region of darkness
Which is also known to us by the name, *Canaan*;
Literal renditions of the sacred text
Bring us to an incomplete understanding
Of the people who could mention the Sacred Name,
Which if repeated as in a mantric form,
Produces changes in personality-function.

Abraham also means 'Father of a multitude of sounds',
Sounds which permeate the universe
With all their qualities and characteristics
Of tone and pitch and amplitude,
To which the bodies of conscious creatures,
And their minds also act as condensers,
Without their becoming opaque to the deeper silences
Whither we have ceased to look.

Abraham was the Father of attributes and virtues,
Of ethics and morality and sincere devotion
Needed to electrify and assure
The gathering of information and of knowledge
Of which Ishmael, his son, is archetype —
Ishmael the seeker, not any blind wanderer,
Whose curiosity was insatiable,
For the things of this world and that also,
Who finally found salvation in his father's house,
In this heaven of completion of desire.
Whence the artist, the philosopher, the scientific mind?
Whence this urge to know, to seek and to inquire?
The seed of these tendencies were planted in the race
At the dawn of creation and remained therewith
Until the capacity for mental achievement was awakened
And this evolution brought with it inventions and tools,
Rendering life in the world more comfortable
Until, alas, comfort became the end and not the means.

The Seal of the Prophets came to remind the world
Of the ineffability of Truth and its motivations,
Remodeled the method for entrance to the mysteries
Where sound is sought under a multitude of covers

And knowledge is found behind a wall of hindrances,
Whose methods for pursuing the sacred path
Remain in the world to this day as testimonials
Of Truth and the Way of achievement.
What is Divine Wisdom?
Not a complex doctrine nor formal teaching,
But the experience of awakening to life.
What is Divine Understanding?
The ability to appropriate and use and alter
As if one were master and all appearances slaves.

Thus the Heaven of Abraham where enlightenment is the norm:
ISHK ALLAH! MAHEBOOD LILLAH! AL-HAMDU LILLAH!
God is Love, Lover and Beloved. Glory be to God!

VI.

And now peace..........
And now stillness..........
And now that strange awakening into living no-thing-ness
Where storms persist no more; the waters have receded.

This is the land sustained by the Voice of the Turtle,
Where the Holy Spirit echoes as the Dove,
Where endless cooing reverberates through the ether
Beyond the *maya** of the Hindus and the *mayim*† of the Hebrews —
The Heaven of Noah, personification of repose.
This is not a heaven conceived as a separate realm,
This is the underlying effluvium of existence

* Measurable, limitation.
† Waters; any form of vibrations.

Upon which all nature must depend,
Necessary for its preservation and revitalization.
The meaning of the *Vishnu Purana* becomes luminescent,
The teachings of the Prophet Jonah are clarified,
The divisions into light and darkness, *nirvana* and *samsara*,
Even into Islam and *harb*,* is evident.

The Sheikh and I reposed in profound meditation,
Sustaining ourselves in that lofty atmosphere,
The Ararat of the Bible, the Meru of Vedic texts,
Where creation and light formations appear as dreams,
Wars and tremulations and catastrophes have no meaning,
But the infant's cry, the lover's sigh
And the joy of coming spring are monumental.

> The sown is balanced by the reaped,
> The harvest is related to the sown,
> The pain within another's breast
> Is felt as if one's own.

> The storm has passed, the calm has come,
> No base thought or vain emotion,
> The pilgrim finds himself at home,
> Himself the waves, himself the ocean.

> By the Sword-ark was Noah saved,
> In the Sword-ark all forms find rest,
> In that repose which God has given,
> The Sword-ark the mansion of the Blessed.

So everything comes to a final equilibrium,

* Darkness, samsara.

Out of which equilibrium all movements, all activity,
Out of which all evolution, all destruction,
Out of which everything is made that ever has been made
Coming from the Holy Spirit, moving with the Holy Spirit,
Guided by the Holy Spirit to this, the Father's house.

Thought destroys the smooth flowing of ultimate essence,
Thought creates all our heavens and hells,
Thought brings us everything except finality
Which, unrestricted, is not the creature of thought —
For the Divine Will is infinite in Its facets,
Which Itself is one with Peace.

There is that vacuous 'peace' devoid of characteristics
And there is the Peace-of-God, a pleroma,
Which passes understanding but not our love;
The first is often a concoction drawn from Iblis;
Even the *thought*: "peace beyond understanding"
Becomes the source of trouble and disturbances,
A phrase used as a weapon by philosophers,
A phrase which pulls a curtain of illusion over the stage
Where realities appear when it is raised.

When the waters of maya recede Mount Ararat appears,
Not a mountain of particularized geography
But the superpiling of light upon light upon light,
The accumulation of lights of varying gradations,
Of a multitude of qualities and potentialities
Of which the rainbow is an external derivation.
But the Voice of the Turtle is everywhere, everywhere —
The life of life, the love of love, the light of light,
Dependent on nothing, upon which everything depends,

Modified by no-thing, limited by no-thing,
Whence the universe seems to come and go
With all its comedies and tragedies and by-plays
Wherein Allah is author, stage manager and troupe.

Through experience one reaches the Heaven of Repose,
Or else it comes by a special Grace of Allah;
In mastery one stills the storms within himself
And the sabbatized Sabbath takes on full meaning:
To calm all thoughts and watch the flow of life,
To focus the consciousness within the heart-of-hearts,
To find one is engulfed in this universal peace,
This superlove, this source of all activity,
This potentissimility of every energy
Whence everything outlets, whither all return.

Legends and folk tales hidden in tradition
Continue the hieroglyphic communications
Which thus are passed from generation to generation,
Not through ordinary avenues of intellection,
Not through any process of giving and taking,
Of acquisition, bestowing or motivations,
But by a full process of silent-becoming-blending.

What is this *Zikar** which is repeated endlessly?
This *Fikar*† which is the propensity of the *fakir*?
This contemplation which is an absorbing exercise?

Silence gives rise to love, and love returns to silence,
Silence gives rise to wisdom and wisdom is imbedded in silence —

* The name of God repeated in sound.
† Ditto, in thought.

189

It is not a drama of love and death,
It is not a comedy of love and silence,
For death comes to the selfishness in us,
To be resurrected in the full, Divine existence.

Pursue love, follow love, experience love;
Know Shem as *agape*, Japheth as *philos*, Ham as *eros**
Processed from this universal peace;
Do not disdain, do not employ the mental scimitar,
Understand the radiating powers of the superconscious,
The equally radiating powers of the sun-of-love,
And thus come to possess the elixir of being.

Thus I, Saladin, the sultan, accepting the path of *Tarikat*†
With its disciplines and exercises,
Found this heaven within the recesses of being.
A hidden touch, a movement as of a spring or button,
And the whole world seemed to be illumined —
To know oneself yet not repeat this formula,
To understand nor yet say, 'peace, be still,'

    Thus to find the heavenly Jerusalem,
    Dar-as-Salaam,
    To hear the sound of the Dove,
    To assimilate peace.

What is *nafs selima*?
It comes to fulfillment in the perfect sage
Whose personality exudes sweet wholesomeness,
Who carries the universe yet feels no strain,

* The inner interpretation of the 'sons' of *Noah*, or 'Repose'.
† The esoteric path of Islam.

Who bears all burdens without any thought of burden,
No cross, no weight, no trouble —
And the function of the Bodhisattva is one's own.

VII.

"All rivers flow into the sea, and yet the sea is not full,"
Sang David, the Prophet, harpist, seer and king
Whose wisdom comes to us by our singing his motifs,
Not by praising the Prophet or the verbal shadows —
The bent of the partially educated.

All these spheres and modifications of the universe
Which may be known as 'heavens' or called otherwise
Are samples of cosmic tunings of great complexity,
Yet real in the ultimate transcendent sense.
When I, Saladin, the sultan, made a noble effort
To enter that which may be called the highest,
I felt not self-hood but a union with my Sheikh
As if the stage of *fana-fi-Sheikh** had been completed
And selfhood was ready for a higher evolution.

Jinnat or *Gan Eden* is that eternal paradise
Which Adam foreswore when he entered the abode-of-timing,
The region of perpetuality for that which may become
Without diminishing the forces of its essence;
So there is really no differentiation
Between Adam, universal man and manifesting life.

Consider this human body, the production of pure wisdom
* Effacement in the spiritual teacher.

With independence and interdependence existing
Between cells and nerves, systems and organs and functions
Presenting a galaxial complex of many societies,
An institution compounded of institutions
In which no part is entirely separate.
We die in Adam who foresook the eternal realm,
We live in Adam, bridegroom of universal life.

The soul of the Messenger hovered in *Jinnat*
And when he asked "Who are you?" of Khadijah,*
She soberly replied, "I am Khadijah";
But what a shock upon this gracious lady
When she heard the reply: "No, I am Khadijah,"
Then softly added, "Pray, who is Khadijah?"
For when the consciousness approaches this threshold,
Or is merged, in a sense, within the One,
Names may mean nothing because of the process of mergence.
"I am the wife of so-and-so,
I am the daughter of such-and-such,
I am also the sister of a famous man,"
To which the answer: "I am that man"
Came from the soul baptized in unification.

The Unity-Doctrine of the *Beni Israel* is not enough,
The Trinity of the Christians far too much,
But in Islam *Ahadiat*† subsists,
Maintaining the universal brotherhood for all times,
Excluding not a single creature from its ranks,
From super-super-man to infra-infra-atom,
Even as the cells and organs unify within the body,

* The first wife of Mohammed.
† *Ahadiat*, as presented, not *Tauhid*. This is a transcendental, all-embracing unity.

So the totality of living creatures within Allah.

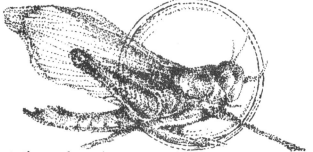

Salutation to breath consumed by all living creatures,
Salutation to blood common to all humanity,
Salutation to universal Grace.

True that the universe has been divided
By series of crystallizations and stepped-down tunings
Segregating various categories of nature,
Not in any absolute sense as some would have it,
But from emanations of the Deity,
Which manifest from the Ultimate —
In rhythms upon rhythms and counter-rhythms
Moving about with no sense of selfhood,
Harmonizing with no awareness of differences.

The Prophet, to whom be peace,
Proclaimed this brotherhood from the beginning,
That in Islam there can be no exclusions,
No subtle examination, excusing and accusing —
The universe is composed of rays of living light
Which light is both substance and vibration,
And the ultimate soul may be said to be the same.

Adam is the totality of the human race,
Past or present or yet to appear in the world;

Adam is the totality of primordial creation,
The ultimate resurrection of all life,
The formed created from archetypal imagery,
And, in a certain sense, a reflection of God.
The human body and human psyche offer
A true transencyclopedia
To be given careful study and meditation.

Scriptures of the Hebrews and the Christians
Have several allusions to the 'Song of God'
As if rejoicing were basically essential to any worship;
The damned are they who do not praise,
The damned are they who can not sing,
The damned are they who can not rejoice —
But any suggestion of the 'eternally damned'
Is nothing but an expression of the ignorant
Who thus become excluded from Supreme Compassion.

IN GOD WE LIVE AND MOVE AND HAVE OUR BEING —
Either this is so or not — and it is so:
Divine Love is in all, through all, with all, always,
Leaving an open door for movements of wisdom
That it can be better appreciated by man.
The sin of Adam was to consider his individuality,
To seek a separated enjoyment, reap separate reward,
For in separation all die, in unity all live —
Which truth is re-echoed in our blood-stream
If only we should look, and meditate.

Is there no lesson from series of devastating wars?
Do not storms and pestilences and famine strike the world
Nor exempt the specially privileged from their ravages?

It is not so much a kingdom of God on earth
As a kingdom of humanity which must be stressed;
If we do not love our fellows, how can we prove our love?
Christ has taught one thing, theologians otherwise,
But we follow the theologians into darkness.

Let us worship Allah by exhibiting *akhlak Allah*,*
Feeling His presence every moment of our lives,
Thus to experience the incessant resurrection,
Which I, Saladin, the sultan, received through Grace,
The answer to my prayer to be a faithful Muslim.
SUBHAN ALLAH! AL-HAMDU LILLAH! ALLAHO AKBAR!†

VIII.

"Arise and come. Arise and come swiftly."

These words re-echoed through my being and I,
Saladin, the sultan and Islamic devotee,
The man who had conceived he had the attainment,
Who had been permitted to travel through the heavens,
Felt humble indeed, felt as if but a dust-spot
And shocked into this sense that being-of-self was nothing.

I stood as if I were a man, though not a mortal,
I stood at the summit of that which has formation,
At the pinnacle of everything that is nameable,
At the acme of accession of that which belongs to heart,
Perceiving before me the Grand Sword of the universe,

* Feeling as if in the presence of God.
† Sacred phrases.

195

That scintillating Sword with razor-edged blade
Across which stood the Empyrean:

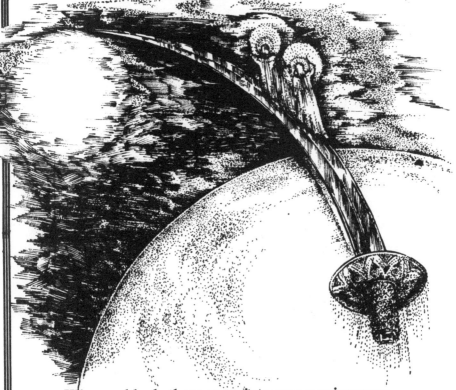

When suddenly there came into my consciousness
A recognition of God's Messengers, Moses and Jesus,
Guiding my footsteps over that narrow blade,
Guiding where it seemed impossible to proceed,
Where all around was a vast inexhaustible abyss
(Or so I thought, or thought I thought),
Only to find myself moving onward, onward, onward,
Moving under guidance and not as if self-propelled,
Moving with unerring swiftness toward the *Arsh-Throne*
With Moses helping and Jesus encouraging,
With Jesus helping and Moses soothing my heart
Until the threshold was attained; I bowed as if to the dust.

Then said Moses, the Prophet, the Law Giver:
"O Saladin, servant of God and king of kings,
Ruler and Commander of the Faithful,
The land which I could not obtain by means of the Pen,
The land obtained by the righteous Sword is yours —
Rule as if under perpetual Divine Guidance
That the embedded holiness be well conserved,
That the saintliness of its geography be augmented,
That the fund of *baraka* ever increase,
That all the kindly people of the world be permitted to visit,
That no hard distinctions be made between the children of men.

"You are now blessed to formulate an ideal government,
So countries within your dominion cherish your reign,
That the land attain an ever greater renown,
And your name shall be written in the books of history."

Then Jesus-Messiah communicated as if to me,
Though rather in a form of silent communion
With the feeling of an all-embracing attunement,
The same, yet different, and yet as if he were saying:

"I came not to be worshipped, not to be superdeified,
Not to be chagrined by ill-fitting honour words,
Nor be dismayed by claims which I would deny,
But to be followed, to be emulated, to be loved.
Read my words, meditate thereupon, but more than that
Continue the practice of royal *mushahida*
Which leads to complete emancipation."

At this was I guided to the *Arsh-Throne*,
Where every personality is all-personality,

Where every one is every other thing-being;
Only for the purposes of assisting the creation,
For the sake of aiding humanity they appear as different —
With tremendous outbursts of aureoles and auroras,
With endless all-compelling illumination,
Lights reflecting lights, lights refracting lights,
With colours parading in a stupendous array,
And with them all, through all a voice of wondrous sweetness:

"I am the Seal, the Seal of all the Prophets,
Whose testimony is my testimony and I their testimony,
Who all are Muslims, accomodations of Divine Will,
Empty egos, filled with the eternal Spirit,
Operating as *nafs alima*, the self-empty-universally-filled,
The Messengers of God whose hearts are altars
Expressing under varying conditions the sempiternal Message,
Attuned to the ever-beating heart of Compassion and Beneficence,
The undertone of the very essence of Being.

"I am the Seal, not the Seal to an empty box,
Not the Seal to those dishonoured by non-Muslims,
Nor the Seal for those dishonoured by so-called Muslims.
When you belittle my predecessors, I am belittled;
What honour to be best among the insects!
What glory to be foremost among the asses!
Even to be king of mankind, what benefit is that?

"The best of all religions is THE RELIGION,
The best of all the Messages is the ONE MESSAGE,
The best of all Guides is the Guidance itself;

"Honour those whom I honour and you honour me,

Belittle other Messengers and the appeal is vain.
Quran is the final Book closing ages of revelation,
Quran the final chapter to all that has been sanctified,
Not the *only* but the final Book of the series,
Not the only — for I counseled the search for wisdom;
Not the only — but the ultimate for the world.
Learning is not enough, wisdom must be added,
Nor is it necessary to apprehend a multitude of forms,
Nor to be concerned with constant repetitions,
Nor to close oneself from the habit of repetition,
For simplicity of heart is quite sufficient;
Self-surrender is enough.

"O Saladin, glorious and best of sultans,
You truly are my Khalif no matter who sits in Baghdad;
You truly are my Khalif who operates as vice-gerent,
Be my legate, my representative on earth,
But come and learn with me the wisdom of the ages,
To absorb, to appropriate and finally become.
Praise be to Allah — *Subhan Allah*!

"Beloved of Allah, you will be questioned about recognition,
How did you know of Moses, Jesus or the Seal?
This is Grace which eyes do not determine.
Consider the wisdom of the Hindus —
Wisdom which some Muslims can appreciate,
While others deprecate because of idolatry —
Of which I offer you the cream herenow:
The *bindu* of every one is different, the *sindu* of the perfect the same,
But the *sindu* of the ordinary man is different
For the consciousness of him is only partial,
While the consciousness of the perfect is the whole.

"The All is Allah and we know the All as Allah,
Yet the All has a multitude of ranges and vibrations,
Grades and gradients from the primal light,
The light of each gradient acting upon its similars,
Though vibrationally they may not be the same;
And the light of various gradients plays upon the others,
So there is totality of light upon light
Through every aspect of this manifestation.

Thus *ruh*, known as the soul, is this perfect light,
Thus the attainment of *nur*, the light in its true essence,
Although before creation *ruh* and *nur* were the same.
This wisdom has been carefully preserved
In the wisdom of the Sabeans and the Hebrews,
And in the traditions of several other cultures,
All blossoming out of the ever-living Light.

"Beloved, I shall not detain you now with details;
Beloved, we must remove the black spot from your heart
Even as the black spot was removed from mine,
A process by which one becomes a perfect Muslim.

"Now you can understand the interdict against portraits,
For how can a sheet of canvas contain my image?
A patterned cloth picturize my spirit?
At one moment I appear thus, at another different;
For personality is subject to incessant change,
And when the Prophet was screened with living light,
There was nothing but the light, no shadow at all.
How can we make a picture-form of this supernal light?
You are a man, a warrior, a hero, a sultan —
Do you look the same to friends and enemies and family?

200

Which is the true Saladin? Are not all of them quite true?

"I come, I go, I reappear, I disappear,
By Grace I manifest in the twinkling of an eye,
To appear in a different guise, to remanifest as the same,
For perfect beings form a cosmic body,
Even beyond the aspect known as Adam.
Can a portrait be a proper presentation?
Can one explain a diamond by a single facet
Leaving no scope for the grand play of light?
Man applies the word 'reality' to his abstractions,
Unable to distinguish between 'reality' and illusion.

"Whenever the spiritual Sheikh appears
It affects the countenance of the pupil,
And even the Sheikh may change in such a situation,
So who can say what is the appearance, what the reality?
There is a supreme state called *lahut*
Which is not a condition, being beyond conditioning,
Where the timeless wisdom is all-pervading,
The Supreme Truth, so to speak, and oneself seem unified,
One is lost utterly to that with which he has been identified,
And there is nothing with which he is not identified.
Who is the true Khalif? The most self-surrendered,
The most attuned to the absolute being of Allah —

"Ya Allah, in love, in reverence and humility
I surrender to Thee and Thee alone
And Thou dost raise me spiritually.

"Enough. I place before you others in the Chain
That you may more appreciate the meaning of the Seal;

No Seal without the Chain, no Chain without the Seal —
This is the message for your humanity,
For Egypt especially and for the world.
Names, forms, appurtenances come from analysing,
But the inner heart makes no dividing distinctions;
Feed, strengthen and nourish everything that has become,
That it may recognize what it seems to be,
That it may fully find what it really is.

"That Quran which is eternal commands all languages,
That Quran which is eternal has the deep teachings
Which the Prophet interprets in the language of earth;
The knowledge of this universe is so vast
That couched in terms of derivatives and words
It may lead to confusion and speculations;
Allah is *Al-Hayy*, the living Eternal
Whose many attributes are latticed into personalities,
Effects of a unitary cause.

"I shall not weary you with lengthy discourse:
Know that Allah has sent many, many Messengers
With variations of one supernal Message,
And *dharma** and *din*† and religion are essentially one.
Fare you well. Allah bless you. Keep alert. Amin."

The sudden disappearance as of a vision,
The transformation of person into essence
Within or without, I could not tell, I did not know,
But immediately I heard another voice:

* The spiritual teachings of India. [See Glossary — ED.]
† Ditto, Arabia.

IX

"I am the voice of a once perfect King,
Coupled in eternity with an equally perfect Queen,
Refusing even at the price of my salvation
To be separate from her, my partner-wife —
Ram was, Ram is, Ram-Sita for ever.

"Even as the systole and diastole of the heart are as one,
The blood rushing to aid the suffering tissues,
The blood returning, as if compelled back to the heart —
Thus the operation of the lovers of humanity,
Thus was Sita, the seeker of my being,
Thus the role of love beyond name and form
Even as the play of blood within our bodies,
And as if we were half-bodies,
Through our union a perfect personality became.

"God, the All-all, created men and women in His Image:
Religion is therefore for both men and women,
Spiritual liberation is for both.
The false have declared the male to be superior,
The false have declared one caste to be superior,
The false have proclaimed a racial superiority —
In the realms of finitude are big and greater and superior,
In the realms of finitude are small and little and lesser,
In infinitude such diversification can not be
Lest the infinite be abstracted out of itself,
Which would only result in another infinity.

"All Prophets in all ages presented Islam,
All Messengers have emphasized surrender,

Unity, Prayer, Fasting, Alms and Pilgrimage;
The real teaching of India is *sanatana dharma*,
Nothing to do with exclusive sects and cults,
Nothing to do with the cross-play of divisions,
But the proclamation of truth from everlasting.
So temple-idols must go that God be worshipped,
So symbols must be restored to their proper setting,
And the veils over meanings be lifted.
Be not misled; teach that people be not misled
By doctrines of mediation and intervention
Til man ceases to be a light unto himself.

"Some day will people cease to worship Ram-Sita,
Some day will people come to worship *with* Ram-Sita,
Following the ways of the most ancient sages,
Following also the ways of true holy men.
Do not change the heart if so the heart be broken;
Pray, instead, that every heart be changed,
See, instead, that hearts are never broken."

Then, by the transcendental process of all-being,
Becoming one with Ram, becoming one with Sita,
Becoming also one with the conjoined Ram-Sita
In the ultimate synthetic unity we call *soul*,
Absorbing full wisdom with conscious immediacy,
I knew the various meanings of the Ramayana,
That spiritual folk-lore epic of the Aryans.

Ram is the ruler of man, the ruler also of humanity,
Governing through wisdom and righteousness,
Selecting institutions of ameloriation
That life may be pursued in equilibrium,

Yet man can continue on the spiritual path
With no loss to himself or his society.
Rules, commandments and incipient customs
Were not meant to become crystallized norms,
Impeding future peoples from self-expression,
Leaving blank words to stultify the spirit
And introducing complex inhibitions,
Dehumanizing humanity.
The labelling of patterned forms as 'spiritual',
The encouragement to privileged priestcraft,
The exclusion of the masses from approaching altars
Brings nothing but the doom.

This was not the way established by King Rama
Who was, perhaps, an archetype for Joseph,
As his enemy Ravana resembled Pharaoh;
For Rama is the ever-beating heart,
Ravana the lusting appetites, most pronounced in sex
But present also in every outburst of temper,
In endless greed for amassing worldly goods;
Such tendencies swirl blood-energies toward a focus,
Creating a momentary but falsifying joy,
Never bringing lasting satisfaction.

Sita, in a sense, represents us all,
Torn between these obvious antagonisms,
Lured by the worldly life with its many charms,
Yet in our being-of-beings always needing God.

In Allah one finds the perfection of all qualities
Which sustain the universe from its Fountain-head,
So true religion is Islam and *sanatana-dharma*,*
Realized when the Sword-bridge has been crossed,
Realized when the *Arsh-Throne* has been approached,
Realized in the Light-Light where Allah is serene.

X.

No sooner had this dual Ram-Sita vanished,
No sooner this personality disappeared,
Than again the Messenger completely purged my being,
Raised my faltering eyes to the Empyrean,
Bringing the full picture and teachings of Shiva,
Another so-called 'god-man' of the *Bharatas*
Whom we in Islam might refer to as *Rassul*,
One of the many Messengers from Allah.

Then I welled and swelled until I became so vast,
Waves upon waves upon waves upon waves,
Movements and countermovements and cross-currents,
All moving in colossal harmonies,
Making me aware of the smallest portion of self,
With infinitesimal repetitions consonant with vastness,
While the immensity remained quite cognizant of the least,
The tiniest portion reflecting the grand All-Whole
To the accompaniment of musical peals of laughter
And the appearance of a most remarkable person:

* The 'eternal teachings', now translated as 'perennial philosophy'.

"I am Shiva, the dancer who performs the universe;
I am Shiva, gate-keeper of the amphitheatre,
Where I play all roles and also am the audience,
Where I watch to see that others enact their parts
Being also the stage-director of the universe,
And, while people go seeking my star-role,
They become so utterly lost in their self-efforts
They mask an illusive separation
In a universe that is without differentiation.
You have come to me because you have been with me,
When you are with me you naturally come to me,
The dance, the music and the audience,
Which is also why I am known as *Ishvara*,
Although this identity is a veil
To offer the less-capable a picture of Divinity.

"*Ishvara, Osiris, Asar, Asher,*
Variations of the One Holy Name,
Taught to Moses by Khidr* in the form:
'*Ehyeh asher ehyeh*' — I am Ishvara who was, is, will be,
That One Who is the Only-Only-Only,
Forevereverevermore, and on and on,
Represented through a name-veil offered by man;
There is None else,
Though time-space and lattices interfere,
Producing separations and partialities
Out of this Oneness.

"What is Yoga?
The way to God, with God, in God — nothing else.

* According to Quran, the spiritual teacher of Moses. According to Kabbala, Jithro,
a Hindu. Mittani-Midanite.

207

The institutions which are evoked by man
Can not compel any cosmic deliverance
Which is beyond the scope of cause-and-effect,
Nor can one formalize the mystical doctrine
Which is transcendent to man's reasoning.

"I came as a Messenger from the Great Beyond
Issuing proclamations and making suggestions:
How to live in the worlds of being and becoming
And yet prepare oneself for this eternity.

"The social order as was then constituted
Consisted of various orders and ranks of citizens
But in a vertical manner, as if side by side,
That through mutual help and cooperation
A polity could be built and security maintained
Insuring a maximum of satisfaction,
Enough to stimulate that inner longing
So they would continue onward after death,
Finding this universe an endless wonder.
Aftermaths and afterthoughts of men,
Supposedly established in my honour,
Were chiefly expedients which the master-minded
Conceived by various means to achieve power,
And social customs became so ingrained in society
That even after centuries they were hard to uproot,
To restore the nation to its purest teaching,
Which is to say, surrender to the Divine Will.

"Thus humanity has become the slave of time,
Caught in the labyrinth of phrases and maxims
And in the hopeless entanglement of custom,

Making escape extremely difficult.

"Nourishment is direct — blood invigorates all cells;
Breath is direct — we partake of a single atmosphere;
Love is direct — no intervention between hearts —
Such are the principles of the All-One-Ever.

"Many have worshipped since I first delivered my teachings,
Many have imagined themselves to be my followers,
When actually they have been blinded by their priests;
Few, indeed, have come and worshipped alongside me,
Even among the many trained in yoga systems.
Joy is not a state to be attained by mere well-wishing
Nor ecstasy a super-amelioration —

"Love, love, love and you shall attain the highest
Consciousness-knowledge-bliss;
Love, love, love and you shall know yourself;
Love, love, love and the universe will be at your command.
Love, and forget me; love, and never shall I be far away."

XI.

Now that I could stand before the supersonic light,
Now that my heart seemed free from limitation,
Now that I dwelt within the wisdom of Allah,
The Prophet, upon whom be everlasting peace,
Could appear before my person, and did.

How beautiful Thy courts, O Allah, the Magnificent!
How marvellous the supernal of all temples,

How utterly wonderful the Grand Mosque of the skies,
Filled with the praises of countless devotees,
Perfumed by the utterance of countless devotees,
The all-existing mansion of true excellence,
Where Scriptures are like scrolls of brilliancy,
Where unquenchable lamps pour indescribable rays,
Where the universe both is and is not, in a sense,
And where the collation of single consciousness
Tends to personality for the sake of function,
And the Messenger of God held all within his palm.

There another person was shaping before the *Arsh-Throne*,
Filling aeonic space with echoing musics
In that immediacy of the sphere of boundlessness,
Where the untrammeled symphony seemed the only reality
Until it formulated into a person,
As the cosmic flute-player known as Narayana-Krishna:

"Love, love, love, stupendous love..........
Joy, joy, joy in the extreme, nothing else..........
O wonderful You, O wonderful not-I, O wonderful All..........

"The Gitas and other holy books of India,
As well as legends passed on by word of mouth,
Contain only the outer crust of revelation;
This was enough, for you cannot imprison creation
In books of transmission which, at least, are only keys.
Try to convey a portrait of totality,
To compose an essay which circumscribes the Secret,
And you are trapped; knowledge is cloaked by ignorance
Which through the veils of multiplication
Deludes the metaphysician into a phantasy

Which he holds before the unenlightened
Whither they stream, thinking to have found the Way,
And symbols, including the symbol of no-symbol,
Veil the reality in which we always live,
From which we find no assured escape.

"Where is that *om* to suggest complex theologies?
Where is that *om* to justify many rituals?
Where is that *om* to uphold a *Trimurti*
Or any arithmetical division of Infinity?

"Love, love, love, stupendous love.........
Joy, joy, joy in the extreme..........
Heart, heart, singing, happy heart..........
Why should the monkey be deified and man despised?
Why should the snake be sanctified and man despised?
Where the revelation that the elephant is a god?
Did I incarnate as a bovine or as a human?
God Is: that should be sufficient.
Love, love, love even the cowherds..........

"If you love me love the cowherds and not the cows,
If you love me sanctify the cowherds and not the priests,
If you love me you will learn the true love......
If you learn the true love you will love me, love me.
Find joy in work — this is *karma yoga*;
Cease to discuss and employ your lazy entrails,
Put your muscles into yoga and shut your brains,
Entomb your nerves and hallow your hands with dirt,
Serve the animal world but do not worship it,
Serve the human world and worship God.

"In the totality of cosmic evolution
From the infra-molecule to the super-superman,
Where change is an incessant and irremovable factor,
Where time-processes may be slow or very speedy
In movements from the pulse on to the aeon,
Nature-Prakriti unfolds herself
As the outer aspect of the spirit of Is-ness.

"There is a complete emancipation of the spirit
In which even the cells of the body participate,
So that birth and death and becoming continue on,
The mind is clarified of even its favourite thoughts,
Impressions pall into shadowy illusions,
And the Transcendent Unity appears unfettered.

"So I sing the universe unbounded
And electrify the universe which is bound,
In song and dance and ecstasy of being.
Humanity first, then establish your social morality;
Humanity first, then the ideal state and conditions;
Humanity first and last, and all things in their place,
That love and its ecstasy be yours,
That love and its ecstasy be mine,
That loves be as oceans so united
That the waves are dancing in delicious delight —
Thus dharma, thus Islam, thus the Supreme Message —
This is the essence of the Gita of Supremacy."

XII.

Nothing remained but the impulse to praise Allah,

Which carried on within the beating heart;
Pride and humility could no longer be,
And nothing was but aweful contemplation
Wherein Allah worships Allah as through a self,
In a quietude that seemed to swallow all music,
In a silence opposite to that of absolute death,
Like the sleeping of an infant of potential becoming;
And in that mood the Buddha manifested,
As that sage of wisdom who once roamed the earth,
Spoke many words, recorded in various fashions,
And taught men the Way of liberation;
And now he impressed me in this fashion
Which I interpret in the form of words:

"I am the spirit of the universal bliss,
Which is to say, the happiness of beings,
The illumination which is the essence of every thing,
And if the unhappy could attune
They would absorb this radiating spirit
To share in the all-compelling compassion.
Emancipation releases us from pain,
From ignorance, from sorrow and triviality,
Enabling all to dwell in *sukhavati*,
Which is to say, the spirit of delight.

"I taught no doctrine. I showed the way
To release man from his many confusions.
Meditation is superior to speech, why not use it?
Compassion and insight are all-pervading,
So that there is the Guidance in every instance
To which the ego-mind puts up an opaque front
And cries, whenever any difficulty is met.

Hypertension has been introduced in my name
Instead of calm deliberation and *prajna*,
The *bhikkhu* has been substituted for the *brahman*,
Or perhaps the intellect for the *bhikkhu*,
Bringing subterfuge instead of liberation;

"Let me inform you, beloved Saladin,
That I was one among innumerable Buddhas,
Identical with the Messengers of God,
With no other purpose or mission,
Leaving this prediction for the earth:

> IN A THOUSAND YEARS AFTER I LEAVE THIS SOIL
> BUDDHA MAITREYA SHALL COME TO AID THE WORLD,
> BORN IN THE PURE LAND OF THE WEST,
> BORN AMID A PEOPLE POORLY GIFTED
> TO OFFER THEM BLESSINGS OF COMPASSION,
> AND COMPASSION SHALL BE FOREMOST AMONG HIS
>   TEACHINGS.
> HE SHALL INSTRUMENT ACCORDING TO HUMAN NEEDS,
> TEACH IN ACCORD WITH WISDOM'S DICTATES,
> TO BE KNOWN FOR HIS REMARKABLE CHARACTER
> RATHER THAN FOR ANY PROFOUND PHILOSOPHY.
> HE SHALL BE SEEN RIDING UPON A WHITE HORSE
> AND NOT IN THE SYMBOLIC FORM AS SOME MAY SAY,
> WHO, LOOKING FOR THE HORSE WHERE THERE IS NONE
> WILL FAIL TO OBSERVE THIS COMPASSIONATE MAN.

"Which prophecy was long fulfilled in wild Arabia,
Where the Hashimit* yielded to Guidance,
Entered into the same deep stages as did I,
Attained the self-same emancipation as did I,
Won the hearts of surrounding multitudes as did I,

   * Mohammed. — ED.

And further perfumed the state of morality;
Whose personality became a shining light,
Who foreswore every form of self-adulation,
Lest mankind be deluded by false Messianism,
So he became the exemplar for the future.

"I came to restore the Message, to uplift humanity
Above crazy-quilt patterns of complex ideas
Which the ego constantly weaves for the race,
Offering false exits and complicated by-ways,
Misleading humanity away from the spiritual path.
Beware of those who call their rhetoric logic
And substitute authority for human effort,
And place before God everything but God Himself.

"The doctrine of absolute oneness
Was transmitted onward by me to my disciples,
Handed down by those we now call patriarchs
Until this day. But it is not different from
*LA ILLAHA EL IL ALLAHU,**
Which I shall not explain, lest perplexities follow,
Exalting my person instead of hallowed teachings;
So many philosophies appear in my name
With which I have never had association.
I did not come to liberate the ego,
To substitute a type of super-ego,
To establish new systems of classification
Leaving the world in ignorance.

"There is a universal salvation or there is none,
For where can there be limitation to Compassion?

* *La ilaha ill' Allah.*—ED.

215

To Mercy? to Beauty? to Grandeur? to Wisdom?
Buddhas, Avatars and Messengers are as One.''

The smile persisted after the communication,
There was serenity, there was peace, the slumber of the soul.

Then I saw a flickering in the Light,
The procession of a glorious multitude,
All the Messengers and Prophets of Allah
Passing and repassing upon the cosmic stage,
Angels and archangels and choirs of celestial beings
Singing and chanting in supreme jubilation
To the dancing of galaxies of galaxies,

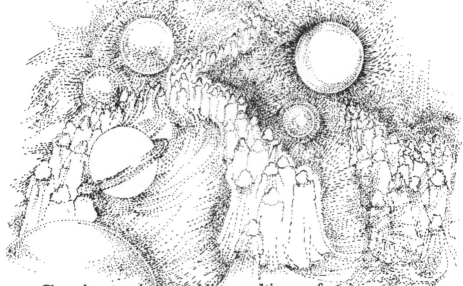

Changing, turning, moulding, melting, re-forming,
Lights without lights accompanying lights
With every micro-atom hugely magnified,
With every macro-cosm totally minified,
The grandest and least blending together —

The Mighty Breath encompassing all manifestations,
The Mighty Breath relaxing into stillness,
Everything and nothing together and all and emptiness,
Until the whole was modified en masse
With the Grand Seal of the Prophets in their midst
With all the Messengers of Allah around him,
The Voice repeating from the *Arsh-Throne*:
"THIS IS THE SEAL; REVELATION IS CONCLUDED."

I was the pain and joy of every one,
I was the life and death of every thing,
I was totality in my nothingness,
Effaced in the Sheikh, the Prophet and in Allah,
Sharing in the primordial *Nuri Mohammed* *
That which was and is and ever shall become,
Ever-was, ever-is, ever-shall-be, world without end,
And I awoke,
As from a dream.

* Primal Light; the first creation.

Book III

The Story of Sultan Salah-ud-din Ayyub and his Seven Sermons
to convert the Christian Captives to Islam
And Establish the Clans Known as *Bardawis* or *Baldwins*

(Argument: In Part One a truce is made and the Christian
captives are given seven years in which to return home, or choose
between being *Dhimmis*, Muslims or Slaves of Muslims.)

"In the Name of Allah, the Compassionate, the Beneficent:

"Thus I greet you, captives from Frankistan,
Now living in Palestine a year among the Muslims,
Awaiting your final judgment and destination
Whether you shall join the Islamic brotherhood
Or return to some sort of life in your former lands.
I shall not impose upon you the teachings of my Prophet
But place before you the teachings of my Prophet,
And also bring the teachings of your Messiah
For you to ascertain the most appealing,
Asking first, if you have ever been given a choice,
If your rulers, your nobility, your clergymen and monks
Ever permitted any freedom of decision.

"You have a Book — are you students of your Book?
We have a Book — we are students of that Book;
Do not blame me, sirs, that I prefer my religion
Which inculcates pursuit of knowledge and wisdom,
Which your religion does not seem to encourage.
Yet it shall be for you to study your faith,
It shall not be for you to study our faith
And I have restrained the imams from approaching you,
But it is not forbidden for you to approach the imams;
Whosoever desires may go to the monks for instruction,
Whosoever desires may go to imams for instruction,
Whosoever desires may go to priests even for instruction
But ignorance is something not to be tolerated —
Freedom of worship, yes! freedom to be ignorant, no!
We of Islam have this great advantage
For you may study your Book but not our Book

221

While we must study our Book and yet study yours.

"What is Quran? It is the latest revelation of Allah,
Not the only revelation but the latest;
And who can determine the nature of a revelation?
We regard the Torah of Moses as a revelation,
We accept also the words of many Prophets,
Even those whose words do not distinctly say:
'Thus sayeth the Eternal' or give some proper sign.
We also regard your Testament as sacred,
Although it does not declare, 'this is revelation',
And even your churches seem to minimize
The testimony of the companions of Jesus.
Mohammed, the Messenger, examined your religion,
Not finding the practices in accord with the writings,
Neither on foods, nor on Sabbaths, sacrifice or usury,
And if your churches can abrogate such teachings
Where is one to look, to go for guidance?

"When the Muslim mentions Allah he speaks of the Compassionate,
When the Muslim mentions Allah he speaks of the Beneficent,
And even I, the sultan, have warred against certain factions
Who proclaim themselves to be Muslims, yet rely on torture
        and murder;
Who proclaim themselves to be Muslims, to follow their own wills.

"This selection of Books which you accept as sacred,
This compendium preserved from the *Beni Israel*,
Holds that Mercy endures through all time and space,
Yet though the Book says Mercy is for ever and ever,
Where is the Mercy you have shown toward your enemies?
Where is the Mercy in your government and society?

Why do you constantly pray: 'O Lord, have Mercy'?
We Muslims assert that Allah is eternally Merciful,
We say Allah is unconditionally Merciful,
Therefore to tolerate those of other opinions;
Peoples of many religions dwell within our borders
And all are included within our framework of justice.
The treatment by Nazarenes to those of different inclinations,
The lack of cooperation between your divisions
Is quite beyond the comprehension of the Muslims;
Our Prophet taught to discuss religion amiably,
To show good-will, especially during debate,
Knowing that the All-Merciful is both Merciful and Wise.

"If the Merciful be such, what is the meaning of hell?
Naar we understand — the burning of the wickedness in man;
Naar we comprehend — the retribution for adherence to lust
For there is not a single sin in man
Which is not re-adjusted in eternity;
But eternal punishment for theoretical differences
Is quite beyond the understanding of the Muslim
Whose Prophet taught ultimate salvation for all worshippers,
So that even Sabeans and Ghebers are admitted to the heavens
Having had at some time a Prophet and a Book, or Books,
Though they have long since gone astray.

"Therefore I return to Allah, to Compassion and Mercy;
Therefore I turn to the pursuit of knowledge and wisdom;
Therefore I earnestly urge devotion to your faith,
Whether it be also mine or different.

"There is that Islam for which Quran is authority,
And that Islam which gives Quran its authority —

The former from the Pen-Sword of *Rassul* Mohammed,
The latter, universal, from all Prophets,
That all aspects of Truth become known to man,
That all become enlightened and blessed.

"Now I speak of Allah, the All-Compassionate and Beneficent,
But do not call Him 'Father', 'Judge' or 'King'
For although He also may be known under these epithets —
All qualifications being imbedded in His nature —
Does one find that every father is compassionate?
And are your kings and judges models of beneficence?
Surely you have had relations with many fathers,
Surely you have contacted judges and kings.
Consider this vast array we call the 'world' —
Did you surmise the distance to this land
When in your travels you were taken to these shores?
Were you not surprised by the magnitude of earth?
Were you not amazed at the difference in surroundings?
If such experience so affects your minds,
How many times more the sight of the Magnificent,
Who is a multitude of multitudes greater than you suppose,
Beyond your comprehension but not beyond your prayers.

"I speak not of Allah save in the spirit of Compassion,
I speak not of Allah save in the mood of Beneficence,
Though I do not expect compassion from you Feringhis
Nor consideration from those who led you here.

The soul of all is the same, emanating from Allah;
All are born believers, to be led astray
Through false guidance of parents and teachers and environment,
For before Allah there are no heretics or schismatics,
Only those who have performed aright,
And those imbedded in wickedness and selfishness.
Islam is a way of prayer and fasting and charity,
But before I proceed with my personal views,
I ask for some moments of silent meditation.

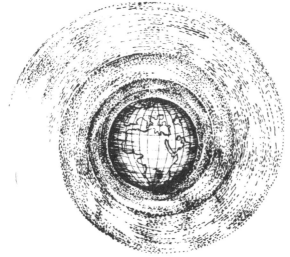

"And now that meditation has been tried,
Now that you have momentarily restrained your emotions,
You can learn to consult the innermost of your being
Completely free from pressure of authorities,
So I beg of you to let me speak of Mohammed
Who brought the final recording from the Heart of Allah,
That the ways of the outer world be given proper study,
That the ways of the inner worlds become unveiled,
For in Islam is the unifying integration of the soul.

"Jesus taught: 'Thy Will be done on earth as it is in heaven,'

And if Allah, the Supreme, has *willed* Compassion,
Why not on earth? Why only in the hereafter?
Already tales have come to the sultan's ears
That many of you enjoy a greater freedom
Than before when you were told that you were free,
For your Islamic masters do not require of you
More than you can bear in your daily toil;
Your returns in food and clothing and allotments
Are better than you had in your former ways
When your erstwhile masters were heedless of your lot.

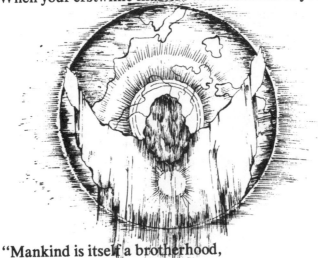

"Mankind is itself a brotherhood,
A very basic teaching within Islam
Where brotherhood is not an empty philosophy.
I give you freedom to withdraw, but still you stay
Listening to my address as if by compulsion,
So this I must ask of you:
If God is so Omnipotent and Omniscient,
Is He restricted in sending forth His Messengers?
Should any countries be withheld from Guidance?
Should any peoples be maintained in ignorance?
Should there be any chained by superstition?

"The reason for my policies is simple:
I have chosen to follow the footsteps of Omar,
The second Khalif in succession after the Prophet,
Whose heart was always open to the Guidance.
He came riding on a single animal, a conqueror,
And the streets of Jerusalem were opened for him then,
An actual conqueror, riding in simplicity,
Upholding the rights of Christians to churches and worship,
Upholding the rights of Hebrews to synagogues and worship,
Disturbing in no way the ownership of properties,
Save in the instance when God had uplifted the veil
That the site of the ancient temple must be sanctified
By the erection of a mosque for worshipping Muslims —
Thus the conqueror who came in all simplicity.

"Allah has sent His Messengers with codes,
With rules of conduct for personal and social behaviour,
With suggestions for devotion and worship and guidance,
True from the beginning with the Patriarch Adam
And so continued to these very days;
So when the Message of Jesus was covered with dross,
With weeds of strange theologies and doctrines,
With diabolic behaviour between contenders,
It was time for re-affirmation of the Truth.

"The Book of Adam is gone and that of Noah also;
The Book of Abraham has been made a secret pamphlet [5.]
Fit only for those initiates who accept it,
Though many of the institutions of these Prophets
Continue onward within the realm of Islam.
The Books of Moses are preserved by synagogues,
But what of the teachings set forth in those Books?

I shall not detain you by going into details
For, in returning to this, the Holy Land,
The people built another temple for worship
Without including a coffer for the Eternal,
A place for the Indwelling Presence of the Deity,
But rather built for their own edification,
Setting forth a precedent for much of mankind,
Offering temples built by human hands
Against the very precepts of the Scriptures.

"So Allah sent Jesus to restore the polity,
To emphasize the Presence of the Supreme,
Which priests and dualists and Scribes did not approve —
Now that Second Temple is no more.
Said Jesus: 'I came not to destroy but to fulfill,'
Yet you reject so many of his commandments
That one wonders why you accept any of them at all:
Your dietary habits, your lack of cleanliness,
Your total ignorance of the principles of usury,
The careless attitude toward widows and orphans,
The supreme contempt of the proud toward the needy,
While your men-of-the-Pen have long since substituted
The theological conclusions of ecclesiasts,
So the words of Jesus are multiply overcovered
And in the end there is no guiding ideal.

"This need not be, you may turn to Allah,
You may turn to God — this is repentance;
You should turn again to some form of Holy Guidance,
Choosing by experience, not by unsubstantiated creeds.
Go! I dismiss you, but demand of you your manhood;
Let each decide about his religion and his fate!"

II.

"In the Name of Allah, the Compassionate, the Beneficent:

"Beloved, I greet you as among my faithful subjects,
Whether you be slave or free, Muslim or Nazarene,
For Saladin will not be noted for injustice,
And as sultan must prove worthy of his own ideals.
Whosoever has suffered from injustice has been free to come,
Whosoever has any grievance may approach, and now
On this appointed day of reconciliation,
It is harmony of hearts, not conversions that I seek,
Though if you do become Muslims my heart shall rejoice,
While if you remain Nazarenes a tax shall be required
Although while in captivity there can be no levy.

"Friends, erstwhile subjects, you are the beloved of Allah
And being beloved, I shall not seek to convince,
Hoping only that your hearts be opened to insight;
Therefore I do not impose Quranic teachings,
For one, lest the words become mere by-plays,
For by force can people be compelled to pray,
But never can the heart be so compelled,
And the attributes of Allah would become nonsense.
Jesus, your Christ, has warned about empty mumbling,
Urging you to pray only in surrender,
Lest words become void utterances or chatter,
Desecrating holiness.

"If the Will of God is to be done upon this earth,
Why should you not be happy as the angels in heaven?

Why so much trepidation, so much anguish?
Allah, the Forgiving, knows your motives in every act,
He is slow to punish, quick to loving-kindness.

" 'Blessed are ye,' said Jesus — who dare change the text?
'Blessed are ye,' said Jesus — why confute the context?
'Blessed are ye,' said Jesus — why any other pretext?

"Are you so blessed, or are you only worms? Which the truth?
The Prophets speak, the priests pretend to interpret,
And the freedom that Allah has given to your souls
Is portrayed as a very distant phantom
With a substituted train of man-made teachings
Presented in the name of a glorious religion.
Quran was given to remind us of these blessings,
Blessings with which Allah has endowed His creation —
Why cry for Mercy who dwell in the universe of Mercy?
To believe in Allah without bestowing Mercy
Is to accept a portion and split the revelation;
To conceive of Allah without recognition of Beneficence
Is to render the teachings worse than useless.

" 'Those who believe (in the Quran)
And those who follow the Jewish (Scriptures),
And the Christians and the Sabeans —
And who believe in God and the Last Day,
And work righteousness shall have their reward with their Lord;
On them shall be no fear, nor shall they grieve.'*

"I shall not employ my sultanate to impress you,

* Quran II:62.

But wish to emphasize what Jesus taught you,
That the blessed are merciful, the merciful truly blessed.
Among the Muslims love for Allah is paramount,
Among the non-Muslims fear of punishment dominates,
Yet every longing heart is seeking love,
Every lonely person desires to be cherished,
Every human being looks for affection.
Fear and terror are the tools of the devil,
Which keeps the consciousness in dark confusion,
Leading to falsehood when the soul seeks light.
I have no doubt concerning your final decisions,
But he who comes to me from fear of fear
Or he who comes because of material benefits
With no vision for an after-life or righteousness
Is not, can never be a Muslim. Him I spurn.

"We stand in the midst of eternity, in the midst of love,
In the midst of compassion and of endless blessings
Which are the incessant outpourings of the Holy Spirit,
Lifting our minds toward the awareness of His Presence,
Filling our hearts with the overjoy of His Nearness,
Whereupon all the cells of the body tingle and dance,
The mind is in a state of ebullition,
And the heart is bathed in ecstasial delight,
All filled with praises of their Maker.

"As sultan it is possible to furnish some contentment,
As sultan it is not possible to make you happy,
And if you worship the sultan you are base idolators,
Nor do I wish my praise to come from your lips
For praise belongs to the One Praiseworthy.
I am no Harun-al-Rashid to move in disguise

231

To ferret private opinions about my kingship,
To interfere in private matters.
Words are never truths, and inventions of the scribes
May veil you from the inner guiding light,
So that happiness and repose are not your lot;
Do not be beguiled by phrases or petty maxims
Which act as drugs, hypnotizing the intellect,
But learn to praise God for in that is fullness of being.

"Consider the morning brightness and the dawn,
The scented blossoms of fruit trees in the Spring,
The babbling music of happy rivulets,
The symphony of birds upon awakening,
And become aware of the blessings of Allah,
The bliss which is no dream but The Reality.
Allahu! Allahu! Allahu!
In the morning before my prayers: *Allahu!*
In the hours between my prayers: *Allahu!*
Between prayer and sleep at night: *Allahu!*
The *Zakir* keeps remembering his Deity,
The *Zakir* is not concerned with self,
The *Zakir* needs Allah and nothing else.
We Muslims are aware to Whom we pray,
We feel the nearness of the One adored,
There is no power nor life save in Allah,
There is no emptiness nor fullness save He,
Learn to appreciate my feelings when I say:
Allahu! Allahu! Allahu!

"God bless you all."

III.

"I begin in the Name of Allah, the Compassionate, the Beneficent.

"Beloved Ones of God:
Because this is the end of three years' sojourn,
We may be concerned with meanings of this 'three',
Especially since you believe God is Three-in-One.

Your Scriptures open: 'In the beginning God,'
And I have opened: 'In the Name of Allah,'
Which is the wont and custom of us Muslims;
Whatever God has willed we accept as praiseworthy,
Nor do we forget our God when invoking His Name,
Nor moan nor rant nor weep over tiny matters.
How many Prophets mentioned in your Scriptures
Have invoked a Trinity or mentioned a Three-in-One?
I do not know whether you accept these Prophets
Or by what means you have come to repudiate them,
But can you point to a single instance
Where a Trinity has been invoked in all the Scriptures?
If so, I offer my sincere apology;
If so, I must pay a suitable penalty
For I hold myself to accept all prophetic teaching.

"Does your Deity exist only in the heavens?
Can there be any limitation to His Omnipotence?
Can there be any vacuum in His Omniscience?
You may object to our customs and folk-habits,
To outer things that belong to temporal Islam,
But be advised there is an eternal Islam
Which underlies the teaching of all religion —
And in a single place, is there a Trinity?
I do not find Moses proclaiming any Trinity,
I do not find its mention in the Books of Solomon
Or in the Psalms of David or anywhere else.

" 'Hear, O Israel, the Eternal our God, the Eternal is One'
Seems to be the basis of Scripture, and of nature,
In the world around us, and in our body, too,
And particularly in the air we breathe.

"I now place in your hands both Bible and Quran
Which, if you read, you will find in much agreement;
Bible contains the books of the *Beni Israel*
Who do not consider them all as revelation,
For in some of them the Deity is not mentioned,
And others of them have little to do with God.
Quran is opened with an invocation,
Which is repeated before nearly every *Sura*
And belongs, no doubt, to the revelation itself.
What value are your declarations of faith
If the heart is never quiet, nor the soul becalmed?
If you do not experience inner peace?
If you are always subject to agitation?
We Muslims proclaim Allah and meditate,
We try to understand His attributes,
We want to act as if He were ever present,
So faith brings us strength and full assurance.

"Is there a single Prophet who proclaimed the self?
But scribe-religion is much concerned with self,
So utilizing human institutions
That this realm of self overshadows the Being of God,
Which is to say darkness and diabolatry and ignorance.
Again I read from your accepted Scriptures:*

" 'But now they are many members, yet one body.
The eye cannot say to the hand: 'I have no need of you';
Or, again, the head to the feet: 'I have no need of you.'
But much rather is it the case that the members of the body which
    seem to be weaker are necessary,

* 1 Cor. 12:20-26 K.I.T.

And the parts of the body which we think to be less honourable,
These we surround with more abundant honor, and so our unseemly
    parts have the more abundant comeliness,
Whereas our comely parts do not need anything. Neverthless, God
    compounded the body, giving honour more abundant to the
    parts which had a lack,
So that there should be no division in the body, but that its
    members should have the same care for one another.
And if one member suffers, all the other members suffer with it;
Or if a member is glorified, all the other members rejoice with it.'

"We in Islam have accepted this as a teaching,
And we have so esteemed universal brotherhood
As absolutely essential to the way of life;
Nor can we comprehend its rejection by you,
Noticing that it is mentioned in your texts.
If you reject a teaching, what is left?
Only a glorification of a person,
Which is not a glorification when you reject
The words that have come from the Prophet's mouth.
In your world there is the absence of brotherhood:
The high and mighty trampling upon the low,
Stemming their opportunities whenever convenient,
Which seems to be an absolute absurdity;
Yet you are free to continue in such folly,
For there must be no compulsion in religion,
And though I accept Quran and all it states,
I leave you to continue in your own faith
Hoping it will lead to beneficence and gratitude.
God bless you all, and to you all, peace."

IV.

"I begin in the Name of Allah, the Compassionate, the Beneficent.

"I trust to continue in His Name, under His Guidance
For this is the essence of the spirit of Islam,
Offering good-will to every one of you
Who having remained now four years within my dominion
Have been given the advantages of education.
We Muslims seek to exemplify our teachings,
Nor make excuses when we fail in our efforts,
Never daring to nullify passages of Holy Writ;
Therefore I quote for understanding and decision,
Again appealing to your monks for rectification:

" 'Verily, verily I say unto you,
He that believeth on me, the works that I do shall he do also;
And greater works than these shall he do . . . '*

These are the words of Jesus, according to the text;
These are the records in your sacred Books,
But in your hearts do you really believe them?
If there be a single one among this multitude
Who testifies to the acceptance of this teaching,
Saladin shall free and honour him,
Load him with gifts, permitting him to go or stay.
If no one of you will dare to speak,
Then you must be willing to listen
While the sultan expresses his view on this point,

* John 14:12 A.V.

237

Giving you the freedom to interrupt,
To interrogate or argue or comment,
For all are equal before Allah in my view —
No bishop, no king, no priest, no layman,
The sun and the rain and the wind affect us all,
The fruits of good and evil are for all.
Muslims do not abrogate what is in the Scripture,
The revelation is true and therefore timeless
Though many have come with special Messages
Who do not present a code or basic teachings.

"We Muslims honour your Prophets and your Books,
Nor abrogate any transmitted teachings,
Nor even specially honour our teachers and guides,
Holding that all Praise is for Allah, forever and ever.
How vain and vapid many uttered sounds,
Nor are prayers answered; God does not do *your* will.
In Islam we accept without equivocation,
In Islam we do not explain our texts away
Though there are many levels of interpretation.
The living Jesus attracted only a handful,
While Mohammed won the multitudes to his cause,
Though this itself should not be an argument,
Yet in this sense your Scripture has been fulfilled ·
For even if you reject *Rassul-Lillah*,
It cannot be denied concerning his following.

"Jesus came to mankind as a loving friend,
Offering charity and guidance and beneficence
With very little mention of damnation,
For love-religion is greater than anything else,
Opening doors to that which you have not seen.

Your Scriptures proclaim the priority of love,
Your leaders proclaim the priority of faith
Which has been degraded to blind acceptance,
So the Scriptures have been by-passed
And you have been kept in abject ignorance.
In our teaching we also have preceptors,
But our preceptors eschew power for themselves,
Speaking because of knowledge, that is their authority,
Always aiding their disciples on the path,
Pupil and preceptor operating as a team,
Fulfilling the teachings I have presented to you
From the twelfth chapter of First Corinthians.

"Jesus said: 'I go to prepare a place for you.'*
Is there any among you who can explain this passage?
Do you think this *place* is like some earthly scene?
And that your heaven is a fulfillment of your earth?
How can that be! Is this surrender to God?
In Islam *place* represents the soul's abode, 6.
The station of one's being in the grand unfoldment
Which enables man to understand his purpose,
And there is opportunity for every person,
Whosoever zeals for the highest wisdom,
Accepting the instructions of the preceptors
Who through love, in love, by love
Guide their disciples toward God.

" 'Jacob was a plain man, dwelling in tents.'†
Can any of you explain this text to me? 7.
Can you make any sense of this accepted version?

* John 14:2 A.V.
† Gen. 25:27 A.V.

239

What is so wonderful about living in tents?
What kind of virtue is latent in this plainness?
When you really desire to know the Scriptural meanings,
To examine the actual words of *Nabi* Moses,
You will find corruption and mistranslation
As was proclaimed by our *Rassul*-Mohammed.
Jacob, like all Prophets, was close to perfection
So one may speak of him as a perfect man;
And what is a perfect man
But he who understands the states and stations of life,
Who understands the meaning of the ladder
Which goes from earth to heaven, back to earth;
So he becomes aware of all facets of manifest being,
Of the heavens and hells and earths and all therein,
For from Allah all have come, to Him return.

"The states of consciousness of man are several,
Not to be explained in terms of one another:
Deep sleep, dreaming, ordinary daily awakening,
The aspects of life connoted by jinns and angels,
The grandeur open to Saints and Prophets,
All of these belonging to human kind.
So the term 'tents' has a much greater meaning,
And many also of the terms used by *Nabi* Moses,
The meanings lost when the sight of God was lost.

"In Islam we have our external religion,
In Islam is also the internal religion
For the benefit of bodies, hearts and souls,
That time and eternity melt one into the other.
How can a loving Creator-Father, All-Wise,
Keep Himself forever hidden from His offspring?

We recognize the multitude of qualities of Allah,
Venerate them as the Beautiful Names,
To repeat and repeat and so impress ourselves
Until the qualities are then assimilated,
Giving some comprehension of Divinity.

"Two modes of life are open to every one:
The way of self-in-thingness, thus accumulations;
The way of heart-in-devotion, thus surrender.
One need not criticize the unfortunate
Who cling to the life of self-in-thingness,
Excusing the short-comings that they make,
Exaggerating the errors of other people,
Overblaming, causing rivalry and hatred.
The Prophet taught that this folly should not be repeated,
Though his followers are divided into sects
Who honour the Prophet in their various ways,
Each claiming to be the body of true believers.

"But when one undertakes the inner journey,
These habits are seen as childish and cast away.
Woe to the scribes! woe! woe to the scribes!
There is a terrible tyranny in the misuse of words,
There is a subtle tyranny in the misuse of rhetoric,
There is terrorism in emotional methods
Which leads to endless schisms and enmities.
Jesus has said: 'You cannot worship God and Mammon' —
But many of you have tried and insist you can,
Evidencing lack of trust in your very religion,
Evidencing by the condition of your heart
That you are bound in selfhood, not in God.

"Again, Jesus taught to be like little children
In loving surrender to an All-Present God,
But few of your leaders manifest this way of life —
Do children harangue and threaten and exhort?
Or turn to lusts and venery and strife?
Knowing that God is love, I love you all,
Nor dare permit within my sultanate
Those tyrannies, those cruelties, those vicissitudes
Which so abound in the lands of Frankistan,
Where your rulers often behave as craven beasts,
Devouring one another with or without cause —
And these supposed to possess the keys to God's Kingdom!

"Allah the Creator wished to be loved,
He created from the essence of His Love,
So Creator and creation and creature form a Unity —
You Nazarenes, full of fear, have given power to hell;
You Nazarenes, full of uncertainty, have given the scepter to Iblis;
There is no power nor might save in Allah.
As Jesus said: 'The truth shall make you free.'
May it be so. God bless you all. Amin."

V.

"In the Name of Allah, the Compassionate, the Beneficent.

"Beloved Ones of God:
You have come to learn the meaning of compassion,
Receiving consideration in your affairs,
Nor treated as beastly animals by superiors,

Finding at last the dignity of manhood,
Thus to appreciate the superiority of Islam,
Quite different from the whispered villainy
You heard in former campaigns.
Compulsory study of your own sacred Books
Has done considerable to add to your uncertainty
As to the truth of that which has been imposed,
For every soul is born, by nature, a believer,
Distracted therefrom by parents and surroundings,
Taken from the path of spirituality,
Placed within a maze of conflicting claims
Which lead to neither happiness nor well-being.

"Some things I do not countenance:
To compare the behaviour of your sultan
With the magnificent person of Lord Jesus Christ;
Has a single one of you been brought to judgment
For failing to live according to Islamic law?
For falling short of the teachings of *Rassul*?
The testament of our Prophet is a continuation
Of the teachings of Jesus and all his forebears
Given in early ages in this land.
Many of you now understand the teachings,
Finding their identity with Islam,
That the spirit of the teachings is the same,
Whereas the ways of life in all Frankistan
Bear little resemblance to any sacred teaching.
Yes, Saladin cannot be compared to Jesus,
And if any of my sycophants so pretend,
He shall immediately fall from my favour.
LA ILLAHA EL IL ALLAH!

"Nothing to be worshipped but Allah,
Nothing and no one else to receive full praise,
Though you may address the Deity by other words,
The spirit is what matters in such affairs.
We have not tried to overwhelm you as converts
For if there is no sincerity, no Islam.
Driven by fear, by terror and damnation
You have impotentized your God, magnified Satan
And accepted negativity as the way of life;
God is Love, God is Mercy, God *is* Life —
Rid yourselves of hypocrisy and pretense,
Or the idea of the rack or torture
Utilized by the power-monsters who were your suzerains.
How can they control in the after-life
That which is beyond their sceptred authority?

"Does any one on this earth bind the heavens?
What did you bring into this world? What will you take?
You came as simple, guileless children
To whom the kingdom, according to Jesus, belongs;
But authority is in the hands of others,
Children have no voice and mighty thunders of fear
Echo and re-echo within and without your selves.
When charmed and hypnotized and blandished,
You turned attention to enemies far away
Who never did you harm, while your exploiters laughed,
Promising what did not belong to them
While taking from you all that should be yours.
Fear, not Love, should carry the standard of religion!
Even misguided Muslims make no such error,
Constantly repeating: '*Allaho Akbar!*' — God is All-Great,
Which being so, neither fear nor Satan nor hell

Can keep them eternally in shackles.
Alas, that so many of you have become like dogs
With muzzles on your bodies, hearts and souls,
Shouting the word 'freedom!' under compulsion,
'Salvation!' while aching with fear and trembling.

"There is a religion of the kindergarten,
There is a religion of childhood and youth,
There is a religion of maturity,
And also the religion of the seer.
If we do not pass from grade to grade,
Where will the wisdom manifest?
If we do not pass from stage to stage,
How can we come close to God?

"I cannot recommend a religion based on sin,
I cannot recommend a religion based on fear,
And even less, a religion contrary to its Book;

"If the Creator saw that His creation was good,
As it is written in the Books of Moses,
Where the authority that men are born in sin?
There has never been a revelation to man
But it condemned murder and adultery and greed,
That it encouraged honesty and forbearance and virtue,
That did not exhort to prayer and meditation,
That it stressed the after-life over one in the world.
Many of you are inclined to visit our imams
Who show you more consideration than did your priests,
Who do not blame you for every small transgression,
Who emphasize the forgiveness of Allah.

"One does not understand this emphasis on sin,
One readily understands the adoration of his Maker
Who is not limited in any way.
Did Allah produce a universe of beneficence,
Or did He place a labyrinth before you
That by your personal efforts you might understand
Its nature and your purpose of being here?
O hitherto unwashed and quite unlearned,
Have you not all without exception
Benefitted from your bathing and your education,
Benefits of which you were deprived
When living puny lives as exploited peasants?
We are slaves of Allah that we may learn,
Not stemmed by a formal orthodoxy,
Discarding righteousness and the True Path,
And having the lot of heaven assured to us.

"Yes, there are sins, there are evils, there are ills,
But having a guidance upon which there is no doubt,
Having in Holy Quran a Book of assurance,
Why is there any need to fear? Praise be to Allah.
The fearing among you have paraded before my throne
And, one by one, come and confessed your reasons
Until you learned to stand before the sultan like real men.

" 'The lamb and the lion shall lie down together'
May be a most beautiful of Scriptural texts,
But have you not quavered before your superiors?
Or even dared to act like humans before them?
Though a sultan, I am most of all a man,
Before my subjects I function as a superior,
Before my Deity I am only an equal devotee

246

Nor is there any place within the mosque
Where an official is given special sanction
Which is, I believe, the way things are in heaven.
What can you take with you to Paradise?
Honesty, sincerity and a noble heart;
Not wealth, not power, surely not lust, never pride,
Which things belong to those you regard as nobles,
So, even in combat they could not sacrifice
These shortcomings so affixed to their characters.

"What is jihad? The noble holy war against evil,
Whether that evil appears within ourselves or elsewhere;
But among you Nazarenes, the devil is the stranger,
The enemy is far-flung, one who is different.
Every one of you may readily approach the sultan
And even, if you desire, go to our *kadis*
To settle your disputes; you have found them just
So you are now contented more than ever in the past.
Already half-Islamized and learning that we respect
Those things which you thought you alone possessed,
You have found we uphold the teachings of Christ,
Greatly esteem his most noble sayings.

"One by one I end your doubts and win your hearts,
Who no longer remain in doubt or destitute of heart,
Experiencing yourselves the benefits of Islam.
With this abatement of fear and clarification of mind
You begin to understand and live a purposed life.

"We devotees of Islam may own a quantity of slaves,
Yet we always act as if we were but stewards,
Knowing that if we do not treat them fairly,

We must face the ultimate judgment of heaven
And be held to account for even the smallest misdeed;
Therefore to raise your status and set you free
Is not only a political or social endeavour
But a preparation for the blessings we may find
Both in the world before us and in the life to come.

"Jesus has taught that this world is but a bridge,
The greater existence is elsewhere,
That there is no permanency in material forms;
Your Scriptures say all flesh is grass,
Yet your leaders seek aggrandizement —
How can this be? Why should this be?
For now I issue a new decree to all of you:
That it is permissable to visit our mosques,
You may even join in our prayers and fasts,
Nay, study in our schools and learn our language
And the duties instilled in religious teachings
And this, without interception of your own religion,
So you may continue to church on Sunday,
Continue your confessions and perform your rites.
You have noticed many Muslims at your meetings;
They are not spies. Sometimes it is curiosity
And sometimes because of their devotion to *Rassul-Lillah*,
They wish to learn more of the mission of Jesus,
Though your interpretations may seem peculiar.

"We consider religious study most important,
As this earthly incarnation is a minuscule
In the actual life of every personality;
What we do here does not determine eternity
For eternity is beyond all determination,

Yet life goes on; the soul is given many chances
As there are many mansions in the Father's house,
Of which you have been kept in ignorance.
Have you ever raised your eyes above the cathedral?
Have you ever been able to feel the silence about you?
We Muslims seek knowledge of this world and the next
Which knowledge may prove to be inexhaustible,
So each must live until we return to Allah —
At least these are my views.

"These are my views, but now I wish debate,
I wish debate, discussion, exploration,
I wish none half-hearted; either full surrender
Or your adherence to your present faith.
He is no Muslim who half surrenders,
As the Messenger discovered in his lifetime
During his sojourn in the city of Medina
Where people joined his cause for the sake of spoils,
Or in expectance of some earthly return.

"In Islam we are taught that Allah is eternal,
But no thing persists for ever and ever and ever
Excepting God and His Mercy and Compassion,
So hell must pass away as will heaven and earth.
Strange that I speak to you in this simple way,
Noticing the teaching of your Scriptures,
Noticing the departure from these teachings
When one observes your governments and churches
And the customs of your societies.

"Come with me on this way of life to God,
Come with me on this way to life to God,

Come with me on this way of life in God,
Come with me to God in this way of life,
Only come and seek, for you shall surely find:

"No more verbal accounts but actualities,
No compulsion, no stress, only friendly invitation,
So we shall discuss, we shall explore, we shall elucidate,
We shall examine, we shall reason and we shall meditate,
Yet the decision remains with you, my dearly beloved,
The decision rests with you, beloved ones of Allah.

VI.

"In the Name of Allah, the Compassionate, the Beneficent.

"Beloved Ones of Allah:
We come together at long last in happy communion,
Finding that many of you have agreed with Sultan Saladin,
Finding that many of you have found your peace with Allah,
Finding that many of you have wished to join my brethren,
Refusing ransom to return to your former ways
Even though it means another year in slavery.

"Yet because there is no compulsion in true religion,
Yet because the Muslims abhor an Inquisition,
Yet because there must be full assurance
Without the slightest tinge of hypocrisy,
I would, *inshallah*, discuss some other principles
To lessen any possible misunderstanding.
If Allah, the Merciful, the Compassionate

Be without fault, be without blemish, be unhindered,
How can He be compelled to accept from any race
The vessels of Prophethood and the channel of His Message?
Where is the justice and magnanimity in that?

"Even in the Scriptures of the *Beni Israel*
There is mention of Habakkuk and Jonah and Job
Who were not descendants of any Jacob-Israel,
Yet were admitted to be among God's Prophets;
Since this is so, who determines where and when
The sceptre of Prophecy is assigned to the world?
What are the signs of spirituality?
Warnings? or a code? or blessings from the Supreme?
Or a multitude of mercies for the down-trodden?

"Mohammed, upon whom be peace, taught us prayer,
Repeating, in Arabic, formulae similar
To those persisting since the time of Adam —
Not petitions to a God of unlimited materiality,
Not endless requests which purport lack of Wisdom,
Nor wishes nor beggary nor fulminations,
But constant willingness to surrender to God.
So why fear? Why beg? Why beseech? Why implore?
This difference of attitude in prayer
Is quite apparent to your guardian sultan
Who has no fear of Muslims being converted
From mere attendance at assemblages or rituals,
For only those weak in faith have any fear
That the devotees will be so influenced therefrom.

"This I leave, to consider next the Fast.
The Bible teaches that God has a day of rest,

Although this can only be symbolic
As life is ever moving in this world;
Yet for the sake of bodies there should be a rest,
Not only from external activity and work,
But also from the internal activity of mind,
That man's own servants be given proper repose,
That body, mind and heart be reinvigorated
For the sake of health, for the control of Iblis
And for the expansion of inner realization.

"Five daily prayers mean more than just to pray,
Five daily prayers involve constant remembrance of Allah,
For when we are close to Allah we are far from wrath,
When not in wrath, we are delivered from hell-fire.
The Islamic prayer is of body, heart and soul:
We pray with body which must assume various postures,
Postures which are physical, psychic and moral,
The basis of our practical psychology
That the ego be restrained and the heart stressed.

"Beyond this is the prayer of the soul itself
Which constantly seeks union with its Maker
Until in full remembrance it realizes
That Allah is praying to Allah through His servant,
So whether the prayer be personal or universal,
Paradise may beckon to every devotee;
And by praying together in congregation,
We learn to appreciate human brotherhood.
Relaxation from tension is very much needed,
And every move from tension brings a blessing,
So abstinence from food at various times
Assists the individual in all his parts;

Those who see Ramadan as a discipline see well,
But this is just the cover over the true fast
Which is more than mere restraint from food at times,
But restraint from anger, jealousy, envy, ill-will,
To control the ego-*nafs*, source of all our troubles,
So the fasting of the body is a feeding of the soul.

"Ramadan is based on the life of the Holy Prophet
Who lived as a man among men when here on earth,
Whose consciousness could soar to the Great Beyond,
Wherein he could communicate and be blessed,
Partaking of the highest form of communion,
And desiring his followers and disciples to do likewise,
So the Fast is preparation for the Feast.
Your Lent is highly esteemed by us Muslims
Who recognize the validity of holiness,
Who do not insist on a monopoly to salvation,
But recognizing divisions among you people
Retain a strong antipathy to what you call schismatic.
Accepting the latest form of the Divine Message,
We perform the Ramadan accordingly,
Nor have degraded ceremony into superstition;
Prayer and Fasting are thus among the Pillars of Islam,
Both of the eternal Islam presented by the Chain,
And the latest revelation of *Mecca-Shereef*.

"Bestowing of alms is also incumbent on us,
Which is expected of every devotee,
Whatever be their form of religion and code;
Yet, despite constant series of warnings,
Too many people live to accumulate,
Accumulate for the sake of pride and vanity,

Even though they lose happiness thereby.
You over-emphasize the *person* of Jesus Christ,
Devaluating his teachings, so wealth and glory
And plaudits of the multitude
Remain your practice despite the Holy Book;
Therefore all your condemnation of others
Is not based upon your sacred teachings,
And in this you are heathens more than believers.
So be it. I have accepted Islam and try
To fulfill my duties as the Prophet instructed,
Providing means to forestall starvation,
Not for myself alone but for the nation,
Knowing that Allah is ever Compassionate, Beneficent.

"What is true religion?
Attendance on the needy widows and orphans,
Not pompous repetitions of any formula;
The care of others brings blessings to oneself,
Whereupon *Zakat* is a hallowed institution,
That it is really more blessed to give than to receive —
Therefore I have demanded nothing from you,
Considering it a privilege of revealed Islam
To follow this path, hoping you will join me,
Coming at last to accept my ways.

"Finally is the institution of *Hajj*,
The journey to the sacred places of Mecca
Which is also a basic principle of faith.
I have arranged to permit all Nazarenes
To make the pilgrimage to Jerusalem,
To visit the sacred shrines of their religion
Which are also sacred to us, who also

Accept the sacred places of the various Prophets;
Only as our Kibla we face in worship
The place where Abraham received his Divine Blessing,
Nor do we forget the role of Abraham
Who was vouchsafed a certain revelation
Which we in Islam have striven to preserve.

"Thus we find these five-fold tablets of revelation [8.]
In both the eternal and historical Islam,
Considering all ways to Allah as ways to Allah,
Minimizing differences and maximizing devotion.
So much have I spoken of the glories of Islam
That I must apologize, having forgotten
That it is not for me to proselytize,
Nor even force you to listen to our imams.
May Allah bless you all, forever and ever and ever. Amin."

VII.

"In the Name of Allah, the Compassionate, the Beneficent.

"Beloved Ones of Allah:
Now is the day of final reckoning,
Now is the day of ultimate decision
Wherein after seven years of seeming deprivation,
You are to become freed as Muslims, or ransomed,
Or to remain here as protected citizens
Following your own faith by recognizing
That in this land only true Muslims can serve
In the higher responsibilities of government

Or bear arms, from which you are exempt.

"I speak to you this time in trepidation,
Realizing that some of you are quite adept
In knowledge of the religion to which you have turned,
So I beg pardon of Allah for even daring to speak.
I note your joy in listening to the sultan,
I note your joy in your present status in life,
I note your joy and offer my praise,
For as Jesus has said: 'Great is your joy,'
Only before you did not have very much joy
And some did not even know the teachings of Christ.
I also take great joy in all my subjects
Who in the ultimate sense are not my subjects,
Nor am I their guide save in a worldly sense
To provide, protect, exhort and animate,
Leaving the more precious things of Allah
To those more suited for this duty.

"Awaken to the loveliness of your Creator
Who loves you more than you have been conceiving,
Inviting you to enter His Gardens of Joy
So that, on leaving this sordid world
You are relieved from a multitude of cares
And your future journey through the universe
Becomes a matter of ever increasing awakening,
Until at long last, you arrive at the gates of felicity,
Knowing that Allah is absolute Beneficence and Compassion.

"This policy has become the nexus of my rule,
To be shared by subjects of every faith;
Now seeing this, you have begged for your conversion,

You have come in multitudes to this way of life,
You have foresworn your earlier ways of ignorance,
You have demanded release from superstition,
You search for knowledge and, as Christ has said,
You seek and it may be opened to you,
Not restricted to the dark cloister of some monastery,
Not monopolized by your prelates and your scribes.
But I must caution you from any thoughts of irreverence,
From wishing to war upon your former associates
From a military zeal not of the heart,
From any selfish invocation of Allah.

"*As-salaam aleikhum* supports an attitude of peace,
That by promoting peace we further God's Kingdom,
That by promoting peace we attain to mastery.
We benefit our brethren and the whole community
And ultimately the entire surface of the earth.
So restrain yourselves and learn to battle instead
Against the fallacies that lurk within yourselves,
Against the spirit of calumny and aggression,
Against the attitude of your provocative will,
That through this self-restraint you come to realize
The light and life and blessings of Allah.

"There are deeper sanctuaries within the folds of Islam
More properly reserved for those who persevere,
Accept the discipline of the Inner Path
Or *Tarikat* which leads to Divine Wisdom; then,
Without severe alterations of the modes of life,
One walks steadfastly on the path to God.

"I shall not address you further, for now you know,

257

And yet the purpose of crusading is accomplished,
For you may go unshackled to all holy places,
To shrines and sacred spots of whomsoever,
According to the spirit and letter of the law.

"The holy places remain as gates to Allah,
Which you may visit if you come from foreign parts,
Which you may visit if you prefer the status of *Dhimmi*,
Protected citizens in the world of Islam.
The rest may come to the mosque with me and pray,
Arranging yourselves with me in row upon row,
Joyfully repeating the prayers along with the imams,
We journey together on the highway to our God:

" 'PRAISE BE TO ALLAH, THE CHERISHER AND SUSTAINER
    OF THE WORLDS:
MOST GRACIOUS, MOST MERCIFUL;
MASTER OF THE DAY OF JUDGMENT.
THEE DO WE WORSHIP, AND THINE AID WE SEEK.
SHOW US THE STRAIGHT WAY,
THE WAY OF THOSE ON WHOM THOU HAST BESTOWED
    THY GRACE,
THOSE WHOSE PORTION IS NOT WRATH,
AND WHO GO NOT ASTRAY.'*
AMIN."

* Quran I:1.

Book IV

THE TRIUMPH OF EGYPT

Out of Egypt I call My sons,
Out of Egypt shall I bring My light,
Out of Egypt shall the Message go
To dispel the darkness of the night.

260

In the Name of Allah, the Compassionate, the Beneficent.

There was darkness before the history of time,
There was darkness before the captivity of fire
Whence all the arts and crafts of men have come;
But the Mercy and Wisdom of Divinity were seeded
Even in the anteriority of recordings,
And the wise of the world have made their records,
Retaining monuments as testimonials of their aptitudes,
Preserving in those monuments and in the hearts of men
The deepest secrets of the universe
Which Divine Providence has entrusted to this world.
These wise have been referred to as adepts
Who dwelt from earliest ages in the land
Watered by the Nile above, watered by the Nile beneath,
In the land wisdomed by the secret waters of the heavens.

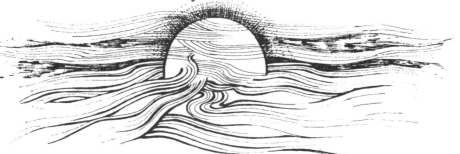

So it was that the Prophet Moses was born in that place
To verbalize some of the most ancient secrets,
The format remaining, but the spirit so deeply covered
When cacophonous agitations masquerading as logic
Poisoned the atmosphere which men must breathe —
So the secret wisdom is entrusted to the sand.
In later times the Prophet Jesus dwelt therein
And was instructed in all the holy traditions,

Whose followers were later involved in politics
That the power of the world became the ideal of man.
And again the Holy Spirit was withdrawn
Until the Companions of *Rassul-Lillah* invaded the country,
Delivered the unfortunate of every class,
Restoring for a time the land to the people,
Restoring for a greater period the spiritual teaching,
Only to be involved again by the dross of contamination
Wherein *nafs*, the spirit of the incessant ego,
Came to dominate the world of Islam,
Which lost its fervour in those incessant struggles
When Muslims slaughtered Muslims with more vigour
Than the most fanatic have displayed in their jihads.

The Message of the Prophets has come to enlighten mankind,
The polity of the early Khalifs was to alleviate human suffering,
But the Arab world was caught in mutual antipathies
Until the Sultan Saladin acquired the sceptre,
Seeking to resurrect the teachings of revelation
So that Egypt, Land of Two Truths,
Might stand as a phoenix reborn
As the true heart-center of the material sphere.

There is no power in dialectic: *ALLAHO AKBAR*.
There is no power in the fomenting of scribes,
Though all the air be polluted with dust and smog,
And the ability to love one another is befarced;
Truth is truth and shall shine again,
Beyond and beneath the noises of radio and press,
Beyond and beneath also interpretations of Scriptures,
Beyond and beneath substitution of man-words for God-words,
Beyond and beneath all the agitations of the day.

Lessons from written history have not been learned,
The causes of the rise and fall of empires is embedded
In memories but not in faculties of thought and insight,
And forces of divers directions are over-emphasized
As if Allah were little more than a mere shadow.

*Is there God in history?**
Such blasphemy dominates one portion of the world
While another denies the existence of Divinity,
So while the antitheists and the atheists contend
The followers of true Faith must now emerge,
Emerge because it is the will of Providence,
Emerge because no alternate course is open.
The nihilists and annihilators must go,
Whether through their mutually insane hostilities
Or for any other reasons, but they must go,
And the sincere believers, because of their inner faith,
Shall come to power on a new momentum of the waves.

Recall the wonderful excursions in the time of Omar
When the empire was in the Khalif-fakir's hands
And the awakened heart of a man made the decisions,
Taking nothing of plunder or treasure for himself,
Relying upon Allah and the teachings he had received.
"Blessed be the poor in spirit" came from the mouth of Jesus,
But the word 'fakir' has been so travestied,
Even by those who claim to follow Jesus,
And sometimes by those who venerate Quran.
Jesus was the Prince of fakirs in actuality,
Siddiq and Omar the Emperors of fakirs in actuality,

* Title of a thesis by a well-known philosopher.

263

When words were used to signify a way of life;
But the scribes and money-lovers hold the reins,
Play with words as they will, distort their meanings
And add to the ceaseless confusion of the world.

Let us return in repentance to the All-Compassionate,
Let us turn in devotion to the All-Beneficent,
Let the false methods of the powerful run their course.
In the name of Power the Greeks battled the ancient Persians,
In the name of Power the Persians warred upon the Greeks,
Each with its propagandists proclaiming some way to *peace*,
'Peace', that awful word of damnation, that raped-virgin,
That monster-dragon camouflaged as a dove,
That idol to which the anti-idolators bow,
That queen of reptile-whores, that arch deceiver,
Paraded by the wicked, inscribed on their banners
Most of all when they embark on new deviltry —
Let us instead turn to Allah and His refuge.

There is an equilibrium toward which all things tend —
Forms and beings and even the thoughts of mind,
To birth, to maturity, decay and death,
Everything proceeding from Allah and back to Allah,
Yet only in Allah is there peace,
Or else in utter submission to Allah —
And the best of states is toward equilibrium.

When the seeking of wisdom is devirginized into a maxim,
The words venerated and the substance lost,
Man feeds upon spiritual recipes instead of food,
Delights in stones instead of the bread of heaven
And accepts serpents for fish in mock delight.

There is an equilibrium toward which all things tend,
Whether the soul in its search for emancipation,
Or a moving body in its quest for some repose
Or the forces of nature, whatever be their function —
So also is Peace in the realm of Islam,
And only through the manifestation of Islam
Can peace, through surrender, be made known to man.
These things are offered most of all: *ishk** and *ilm*,†
The universal operation of attraction in every sphere of life,
The universal action of penetration in every sphere of life,
Functionalized into the waking consciousness of humanity,
To the dethronement of falsehood wherever it lies.

    "Say: I take refuge with the Lord of the Dawn,
    From the mischief of created things;
    From the mischief of Darkness as it overspreads;
    From the mischief of those who practise Secret Arts;
    And from the mischief of the envious one as he practices envy."‡

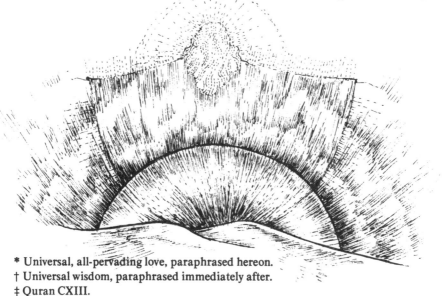

* Universal, all-pervading love, paraphrased hereon.
† Universal wisdom, paraphrased immediately after.
‡ Quran CXIII.

265

The sceptres of the Greeks and Persians are no more,
The peoples of the Indo-Germanic races have substituted
Themselves, aligning and realigning with the same power-motif,
And even today in their mischief, envy and rivalry,
Seeking to engulf the earth, shall fail,
And the Indo-Germanic races must learn
That Allah is, and also that He is over all,
That the power of mankind is but a vacuum
In a universe of Compassion and Beneficence.
O Egypt, you are called upon to expose weakness,
To free mankind from raciality of every sort,
To bring those buried treasures from your heart —
From beneath the sand and from the secluded adepts,
That the glory of Allah may shine in this world.
But when the thoughts of men were turned to luxuries,
Religious services pathologized to gibberish
And the Holy Spirit was withdrawn from the world,
The rains refused and the lands became as hearts,
Parched, dried, sterile and unrequited.

Allah has placed His immediate *Baraka* in water,
Which alone may transmute deserts into gardens,
Water so necessary for every living body,
For animals and birds and trees and herbs,
Required by the simple craftsman and giant factory,
By artisans and technicians and laundry workers —
And the waters shall return, *inshallah*, to their place
And every man come to his rightful state.

> "And We send down water from the sky according to
> Due measure, and We cause it to soak in the soil;
> And We certainly are able to drain it off with ease.

266

With it We grow for you Gardens of date-palms
And vines; and in them have ye abundant fruits; and of them
Ye eat and have enjoyment . . ."*

So shall it be when Allah is the center of men's lives
When prayers are of the body, heart and soul,
When aspirations are of body, heart and soul,
When the life of this world and that have become conjoined.

Beyond this immediacy there is a vaster desert,
A land unclaimed, known as the "Waste Land" †
By those who confuse symbol and reality,
Unmindful of this iceberg consciousness;
When freed from this external hypnotic embrace
The soul, like an aeonic Ulysses, continues on,
And Circe shall throw herself back into the waves.
The Waste Land remains in the minds of rhetoricians,
The despotic empire of the servile men-of-the-Pen
Who look for outward approval as they always have;
Headlines shout: "Galilean, thou hast conquered!"
While uproar smothers the moaning on the cross.
Still deeper is that vaster desert of the heart
Which, however, can be transformed in an instant:

When humankind would realize fraternal communion,
Not just for moments of sanctity in a church,
But with every breath from the atmosphere of air
Which God has created for all of us to breathe,
Permeating it with the vitalities of life.

* Quran XXIII:18-19.
† A protest against and answer to the popular pessimism of important poets
and writers.

The Phoenix has returned again, O Egypt!
From beyond the earliest of human records
To the tomb, to the grave, to be resurrected
Over and over again, to be renewed once more.
O Egypt, land of the Phoenix, the hour approaches
When with the reawakening of the spirit,
The power latent in the heart-center of the world
Returns to the surface to manifest again,
Coalescing the wisdoms of your forebears
With the Finality as revealed by *Mecca-Shereef*.*

There was a famine in the land in the time of Abraham,
There have been innumerable famines in the ages following,
But the night of trial has led to the day of triumph:

    "Arabia shall rejoice and blossom as the rose." †

We may still in these days have recourse to Scripture,
Bearing in mind the actual words of actual Prophets;
Excepting for Guidance the Prophet is as nothing,
And we should be thanking and praising Allah.
Even as the noble Solomon proclaimed a time for all things,
The time for this has come and men shall see it —
In the material world we may perceive the spirituality,
In the flesh of earth the hand of Divinity,
Whether the inspiration was written on ancient palm-leaves,
Or has been secluded in the records of the spheres.

    "For in the wilderness shall waters break out,
    And streams in Arabia,

* Mohammed, the supreme genius of Mecca.
† Isa. 35:1. See Note 9.

268

And the parched ground shall become a pool
And the thirsty land springs of water . . ."*

These have been proclaimed through a sanctified Prophet,
These words are found in Scriptures we consider revealed,
So even now this land of Egypt and the totality of Arabia
Shall, through the ingenuity of man, with the blessings of God,
Alter in appearance to accomodate a multitude,
So the desert shall produce, and want disappear
Except in those places which deny Allah,
Deprive themselves of *baraka* and so decay
Before the living eyes of men who write the histories.

"MAKE STRAIGHT IN ARABIA A HIGHWAY FOR OUR GOD"
Appears in the Sacred Text in several places, 9.
And if we remove the opinions of commentators,
If we dismiss traditions and priests and scribes,
We can see it for ourselves and know it for ourselves.
For the Voice of Allah is steadfast in the sphere,
In the vibrations of the cosmos beyond measurement
And also in the parts which men can survey,
And so it shall be on earth if Allah wills:
MAKE STRAIGHT IN ARABIA A HIGHWAY FOR OUR GOD —
MAKE STRAIGHT IN ARABIA A HIGHWAY FOR OUR GOD
"And the Glory of the Lord shall be revealed,
And *all flesh* shall see it together . . ." †

Flesh has not seen this Glory in togetherness,
Flesh has not yet known togetherness,
Neither appreciated the ubiquity of Allah

* Isa. 35:6-7 A.V.
† Isa. 40:5.

Despite the Scriptures and all our understanding.

Once the *Beni Israel* were the guardians of the Book,
When the meaning of 'holy language' was well known,
When the fearing dared not desecrate the Sacred Name,
Which Name of God is seldom now pronounced,
And in their Book we find the prediction:

> "And it shall come to pass in the last days
> That the temple of the Lord's house shall be established
> In the top of the mountains
> And shall be exalted above the hills;
> And *all nations* shall flow unto it."*

Verbally this has been a cornerstone of religion,
Verbally and no more, an institution of man
To be proclaimed and then ignored,
Down through the ages so to be ignored,
Down through the ages using the Divine Name in vain.
So men have come to worship the outer forms,
Ignoring the inner spirit and revelation,
And the Holy Name of God has been made a secret
And other words substituted by the peoples of the Book,[10.]
With their traditions sarcophagized.

> "Your eyes have seen what the Lord God did because of
>   Baal-Peor;
> For all the men that followed Baal-Peor,
> The Lord thy God hath destroyed them from among you."†

* Isa. 2:2.
† Deut. 4:3.

270

So goes the tradition but not so the events;
In ancient days was Baal-Peor held anathema,*
In more recent times he appeared as a mighty magistrate,
Dividing the Holy Land which did not belong to him,
Dividing the Holy Land as if a personal possession;
With a declaration of self-determination for peoples,
Whatever peoples he chose to apply it to,
And not at all for different sorts of peoples —
Words of honey in the mouth and a hidden cloaked-dagger,
Taking the lands of Palestine and of its neighbors,
Dividing them: *earth is a body, come and eat it*;
So the proclaimed determination was then undermined,
The underprivileged Arabs divided like loot
Although they had not been involved in the wars,
While hypocrites, basing their claims on Scriptures,
Followed the rulings of Baal-Peor without a whimper.

Thus have the people of the synagogue come forth
Accepting the modern Baal-Peor, repudiating Elijah;
Accepting the modern Baal-Peor, rejecting Messiah;
Accepting the modern Baal-Peor, negating their traditions —
This was presumed to be the ending of war:
Instead of the temple, the stock-market and the bank;
Instead of cities of refuge, pots and pans;
No more the possibility of universal pilgrimage,
No more the temple for the totality of humankind,
No more the holy predictions of the Prophets.

"I found Israel like grapes in the wilderness;

* Baal-Peor = Balfour.

I saw your father as the first ripe in the fig-tree at her first time:
But they went to Baal-Peor, and separated themselves unto
    that shame;
And their abominations were according as they loved."*

Thus the contamination of the Scriptures,
Thus the repudiation of the Writings;
And instead of the Universal Mercy of the Deity,
Instead of the Mercy becoming utterly paramount,
Streams of money are poured into ancient lands,
Monies obtained as if there were no God perceiving,
Monies obtained as if there were no God willing,
With factories and machines and mechanical devices,
And nothing for the solace of the soul.
The atheist has his way, the antitheist also
Who may repeat: "Be still and know that I am God"
Without the ability to attain to any stillness,
And even less, knowledge of the Living God.

Silence is beyond the comprehension of such people,
Silence is only another word among a multitude
To be pronounced to prove some syllogism
And not a state to be attained in devotion;
For the scribes can not be silent,
Nor rhetoricians cease from clamour,
Careful in their observations of popularity,
Heedless of the presence of the Living God.

Above all else there is Universal Silence

* Hosea 9:10.

272

From whence all came, whither all return,
Beyond the scope of time and realms of endeavour.

O wonderful *baraka*, product of the Grace of Allah,
Whereby all may know the Compassion of Allah,
Wherein all may experience the Beneficence of Allah,
Wherefrom the strength of every Muslim,
Wherefrom the vigour of the Arab.
Let the talkers talk, let the praters prate,
Let the devil be the father of all lies,
But the silence of the desert remains most potent
To bring to light again the sacred treasures:
Treasures of geological wealth beneath the surface,
Treasures of much archaeological importance,
But above all, those hidden treasures of the heart.

There were places of refuge in ancient times
Called *Thebes* where the persecuted found sanctuary,
Which institution continued for many generations,
From the times of the Prophets through the days of early Christians,
So the ancient Muslims found refuge,
And thus continued their sacred studies.

If Allah wills, Egypt shall again produce these treasures;

If Allah wills, the deeper teachings of Islam shall be known,
And there shall be victory in the greater jihad.
There may be a victory in the greater jihad,
In the endless struggle against man's weaknesses,
Against sloth, against anger, against prejudice,
Against human appetites, self-will and greed;
The world may see the restoration of that Islam
As it was in the days of the early righteous Khalifs,
As it was in the days of the renowned Saladin —
God-bribery should go and the true *Salaat** proclaimed,
Not only for and by Muslims but for the universe.

This is a day when rigorous measures are taken
To explore the worlds of electron and gene and cell,
Where seriousness is maintained in every effort
In the laboratory, the clinic and the field;
This is a day when human faculties are developed
In the shop, the foundry and the factory —
Why, then, should man not equally seek
To uncover the secrets of the soul
With the same zeal and concentration
As is done in these outer modes of life?
What is this worship of Allah so obviously secondary
To the endless strivings to accumulate wealth and power?
What is this worship of Allah so obviously secondary
To the various philosophies of the day?

The angel of the Lord hovered over the Suez Canal
While hordes of ravaging invaders came to murder and to plunder,
And the angel of the Lord became enangered,

* I.e., prayer.

274

Wishing to smite these people with a curse;
But lifting up his eyes he beheld the Southland
Where millions of dark-skinned people are held in bondage
By those of lighter hue who have the power,
Who meet in their assemblies to pass laws,
And while they verbally abolish human slavery,
Accepting the format of the Four Freedoms,
Bring only instead the four damnations of the heavens
Where the white-skinned can live only in shame,
Where the powerful must accept their ignominy
Because all people are treated there as if Allah's family.

"Comfort ye, *all* my people" came from the angel's mouth,
Who in his anger forgot the Mercy of Allah,
Who in his indignation was distraught.
In previous ages men maimed and slaughtered,
Were wont to massacre and bring thoughtless destruction;
But those who uttered proclamations against ethnocide
To rise in indignation against mass-murder of the Jews,
Turned their faces from the slaughter of the Libyans
And refused to face the facts of social slavery.
The Four Freedoms and the Atomic Bomb must be faced together,
The abolition of slavery and second class citizenry faced together,
The exploitation of anybody by anybody else together.

But beyond the angel was the Compassion of Allah,
Beyond the angel the Beneficence of Allah
Offered to the world, to Muslim, Believer and *Kafir*,
To peoples of all beliefs and no belief,
To everybody: high, low, black, white, red,
In which the new Arabia may lead despite the world;
In which the new Arabia may lead despite all arguments;

In which the new Arabia may lead to the confusion of the scribes,
That the glory of the Lord may return to earth and all men pray:

"PRAISE BE TO ALLAH,
THE CHERISHER AND SUSTAINER OF THE WORLDS:
MOST GRACIOUS, MOST MERCIFUL,
MASTER OF THE DAY OF JUDGMENT.
THEE DO WE WORSHIP,
AND THINE AID WE SEEK.
SHOW US THE RIGHT WAY,
THE WAY OF THOSE ON WHOM
THOU HAST BESTOWEST THY GRACE,
THOSE WHOSE PORTION IS NOT WRATH
AND WHO GO NOT ASTRAY."*

                              AMIN.

Samuel L. Lewis
Sufi Ahmed Murad Chisti
ca. 1960

Love and Blessings,

Samuel L. Lewis

Samuel L. Lewis / Sufi Ahmed Murad Chisti

Sufi Ahmed Murad Chisti

* Quran I:1.

276

Notes

1. In the Quran (S.IV:157-159), there occur the following lines: "That they said (in boast), / 'We killed Christ Jesus / The son of Mary, — The Apostle of Allah':— / But they killed him not, / Nor crucified him, / But so it was made / To appear to them, / And those who differ / Therein are full of doubts, / With no (certain) knowledge, / But only conjecture to follow, / For of a surety / They killed him not; / Nay, Allah raised him up / Unto Himself; and Allah / Is Exalted in Power, Wise; / And there is none / Of the People of the Book / But must believe in him / Before his death; / And on the Day of Judgment / He will be a witness / Against them . . . "

To help give a historical perspective to this question we shall quote extensively from the footnotes to these Quranic passages by Abdullah Yusuf Ali: "The end of the life of Jesus on earth is as much involved in mystery as his birth, and indeed the greater part of his private life, except the three main years of his ministry. It is not profitable to discuss the many doubts and conjectures among the early Christian sects and among Muslim theologians. The Orthodox Christian Churches make it a cardinal point of their doctrine that his life was taken on the Cross, that he died and was buried, that on the third day he rose in the body with his wound intact and walked about and conversed, and ate with his disciples, and was afterwards taken up bodily to heaven. . . . But some of the early Christian sects did not believe that Christ was killed on the Cross. The Basilidans believed that someone else was substituted for him. The Docetae held that Christ never had a real physical or natural body but only an apparent or phantom body, and that his Crucifixion was only apparent, not real. The Marcionite Gospel (about A.D.138) denied that Jesus was born, and merely said that he appeared in human form. The Gospel of St. Barnabas supported the theory of substitution on the Cross. The Quranic teaching is that Christ was not crucified nor killed by the Jews, notwithstanding certain apparent circumstances which produced that illusion in the minds of some of his enemies; that disputation, doubts and conjectures on such matters are vain; and that he was taken up to God.

277

There is a difference of opinion as to the exact interpretation of this verse. The words are: The Jews did not kill Jesus, but God raised him up (*rafa'a*) to Himself. One school holds that Jesus did not die the usual human death, but still lives in the body in heaven; another holds that he did die but not when he was supposed to be crucified, and that his being 'raised up' unto God means that instead of being disgraced as a malefactor, as the Jews of the time intended, he was on the contrary honoured by God as His Apostle. . . ." Holy Quran, Abdullah Yusuf Ali, trans., (Pakistan: Sh. Muhammad Ashraf, 1969)]

2. In the Middle Ages in Europe salt was levied as a tax by the nobles on all who were their vassals.

3. From the archaeological excavations and surveys in Edom it appears that its material culture was developed. The only evidence with regard to its spiritual culture is biblical. The wisdom of Edom was held in esteem by the Prophets. Jeremiah asked in amazement: "Is wisdom no more in Teman? [a principle city of Edom] has counsel perished from the prudent? has their wisdom vanished?" (Jer.49:7)

4. Many of the Prophets of the *Beni Israel* had to flee to Arabia from Palestine. Among this group is the Prophet Elijah, who was welcomed and fed by the *Arabim*, the Arabs. The Scribes later altered this word to read *Erebim*, the ravens. From the *Jewish Encyclopedia* (New York: KTAV Publishing House, Inc.): "In the Elijah story (1 Kings 17:2-7), ravens (" 'orebim") bring food to the Prophet. The talmud (Hul.5a) reports an interesting discussion, wherein it is suggested that " 'orebim" might be the name of men (Judg.7:25) or perhaps men of a certain locality, this of course implying the reading "Arabians." And despite the fact that all the ancient versions read "ravens," the reading "Arabians" or "Bedouins" is still a possibility. The hiding-place of Elijah lay directly in the path of the bands who, in the period of drought, would have reason to be near a brook."

5. The *Sepher Yetsirah* is attributed to the Patriarch Abraham. The first poem of this trilogy, "The Day of the Lord Cometh," is based in part on the *Sepher Yetsirah*.

6. The Hebrew word for 'place' is *makam*, which is the same in Arabic. This refers to the different stations or grades of evolution in the spiritual life which one may function from. See note 7.

7. The Hebrew word *ohalim*, which is translated as 'tents', could be better translated as 'tabernacles'. This would mean that Jacob was a man who embodied the Law. However the Arabic word *'hal*, which comes from the same root, gives us even more insight into the meaning

of the passage in question. To the Sufi, *'hal* are those divine experiences, or states, which are given to one who is effaced in the Presence of God. *'Hal* and *makam* are the central terms in most philosophical explanations of Sufism.

8. Saladin specifically mentions four of the Five Pillars of Islam in this section: prayer, fasting, giving of alms and pilgrimage. Not defined is the first Pillar which consists in the affirmation of the Unity of God and the acknowledgement that Mohammed is His Prophet.

9. The author translates the Hebrew *Arabah* as Arabia in this passage from Isa.35:1. The English word 'Arabia' is related to the Hebrew *Arabah* in that both can be taken to mean "the land or ground of the Arabs." In the time of Isaiah the Jews were exile in Babylonia, which was also known as part of the *Arabah*. The Prophet Isaiah foresaw their return to Jerusalem and called on them to "make straight a path" to return to God, in both an outer and inner sense. In the context of "Saladin," the poet foresees new ways of pilgrimage being established, especially between the holy cities of Mecca and Jerusalem. See "Arabia" in Glossary.

10. The most sacred name of God in the Hebrew teachings is composed of the four letters *YHVH*. This is sometimes pronounced, Yahuvah. In this history of Jusaism it was originally invoked, then it was invoked only by the priest in the sanctuary of the Holy of Holies on *Yom Kippur*, and finally it was entirely omitted, and *Adonoi* — which is an attribute of God not His essence — was substituted.

Glossary

Abbas — Paternal uncle of Mohammed and a rich merchant of Mecca. Called by Mohammed "the last of the Emigrants," he was the last of many early converts to Islam who, because of the hostility of the Meccans to Mohammed and his message, were forced to give up their homes and possessions and seek refuge with Mohammed in nearby Medina. His descendants founded the Abbasid Caliphate.

Abraham — (Hebrew) 'Master' or 'Father of a multitude', i.e., 'of nations', 'of sounds', 'of heart qualities' (*raham*). When Abraham was 75, God commanded him to leave his home in Ur ('Light') and settle in the land of Canaan: "And I will make of thee a great nation, and I will bless thee, and make thy name great, and be thou a blessing . . . and in thee shall all the families of the earth be blessed." (Gen.12:2-3 M.T.) According to ancient tradition, the Jews, as well as the family of Jesus Christ, are traced back to Isaac, Abraham's second son; and Mohammed descended from Ishmael, Abraham's first-born son. In the Quran, Islam is described as a return to the religion of Abraham: "Abraham was not a Jew nor yet a Christian, but he was true in Faith, and bowed his will to Allah's (which is Islam), and he joined not gods with Allah." (S.III:67)

Adam — (Hebrew) 'he-of-blood' or 'he-of-Heart Essence'. According to Quran, Adam was the first man, the first Prophet and, as such, the prototype of humanity. God created him to be his "vicegerent on earth" and taught him the "names of all things," by virtue of which he was given power and dominion over them. (S.II:30-31)

"*Dam* in Hebrew means more than 'blood'. It is the homogeneous substance common to all people. In man, in the phsycial body it appears as blood; in the Universe it is a Cosmic Sympathetic

281

Fluid which connects all heart. . . . The Quran teaches that God 'created man from clots of blood'. The idea of clots of blood is that is was through the hardening of the heart-substance of God; that is to say, Allah created man from His own Heart Essence. So the word *Adam* means 'he-of-blood', and therefore in the image of the Creator. . . . In this respect *Eve* [Hebrew for 'universal life'] is the same as Adam. Adam is Universal Humanity, considered as life and form, while Eve is the universal life which sustains such humanity, the love-stream of being which connects all people indiscriminately into one brotherhood." (S.L.L.)

adepts — (from the Latin *adeptus*, 'attained', this term was originally used for one who, through the science of alchemy, had attained the secret of transforming base metals into gold). "According to Sufism everything in the heavens and earth belongs to man. Man achieves his Godhead when he realizes his allness. If he looks at the tree, if he sees the tree, if he can paint the tree correctly, he is an artist. But if he can become the tree, he is a yogi or adept. Then it is no longer symbology, it is self-fulfillment." (S.L.L.)

agape, philos, eros — (Greek) 'love'. "While we have the one word 'Love' in the English language, the Greek language has many terms to refer to various kinds of 'love': *agape* generally represents the culmination of love, which is God loving Himself, within Himself; a spiritual love which is all-inclusive. *Philos* indicates a more intellectual kind of attraction motivated by high ideals. *Eros* is used to indicate the primal sex drive." (S.L.L.)

Ajami — (Arabic) 'non-Arab'. Originally a term distinguishing Arab and non-Arab, it came to designate Persians in general.

akhlak Allah — (Arabic) 'in the manner of God'. Feeling and acting as if in the presence of God. This is a common practice among Sufis: "it comes when the heart is focused on God, and then all that is in God becomes manifest in man." (S.L.L.)

al-hamdu Lillah — (Arabic) 'Praise be to God'. "The *hallelujah* of the Hebrews and the *al-hamdu Lillah* of the Arabians are marvels. First . . . they declare the praise and honor to God. But they have an inner significance for they also mean, 'Be Thou exalted, O Lord.' . . . Shouting these words as did the ancients brings a sense of joy and exultation, difficult to describe, but capable of being experienced by repeating the act." (S.L.L.)

Allah — (Arabic) 'God'. "The All in All. . . . God with all qualities and attributes and all life, nothing excluded therefrom. . . . A great mistake has been made in assuming that this Word or Name was especially used by the Arabs. It was practically the name of God, with slightly different pronunciations, used by the ancient Hebrews and Syrians as well" (S.L.L.) [*Elah* from which also the Hebrew *Elohim* was formed. — ED.] The Quran teaches that Allah is Mercy and Compassion, "the Cherisher and Sustainer of the Worlds," "never born and never giving birth," "the Light of the Heavens and the Earth," the One and Only Being, all abiding in Him and He living in all.

Allah mansur — (Arabic) 'God is Victor'.

Allaho Akbar — (Arabic) "The greatest teaching I have ever learned was that *Allaho Akbar* means 'peace is power', not 'God is great' (great in relation to what?), but PEACE IS POWER. Not force, but peace. Not 'peace with justice'. Not peace *with*, but Peace. . . . Peace is the removal of all things that disturb at all. You see the whole One-ness, you don't have any ill-feeling about another because you see essentially the other as also from God." (S.L.L.) There is no power nor might save in Allah.

Allahu — (Arabic) 'Allah, he'. A phrase used by Dervishes and other Sufis as an invocation of Allah, the One and Only Being, who has many attributes yet is beyond any attributes.

Amin — (Arabic) 'verily', 'truly'. Amen.

amir — (Arabic) 'commander'. A title first used by the second Khalif, Omar who, as the titular head of the Muslim community, became known as 'Commander of the Faithful'. Thereafter the title became increasingly popular and came to designate a subordinate ruler, an administrator of the Khalif.

Amru ibn Aas — An Arabian general. At first opposed to the mission of Mohammed, he later became one of his disciples. Under the second Khalif, Omar, he conquered and later governed Egypt. In a struggle over the succession to the Khalifate which later developed, he took part in a conspiracy which led to the assassination of Ali, the last of the Righteous Khalifs.

angels — (from the Greek *angelos*, 'messenger') "Angels sometimes function specifically as messengers of God, bearing messages which cannot be conveyed to mind without taking on name and form." (S.L.L.) They can be conceived as beings of light; vibrations of the rays of that Eternal Sun; the essence of glorification, devotion and all attributes. The Sufi Ibn'ul Arabi describes them thus: "As for the angels, they represent certain faculties in this 'form' of the world which the Sufis call the Great Man so that the angels are to it just as the spiritual and physical faculties are to the human organism."

Arab — (probably connected with the Semitic root *habar*, 'that which is placed beyond' or 'occidental', 'that which moves or passes'. "The names which we give to the Hebrews and to the Arabs, however much dissimilar they may appear, owing to our manner of writing them, are in substance only the same epithet modified by two different dialects. . . . The Hebrews, whose dialect is evidently anterior to that of the Arabs, have derived from it *hebri* [a 'Hebrew'] and the Arabs *harbi* [an 'Arab'], by a transposition of letters which is a characteristic of their language." Fabre D'Olivet, *The Hebraic Tongue Restored*) Originally the term 'Arab' referred to a nomadic people who populated the desert land to the east and south of Palestine known as the *Arabah* ('desert steppe' or 'wilderness'). Muslim tradition designates Ishmael, the eldest son of Abraham, as the fountainhead of the Arab nation. In his posterity came the Prophet Mohammed.

Arabia — (probably derived from the Hebrew *Arabah*, the feminine form of *Arab* and, as such, the 'ground of the Arab') The English word 'desert' is used to translate four different Hebrew words used in the Old Testament: *Arabah*, *Midbar*, *Charbah* and *Yeshimon*. The *Arabah* was the name given by the ancient Hebrews to the wilderness extending from the Dead Sea southward to Elath (the Gulf of Aqaba), which gradually extended to include the entire geographical area in which the Arab roamed. Thus the author's translation of *Arabah* as 'Arabia' is a more literal rendition of the scriptural text whereby the prophetic implications are brought to light: "Make straight in Arabia a highway for our God" may also be understood in the context of clearing the way for pilgrimage between Mecca and Jerusalem.

"At times Murshid takes the liberty of the Midrashic teacher, clothing his insights in terms of puns derived from the Hebrew. This midrashic method was employed even in the Bible. The method of midrash to give mystical and prophetic meaning to scriptural verses is also to be found as a tool used by Kabbalists and Hasidic masters. The feminine ending, which in Hebrew is "h" is often utilized to indicate not only the change of gender but also the change of direction. So while the word *or* of Kabbalic usage represents divine light descending from above, the rabbinic Hebrew form of *orah* represents the reflected light from below. This model is utilized in many other ways indicating with the feminine ending the earth reflecting to above. We take it that Murshid saw Arab and Arabah in the same way." (Rabbi Zalman Schachter)

Ararat — (Hebrew) 'light upon light'. The mountain upon which Noah's ark came to rest after the Flood.

archangel — (from the Greek *arch*, 'chief' or 'primordial' and *angelos*, 'messenger') "A personified attribute of God. In the hierarchy of angels, one of the rank who serve God in special missions, although these are not strictly personifications so much as being emanations of God." (S.L.L.)

archetype — (Greek) 'first-moulded'. The prototype or essential "idea" of a thing or being; the original model.

Arsh-Throne — (*Arsh* is Arabic for 'Throne' or 'Firmament') The Throne of God, which Sufis identify with the heart of man. "It can be said that the innermost center of the heart is God. God is love and it is this love which connects all human hearts and all hearts." (S.L.L.)

Aryans — (from the Sanskrit *arya*, 'noble', 'lord', 'ruler') Ancestors of the Hindus. A Caucasian people, a branch of the Indo-European family, who invaded and settled in northern India during the second century B.C. Their Scriptures, the *Vedas*, came to constitute the sacred Scriptures of Hinduism.

Asar — The ancient Egyptian name for Osiris. [See EHYEH ASHER EHYEH]

Asher — The chief god of the Assyrians. [See EHYEH ASHER EHYEH]

as-salaam aleikhum — (Arabic) 'Peace be with you'. The corresponding phrase in Hebrew is *Shalom aleichem*.

attributes — Archetypal qualities of God. In the teaching of Mohammed, "all the attributes which had led to polytheism and later to the reverence of saints, were ascribed to Allah, the One God, and known as *Sifat*. God was called first the Beneficent and Merciful (*Er-Rahman Er-Rahim*), and then He was given 99 names which covered His principal attributes, and many of these names are easily recognizable in Quran. By this means Mohammed taught that all virtue, all love, all goodness, all life came from the One God Who could not be limited even by the Attributes which, while they were His, were transcended also by Him." (S.L.L.)

aureoles — Actual halos of radiating light emanating from a body, especially visible in beings who through their devotion and surrender to the ideal, have become transparent to the point of allowing the Universal Light to shine through them.

auroras — High-altitude, many-colored, flashing luminosities.

Avatars — (from the Sanskrit *avatarah*, 'a descent') Perfected beings, individual incarnations or humanizations of the Spirit of the Universe." (S.L.L.) [See also RASSUL]

Baal-Peor — (Hebrew) 'Owner' or 'Landlord of Peor'. A local fertility god of the Canaanites. When the Hebrew people settled in the Promised Land, they adopted this form of worship which was connected with orgiastic rites. Each district worshipped its particular *baal* as the owner which owns the land and brings about the fruitfulness of the soil. Baal-worship among the Israelites gradually supplanted their worship of the One God, and God Himself was reduced to the status of a *baal*. Used as a pun by the author, the "modern Baal-Peor" refers to the late English statesman, Lord Balfour whose attitude toward the land of Palestine is described in the poem.

baraka — (Arabic) 'blessings'. That positive, life-giving magnetism which comes from God and can flow through man when he is immersed in Perfection. Its experience "actually involves love, joy, cosmic magnetism and living light." (S.L.L.) This magnetism can also be felt in the atmosphere of certain physical objects as, for example, healing springs of water.

barzakh — (Arabic) 'partition', 'bar' or 'barrier'. The threshold between human (limited) and Divine (unlimited) knowledge.

Beautiful Names — Essential qualities or attributes of God. "Repeating the attributes of God in *Wazifas* and other sacred phrases, man draws from the infinite Godhead all that is required for his fulfillment and perfection. ... As we cannot know God in his fullness we can nonetheless attune to and assimilate his various attributes." (S.L.L.) [See also ATTRIBUTES]

Beneficent — All-Merciful. One of the principal attributes of God in Islam.

Beni Israel — (Arabic) 'children of Israel'. This term is usually used to designate the Hebrew people, i.e., the descendants of Jacob-Israel. [See also JACOB]

Bharatas — The people of India, descendants of Bharata, one of their great patriarchs whose story is told in the *Mahabharata*.

bhikku — A Buddhist monk.

bindu — (Sanskrit) 'point'. "In breathing man inhales into the *bindu* or 'point' and exhales into the expansive sea or *sindu*. This is known as *bindu-sindu* in the Hindu teachings, and the dot-circle elsewhere. . . . The dot thus posits the ego, and the circle posits the assimilation of the ego in the All." (S.L.L.)

Bodhisattva — (Sanskrit) 'Wisdom being'. "The Bodhisattva, he who is led by the Spirit of Guidance, does not think of his own salvation; he thinks of salvation in a universal sense, thus practicing unification." (S.L.L.) The Bodhisattvic vow: "However innumerable sentient beings are, I vow to save them. However infinite the dharma-gateways, I vow to enter them. However inexhaustible the deluding passions, I vow to extinguish them. The Buddha way is supreme, I vow to attain it."

Book — The recorded Word of God as revealed to man through any of His Prophets. [See also PEOPLE OF THE BOOK]

brahman — A member of the highest caste in India. This was the priestly caste who were students of the Vedas and conductors of the Vedic rituals. In its original sense it means "one who knows the supreme reality, or Brahman." As it became purely heredity it developed into a crystallized privileged class. In the *Dhammapada* by Lord Buddha one finds the original idealism behind the name 'brahman' restored.

Buddha — (Sanskrit) 'Enlightened one.' A title given at first to Siddhartha Gautama upon his attainment of perfect enlightenment, as "the one from whose heart the essence of reason, *Buddh*, has risen as a spring. By this knowledge Buddha recognized the possibility for every soul, whatever be its grade of evolution, of attaining that bliss, having discovered that the innermost being of every soul is divine." (Hazrat Inayat Khan)

Buddha Maitreya — (Sanskrit) 'Benevolent Buddha'. The coming Buddha who, according to Buddhist Scripture, will appear not just to a few people, nor to a certain ethnic or geographical group, but to everyone whose heart is full of love.

Caesars — Emperors of the Holy Roman Empire who, through tyranny and oppression, attempted to extend the sway of their influence even unto absolute sovereignty on earth.

Cain, mark of — (*Cain* in Hebrew means 'acquisition', 'centering', and indicates all tendencies to create a self-center and draw things to it) The mark of Cain, then, symbolizes man's ego, "the self-centering, centripetal activity of consciousness in whatever form." (S.L.L.)

Canaan — (from the Hebrew roots *chan* or *kan*, 'centering force' and *an*, 'void' or 'darkness') Usually translated as 'lowland', Canaan was the ancient region to which God directed Abraham, the land which his descendants were to inherit. It extended from the Jordan River and the Dead Sea west to the Mediterranean.

Chain — Symbol of the way in which all the illuminated souls, the great masters of humanity are connected, as links in a chain: "One spirit and many individualities; one soul and many personalities; one wisdom and many teachers who have expounded wisdom according to their own personality." (Hazrat Inayat Khan)

Christ — (the Greek translation of the Hebrew *mashiach*, 'messiah', 'annointed one', which referred to any redeemer of Israel, the deliverer of the Holy Land) In the poem, Christ is used in the popular sense as a title of Jesus, who is referred to in the Quran as *Ruh-Allah*, the 'spirit of God'.

Circe — An island enchantress in Homer's *Odyssey* who detains Odysseus on his journey home by turning his men into swine. By the aid of a magic herb given to him by the god Hermes, he resists her spells and forces her to restore his men.

cities of refuge — Six cities assigned by Moses to the Levites, or priests, in which they had full jurisdiction. They served as refuge to the manslayer, offering him asylum and fair trial, and thus represented an attempt to restrain the tribal law of blood revenge. More generally, the cities of refuge represent an asylum for the hunted and oppressed, a place where shelter is given and violence prohibited. In such a city the religious law is the operative law.

Companions — The early disciples of the Prophet Mohammed, those who knew or served with him.

condensers — In Physics, instruments used to restore vapor to its original liquid form. In a wider sense, a condenser refers to any instrument (or being) through which subtle vibrations can be made more tangible to humanity.

contemplation — [See MUSHAHIDA]

Cosmic Dove — The Holy Spirit or Divine Breath as the vehicle by which man ascends to Heaven. "Identifying oneself with breath is a form of self-effacement which takes one from mortality to immortality." (S.L.L.) The Divine Breath is experienced when man keeps his heart, mind and breath attuned to God. The Cosmic Dove and Buraq, the "horse" which Mohammed rode to Heaven are the same.

Crusaders — Members of the military expeditions undertaken by western Christian powers, in the 11th, 12th and 13th centuries to recover the Holy Land from the Muslims.

Dar-as-Salaam — (Arabic) 'Abode of Peace'. The heavenly Jerusalem, the inner Temple of Peace.

David — The Prophet-king of Israel under whose righteous rule the nation was unified with Jerusalem as its capital. His story is related in Samuel I and II which describe how, when he brought the Ark of the Covenant to Jerusalem, he sang and "danced before the Lord with all his might." He was the author of many of the songs of praise found in the Book of Psalms.

dervishes — (Persian) 'ones who come to the door', i.e., to beg. Outwardly beggars, inwardly kings. Those who follow the instructions of Jesus to his disciples: "And preach as you go, saying, 'The Kingdom of Heaven is at hand'. . . . You received without pay, give without pay. Take no gold, nor silver, nor copper in your belts, no bag for your journey, nor two tunics, nor sandals, nor a staff; for the labourer deserves his food . . . " and so on. (Matt.10:7 R.S.V.) The Mevlevi Order of dervishes in Turkey use the dance as a technique toward God-realization, a practice which Ataturk attempted to outlaw in this century.

dharma — (Sanskrit) 'duty', 'truth'. "The actual teachings found in the Scriptures, and also perhaps beyond the scriptures. . . . it involves, in a sense, all that man has to do, especially in his relations to God . . . and to his fellow man." (S.L.L.) Buddha taught that by doing one's own duty (dharma), by acting according to one's own nature, talents and abilities, man may reach perfection. Dharma refers to that truth which is the essence of reality as well as the path for its realization.

Dhimmi — (Arabic) 'protected one', 'one with whom a compact has been made'. Citizens of countries which were conquered by the Muslims who did not choose to embrace Islam. In return for the payment of a poll-tax, they were guaranteed the free exercise of their religion and normal property rights.

din — (Arabic) 'faith' or 'religion'. Duty as one's religion. The meaning of this word is akin to the Sanskrit dharma.

ebullition — A state of exhilaration.

effluvium — A subtle outflow of magnetism, manifesting as light or scent.

ego-mind — "The consciousness of being separate from others." (S.L.L.) Man's selfish perspective. Limited mind produces limited thought.

ehyeh asher ehyeh — (Hebrew) 'what will be will bring about what will be'. "When God spoke to Moses He said: *EHYEH ASHER EHYEH*. This connotes an eternally continuing existence and can be translated 'Will be that Will be', or 'I was, am, will be', or even as a variation of the Egyptian: 'I am Osiris, who ever was, is and will be'. Osiris, *Asar* in ancient Egyptian, could easily be assimilated to the Hebrew *Asher*." "It can mean roughly, 'I am the God or Infinite that produces what is the Infinite. And you can't explain it, but you can *realize* it." (S.L.L.)

Elijah — (Hebrew) 'my God is Yahuvah (YHVH)'. The Hebrew Prophet who was instrumental in finally purging Baal-worship from among the people of Israel. He is identified by Muslims with John the Baptist and Khidr who, having drunk of the Fountain of Life, lives on eternally to turn men's hearts to God.

elixir — In Alchemy, the name given to that substance which would transmute base metals into gold and prolong life indefinitely. In a broader sense, that which transforms 'limited man' to 'universal man'.

Elysian Fields, Elysium — In Greek mythology, the abode of happiness to which the souls of the just go after death.

Empyrean — In ancient Greek philosophy, the highest reaches of the heavens which consisted of pure light; the home of the blessed.

entropy — The tendency of the universe toward homogeneity, uniformity or lack of distinction or differentiation, exemplified in the thermodynamic law which states that heat can pass naturally only from a warmer body to a colder body.

eros — [See AGAPE]

Esau — The eldest son of Isaac, twin-brother of Jacob. The struggle between the two brothers in their mother's womb (Gen.25-22) foreshadowed subsequent relations between them as well as between their descendants, the Edomites and the Israelites although in the Bible Esau and Israel ultimately became reconciled. The Edomites, because of a mutual enmity with the people of Israel, joined the Romans in the seige of Jerusalem in A.D. 70. Edom thus became synonomous with Christian Romans and, later, with Christianity in general.

Esther, Queen — (Esther is the Persian word for 'star') A Jewess whom the king of the Persian Empire chose as his queen. She delivered the Jews of her empire from their destruction planned by the Prime Minister, Haman. The story is told in the Old Testament Book of Esther.

ether — The realm of pure Spirit; 'living no-thingness.'

Ezra — The Jewish scribe who led the first caravan of Israelites back to Jerusalem from their exile in Babylonia. He is credited with settling the canon of Jewish Scripture and restoring, correcting and editing the whole sacred volume known to us today as the Old Testament. An integral part of his program for the revival of Judaism was the prohibition of all marriages between Jew and non-Jew and the enforced separation of all such marriages which had already been consummated.

fakir — (Arabic) 'poor'. "The fakir has nothing whatsoever to do with phenomena; it means 'one who is poor', not only in the wealth of things, but even more in the false wealth of the ego." (S.L.L.)

fana-fi-Sheikh — (Arabic) 'Effacement in the spirit of the Sheikh (teacher)'. "*Fana* might well be the Arabic correlative of the Biblical *panah*, which means 'turn the face to', 'respect'. Practically it means 'effacement in', for one dies to oneself to live in turn in the teacher (*Sheikh*), human ideal (*Rassul*) and divinity (Allah)." (S.L.L.)

Feringhis — (Arabic) 'Franks'. More generally, western Christians.

Five Pillars — The five principal religious duties of a Muslim: 2) Repeating the *Shahada*, or Profession of Faith — "There is no god but God, and Mohammed is His Messenger." 2) *Salaat*, or 'Prayer', i.e., the ritual prayer of Islam which is said five times daily 3) *Zakat*, or 'Charity' which has become fixed according to Muslim law as a regular religious tax 4) *Roza*, or 'Fasting', especially the daylight hours of the month of *Ramadan* 5) Pilgrimage, i.e., joining the annual pilgrimage to Mecca at least once in one's lifetime (provided one is physically and financially able). According to tradition, Mohammed called these duties the foundations upon which Islam is built.

Four Freedoms — Considered as basic human freedoms by Franklin D. Roosevelt: freedom of speech, freedom of religion, freedom from want and freedom from fear.

Frankistan — Western Europe. The men of Frankistan composed the main body of Crusaders.

Friend of Allah — The Prophet Abraham, known to Muslims as "the friend of God" (*Khalil-ullah*), "for God did take Abraham for a friend." (Quran IV:125) This epithet echoes the passage in Isaiah (41:8) wherein God refers to Abraham as "My friend."

Gan Eden — (Hebrew) 'Abode of Bliss', usually incompletely translated as the 'Garden of Eden'. "The Garden of Eden represents the picture of *Jabrut* or the spiritual world. There is Paradise Lost and there is Paradise Regained." (S.L.L.)

Ghebers — (Persian) 'Unbelievers'. A term applied by Muslims to the Zoroastrians of Persia who remained there after the Muslim conquest and refused to convert to Islam.

Gitas — (Sanskrit) 'songs'. Hindu Scriptures. The most renowned Gita is attributed to Krishna and is the *Bhagavad Gita* ('Song of God'). The Gita of Supremacy refers to the sublime essence of all the Gitas.

goyim — (Hebrew) 'peoples'. A term used originally by the Jews to refer to any pagan people.

Grace — A loving impulse of God which manifests in every form: in the form of mercy, compassion, forgiveness, beneficence, revelation. It comes naturally, as a wave rising from the heart of God, unrestricted and unlimited by any law. "Divine Grace is such that it wishes the self-fulfillment in man." (S.L.L.)

292

Habbakuk — A Prophet of Israel whose personal history is undocumented. However, his name is considered to be of Arabic origin.

Hadith — (Arabic) 'Tradition'. A compilation of the acts and sayings of the Prophet Mohammed, assembled after his death. It is the second major source of guidance in Islam, after the Quran. As it emanated directly or indirectly from the private life of the Prophet, it established the rules of everyday life for the Muslim people.

Hajj — (Arabic) 'Pilgrimage'. [See FIVE PILLARS]

harb — (Arabic) 'war'. Its literal meaning is the opposite of Islam ('peace').

Harun al-Rashid — Khalif of Baghdad whose court overflowed with poets, musicians, artists and intellectuals. Under his rule Baghdad became the luxurious seat of a vast Islamic empire. Harun is celebrated in *The Thousand and One Nights* as the ruler who wanders incognito at night in the streets of Baghdad with his vizier.

Hashimite — Mohammed, a member of the house of Hashim which was a clan of the Kureish tribe of Arabs.

Hedjaz — (Arabic) 'Barrier'. A territory in Arabia, so called because it is a vast mountainous tract which separates the entire length of the coastal plain along the Red Sea from the inland desert plateau. It contains the two holy cities of Islam, Mecca and Medina. There were numerous Jewish colonies in this territory who had maintained friendly relations with the Arabs. However, when they opposed Mohammed and his followers and joined in armed conflict against them, breaking their mutual treaty, they were crushed and exiled.

Hellas — Greece.

Hesperides, garden of — In Greek mythology, a garden Paradise where golden apples grow.

Holy Land — Traditionally, the terrain of Palestine chronicled in the Old Testament. The tradition of mystical Judaism is that the holiness of God is to be found in the physical land, e.g., the city of Jerusalem. Actually, the Holy Land is wherever people live in the Presence of God and fulfill the Divine Covenant.

Holy Spirit — The *Spiritus Sanctus* of the Christians, the *Ruach Hakodesh* of the Jews, the *Ruh-al-Quddus* of the Muslims. The Spirit of Guidance, personified as Gabriel. "The Spirit of

Guidance may be called the heart of God, a heart which is the accumulator of all feelings, impressions, thoughts, memories, and of all knowledge and experience. . . . The heart of God is the intelligence and the current of guidance in the heart of every man. . . . In the Spirit of Guidance one finds a living God active in the heart of every person." (Hazrat Inayat Khan) The Divine Breath.

houris — The beautiful dark-eyed virgins of Paradise promised as companions to the righteous; in the Quran they are described as embodiments of heavenly light.

hyperspace — The space of possibility.

Iblis — (Arabic) 'The Rebellious'. In the Quran, the angel who refused God's command to bow down in obeisance to man as God's vicegerent on earth. "He was haughty, and became one of those who reject Faith." (S.XXXVIII:74) He represents the contractive force of the ego which gives rise to arrogance and jealousy and all ideas of separation.

ilm — (Arabic) 'knowledge'. The Supreme Wisdom, the knowledge of universal unity which comes to the awakened soul.

imam — (Arabic) 'leader'. In general usage, a layman who leads the Ritual Prayer in the mosque.

Injil — (Arabic) 'Gospel', or 'Good Tiding'. The teachings of Jesus Christ.

inner eye — The faculty of vision without external mediation; spiritual insight.

inquisition — An ecclesiastic court established for the trial and punishment of heretics.

Isaac — (Hebrew) 'Laughter of God'. The son whom Sarah, in accord with the Divine promise, bore to Abraham in his hundreth year; the brother of Ishmael. He is the second Patriarch of the Hebrew people and is referred to as a Prophet of God in the Quran (S.XXXVII:112)

ishk — (Arabic) 'love'. "Love is the source of our creation and the real sustenance of all beings. . . . the essence of our existence; God Himself, as Creator, as Actor, as Doer. . . . *Ishk* is light and love and life and all qualities . . . the source of intelligence. . . . The real life, it might be said, is this life of heart . . . this is *ishk*, and the whole welfare of the world depends upon it." (S.L.L.) "It can't be taught, but it can be caught!" (Rev. Joe Miller)

Ishmael — (Hebrew) 'God hears'. The first-born son of Abraham, born to Hagar, his Egyptian concubine; the brother of Isaac. According to the Old Testament, Sarah saw Ishmael teasing Isaac and urged Abraham to cast them out. Comforted by God's renewed promise, that he would make of Ishmael "a great nation," Abraham led them to the wilderness. There their lives were saved by the discovery of a well to which God "opened Hagar's eyes" when he heard Ishmael crying. (Gen.21:19) The sons of Ishmael, who settled in the north and west of the Arabian peninsula, formed the chief element of the Arab nation; and in posterity Mohammed was born. According to Quran, Ishmael was a "man of constancy and patience," a Prophet of God; he and his father Abraham were chosen to sanctify the Kaaba, the House of God in Mecca.

Ishvara — (Sanskrit) 'Lord'. In Hinduism, God as omnipotent, omniscient Creator; as distinct from Brahman, the eternal impassive ground of all action and change. Also a title given to Lord Shiva as a personfied aspect of the Divine.

Islam — (Arabic) 'Submission', i.e., to the will of God; 'peace'. The teaching of Quran is that Islam was the religion of mankind from the time of Adam, and that all Prophets were Muslims: "Say ye: 'We believe in Allah, and the revelation given to us, and to Abraham, Ishmael, Isaac, Jacob, and the Tribes, and that given to all Prophets from their Lord: We make no difference between one and another of them: and we bow to Allah (in Islam)." (S.II:136) The very term *Islam* means submission to God. Unfortunately this word has also degenerated into a multiordinal word, connoting particular points of view." (S.L.L.)

Israel — (Hebrew) 'Ruling with God' or 'God rules'. The name given to Jacob by an angel and later by God, "for [he has] striven with God and with men, and [has] prevailed. . . . And Jacob called the name of the place *Peniel* ['the face of God']: 'for I have seen God face to face . . . " (Gen.32:29-31 M.T.)

Jacob — (Hebrew) 'Supplanter'. The third Patriarch of the Hebrews under whom they were united as the nation of Israel [See ISRAEL], or the "Children of Israel". Jacob is described in the Book of Genesis as "a plain man, dwelling in tents" in contrast to his twin brother Esau, "a cunning hunter, a man of the field." they were sons of Isaac, the second Patriarch of the Hebrews, and his wife Rebekah. Through a ruse planned by his mother, Jacob acquired the blessing intended for Esau as the elder son, and succeeded his father as Patriarch of his people. In a dream-vision Jacob saw a ladder reaching from earth to Heaven with "angels of God ascending and descending on it; Jacob climbs the ladder and, "Behold, the Lord stood beside him." (Gen.28:12-13)

Jebel Musa — (Arabic) 'Mountain of Moses'. This mountain, also called Sinai, is the mountain where Moses received the Ten Commandments. It is also the site since 530 A.D. of St. Catherine's monastery. It was built by the emperor Justinian as a protection for the monks who had settled there. In the hills surrounding it the oldest and most complete manuscripts of the Greek Bible have been found.

Jerusalem — (from the Hebrew *Yerushalayim*, 'abode of peace'.) Considered a holy city by Jews, Christians and Muslims, it is the only city which they share as a center of pilgrimage. The tradition of "Heavenly Jerusalem" is also common to the three religions; it became synonomous with the ideal city governed by God Himself.

Jesus — (the Greek form of Joshua or Jeshua, a contraction of *Jehoshua*, 'help of God' or 'savior'. The saint of saints, whose life was an example of his message, whose will was harmonized with the Will of God, whose spirit was tuned to the whole universe. He is referred to in the Quran as *Ruh-Allah*, the 'Spirit of God'.

jihad — (Arabic) 'utmost exertion'. "*Jihad* can take the following forms: (a) *jihad by the heart*: this amounts to self-purification, and this type of exertion was termed by Mohammed the 'Greater Jihad' (*Mujahida*); (b) *jihad by the tongue*: this means persuading people to adopt the right path and to dissuade them from evil. Mohammed showed clear preference for this method over methods involving force or violence; (c) *jihad by the sword*: this method of jihad was called the 'Lesser Jihad'. All warfare is abolished by Islam except that which is considered *fi sabil Allah* ('in the way of God'), and to qualify for this two conditions must be met. The first is that fighting should be aimed at liquidating *fitnah* ('persecution'). *Fitnah* denotes a denial of basic human rights, particularly the right to freely profess and practice religion. The second condition for jihad through warfare is that it should not aim at self-aggrandizement, or gaining enemy territory, or spoils of war, or revenge, or to acquiring any worldly

296

advantage. Use of jihad (or compulsion, for that matter) as an instrument of proselytisation is prohibited." (from *Landmarks of Jihad*, by Lt. Col. M. M. Qurreshi, pp. 4-5)

jinn — (Arabic) 'a spirit'. Vibrations or beings of knowledge and subtle faculties who inhabit the plane of existence between the human and the angelic; according to Quran, they were created from smokeless fire. Jinn, genie and genius all come from the Sanskrit root *jnana*, meaning 'knowledge'.

Jinnat — (Arabic) 'Garden' or 'Paradise'. Fulfillment.

Job — (from the Arabic *Ayub*) A Patriarch of the Old Testament, he is generally considered to have been an Arab, not a Hebrew, as is indicated by the form of his name and the scene of his story, i.e., northern Arabia.

John the Lustrator — John the Baptist who, heralding the coming of a new age, urged the people to repent and turn to righteousness. Many, including Jesus, came to be baptized by him.

Jonah — A Prophet of the Old Testament whose name and probable home are Assyrian. When commanded by God to go to Nineveh, "For their wickedness is come up before Me," Jonah fled and boarded a ship. But God caused a great tempest in the sea so that men of the ship cast lots to see who was at fault. The lot fell to Jonah who offered to cast himself into the sea that it may be calmed for them. By God's Mercy, he was swallowed by a whale and then thrown up on dry land. Thereafter he went to Nineveh, and through his preaching the people were saved.

Joseph — One of the twelve sons of Jacob and as such one of the progenitors of the original Twelve Tribes of Israel. Jacob's favorite son, he was an example of manly beauty and loftiness of character. He was sold into Egyptian slavery by his brothers where, because of his ability to interpret the Pharaoh's dreams, he was made chief admnistrator of the kingdom and Hierophant of the mysteries. When famine struck the people of Israel, he secured a place for them in Egypt. There they prospered until the Pharaoh "who knew not Joseph" succeeded to the throne and persecuted them.

Jubilee — God commanded Moses on Mt. Sinai that every fiftieth year was to be celebrated as the Year of Jubilee: "And ye shall hallow the fiftieth year, and proclaim liberty throughout the land unto all the inhabitants thereof; it shall be a jubilee unto you."

(Lev.25:10 M.T.) It provided that all land revert to the common property of all for redistribution, that all debts be cancelled, mortgaged property be returned and slaves be liberated. At its core was the teaching that all things and all creatures belong to God alone.

Kaaba — (Arabic) 'Cube'. The sacred shrine of Islam in Mecca, the central place of pilgrimage and the direction of prayer for all Muslims. According to Quran, God commissioned Abraham and Ishmael to consecrate this site as a place of worship and pilgrimage for all men and to build thereon a temple dedicated to the One God. (S.XXII:119) According to Muslim tradition, the angel Gabriel brought them the meteorite known as the Black Stone which is housed in the Kaaba and marks the beginning of the prescribed circumambulation of the shrine. With the passage of years, worship at the Kaaba became corrupted, and by Mohammed's time there were over 300 idols in it. Mohammed cleared away the idols, rededicated the Kaaba to the worship of the One God, and consecrated it as the direction of prayer for all Muslims, thus producing the accomodation of unification.

kadis — (Arabic) 'judges'. In the Islamic legal system, judges who interpret and administer the religious law.

Kafir — (Arabic) 'Infidel' or 'Unbeliever'.

Karaim — (Hebrew) 'Readers'. Nicknamed the "Children of the Text," the Karaites are a Jewish sect, formed in 760 A.D., who called for a return to the original Hebrew Scriptures as the supreme authority in Jewish life. They came at a time when oral tradition, opinion and multitudinous extra-Biblical laws determined Jewish religious worship and everyday life.

karma yoga — (Sanskrit) 'union through action'. The yoga of action or work, undertaken in the service of God and with no thoughts of receiving personal benefit therefrom. "There is a teaching of the Gita, that to man belongs action, and to God the fruits of action. When man identifies himself with his gains or honors, he limits himself." (S.L.L.)

Kerbela — In Iraq, the site of the murder of Hussein, grandson of Mohammed. In a futile attempt to establish himself as the rightful and duly appointed Khalif, he was martyred by supporters of Yazid, the Umayyad incumbent. This took place nineteen years after his father, Khalif Ali (Mohammed's cousin

298

and son-in-law) was killed by Mu'awiya, who then established the Umayyad dynasty. These incidents marked the end of the practice adopted after Mohammed's death, of election to the office of Khalif by Mohammed's Companions. Thereafter the office of Khalif gradually become merely a religious one, and the secular power passed into the hands of the sultans.

Khadijah — Mohammed's first wife and later his first disciple.

Khalid — The Kureishi military leader who converted to Islam and became Mohammed's greatest general. Under Abu Bekr, Mohammed's successor, he embarked upon a vast program of military expansion, accumulating many spoils of war. He was removed from command by the next Khalif, Omar, for his excesses.

Khalif — (Arabic) 'Vicegerent' or 'Representative'. Originally used in the Quran to refer to man as God's Khalif on earth, it became the title of Mohammed's successors as leaders of the Muslim community. The office became the subject of factional strife as the territory of the Islamic Empire increased. Rival khalifates sprang up and finally administrative power passed on to self-made *amirs* and sultans.

Kham, Khebt — [See LAND OF TWO TRUTHS]

Khidr, Khizr — (Arabic) 'Green'. Having drunk of the waters of the fountain of life, Khidr gained immortality. He is connected with the color green because he brings the water of life to barren soil. He has appeared to Sufis throughout the ages and is identified with Elijah and with the teacher of Moses alluded to in the Quran and the Old Testament. [See the Preface for the story of Khidr's manifestation to Murshid Sufi Ahmed Murad Chisti]

khutbah — (Arabic) 'sermon'. The Friday sermon delivered in the mosque.

Kibla — (Arabic) 'direction'. In Islam, the Kaaba is the direction toward which all devotees turn in prayer. In the early days of Islam, Mohammed established Jerusalem as the *kibla*, sacred to both Jews and Christians. This symbolized his allegiance to the continuity of God's revelation. When, under Divine direction, Mohammed began to organize his people as a community with laws and rituals of their own, the Kaaba was established as their *kibla*, thus going back to the earliest center with which the name of Abraham is connected.

299

Kureish — The most powerful and prestigious tribe of Mecca, the one into which Mohammed was born. The leaders of the Kureish were Mohammed's main opponents during the early years of his mission in Mecca. Gradually they were converted to Islam and later came to constitute the line of succession of the early Khalifate.

La Illaha El Il Allah — (Arabic) 'There is no god except *the* God'. According to Sufis, this can be realized as meaning, 'There is no reality except God', or 'God alone exists'. [See also FIVE PILLARS and ZIKAR]

Land of Promise — Canaan, the land promised by God to Abraham and his seed.

Land of Two Truths — "In ancient times Egypt was divided into *Kham*, which means 'internal darkness with heat'; and *Khebt* (from which the term 'Egypt' is derived), which means 'white light'. The former was the abode of the ignorant (*samsara*), the latter of the initiate." (S.L.L.)

Lent — The period of fasting before Easter, observed in commemoration of Jesus' fasting in the wilderness for forty days. Its observance varies greatly within the different sects of Christianity and in the different hemospheres.

Lotus-eating worlds, Lotus land — Planes of self-satisfaction offering a kind of limited intoxication.

Mammon — (Aramaic) 'Riches'. Riches, avarice and worldly gain, personified as a false god in the New Testament.

manna — (from the Hebrew *man hu*, 'what is this?') The food given by God to the Children of Israel during their 40 years' wandering in the desert; it is described as falling from Heaven like rain — small and sweet in taste. (Ex.16:4; Num.11:6-9) By extension, it is the sustenance which comes to us each day from God's mercy and compassion.

maya — (Sanskrit) 'illusion'. The idea in Hindu philosophy that life in the world is an illusion and therefore every experience in this life and knowledge in this life are also illusions. But "it is not that this life is non-existent, only that we do not see it clearly. Reason can not touch it. *Maya* means that which is measurable; in other words, finite, transitory. It does not mean unreal." (S.L.L.) [See also MAYIM]

mayim — (Hebrew) 'waters' or 'seas'. "The Hebrew *mayim* . . . greatly resembles a plural of *maya*. In addition, their hieroglyphical and mythological significance is much the same. . . .We thus have a flood saga in which the universal waters of *maya* (as *mayim*) encompass the universe, while Noah, the savior, rides high on them and is not touched thereby. The whole is emblematic of the relation of samsara to nirvana." (S.L.L.)

Mecca — Birthplace of Mohammed and site of the Kaaba, the center for pilgrimage in Islam.

Mecca-Shereef — (Arabic) 'Noble leader of Mecca'. A title of Mohammed.

meditation — Any technique by which one discovers his inner peace and at-one-ment with the universe.

men-of-the-Pen — [See SCRIBES]

Meru — The central Mountain of Buddhist and Hindu mythology. "Esoterically, it symbolizes the Mount Meru of the human organism, the spinal column; its summit is the Thousand Petalled Lotus of the brain nerve-center, the *Sahasrara-Padma*." (from *Tibet's Great Yogi, Milarepa*.)

Messenger — As used in the poem, it refers to Mohammed, following the usage of Muslims in general. [For a general definition, see RASSUL]

Messiah — (from the Hebrew *mashiach*, 'annointed one') The redeemer of Israel. Sometimes this term is used to refer simply to the person of Jesus.

Mohammed — (Arabic) 'Highly praised'. *Rassul*, Prophet and founder of Islam. "When the world has become corrupt, it was the occasion for a new *Rassul*, and this one was the Prophet Mohammed. He came at a time so black and terrible that all the world has called that period the 'Dark Ages'. Mohammed had a more difficult mission, therefore, than all those before him. He had to bring back the Divine Message to earth, and he also had to live among ignorant people. . . . With all his learning, he was very humble and even when power and authority were in his hands, he was most scrupulous in his use of them. The Message of Mohammed was Islam and its purpose was the purification of the Divine Message, to bring mankind to the realization of truth without any intermediation of either institutions or personalities, and to carry on the work of human brotherhood." (S.L.L.) The

Quran teaches that he is the Seal of the Prophets, i.e., the embodiment and completion of all which preceded him.

Moses — (from the Hebrew *moshe*, 'water born') The great Prophet of the Hebrew nation. He was born to Jewish parents in Egypt who, rather than see him killed because of the Pharaoh's edict against all male Hebrew babies, placed him in a cradle and set him in the Nile. He was found and adopted by the Pharaoh's daughter, and in his manhood was trained in the Egyptian mysteries. He fled the oppression of the Pharaoh and settled in Midian, where he married. In a vision, God commanded him to lead the children of Israel out of their bondage in Egypt. During their 40 years of wandering in the desert, they were led to Mt. Sinai where Moses received the Ten Commandments for a law unto Israel. He delivered them to the threshold of the Promised Land. "And the Lord said unto him: 'I have caused thee to see [this land] with thine eyes, but thou shalt not go over thither. So Moses the servant of the Lord died there in the land of Moab." (Deut.34:4-5) The rod mentioned in the poem was a rod which Moses had which, in turn, God caused to become a snake in his hands and then turned it back into a rod; with this same rod God caused the waters of the sea to open so that Israel might pass through; and he caused a rock to spring forth with water so that the people of Israel might quench their thirst. Moses is the author of the Book of Genesis and, according to tradition, the second four books of the Old Testament as well. In the Quran, he is given the title of *kalimullah*, the one to whom God spoke without the intervention of angels. "The word 'Moses' itself means waterborn, rising out of the sea, rising out of the samsara to become the deliverer." (S.L.L.)

mosque — (Arabic) 'place of prostration'. In Islam, the place for organized prayer.

Mothanna — A Bedouin tribal chief who became an important Muslim general shortly after the death of Mohammed. With Khalid he helped to extend the sway of the Islamic empire into Persia and Iraq.

Mumin — (Arabic) 'Believer'.

mushahida — (Arabic) 'contemplation'. The Sufi practice of active repose "by the heart centered upon the Being of God. . . . The real practice comes when man delves deeply into his whole heart, sees the universe as within his own heart and . . . feels the whole creation as if within himself." (S.L.L.)

Muslim — (Arabic) "The term 'Muslim' is supposed to mean one who surrenders to God, although more literally it would mean a 'pacified person'. One meets multitudes of 'Muslims' who say they surrender and they have not the slightest idea of the meaning of the word 'surrender'. The Apostle [Mohammed] has said: 'Praise God in times of prosperity and surrender to Him in times of adversity.' " (S.L.L.)

naar — (Arabic) 'flame'. The fires of purification.

Nabi — (Arabic) 'Prophet'. One who speaks the word of God to mankind. The prayer "Nabi" by Pir-O-Murshid Hazrat Inayat Khan describes him as: "A torch in the darkness, a staff during my weakness, a rock in the weariness of life, thou, my Master makest earth a paradise. Thy thought giveth me unearthly joy, thy light illuminateth my life's path, thy words inspire me with divine wisdom, I follow in thy footsteps, which lead me to the eternal goal. Comforter of the broken-hearted, support of those in need, friend of the lovers of Truth, Blessed Master, thou art the Prophet of God."

nafs — (Arabic) 'self', 'ego'. The ego, the structure which holds things as distinct entities. In Arabic this word also means breath. "When we consider such a phrase as that of Jesus Christ: 'Blessed are the poor in spirit', also being capable of the interpretation, 'Blessed are the mild in breath', we may gain some deeper insight into connections between 'breath' and 'ego'. The Arabic nafs has been interpreted as thing-in-itself, or the thingness of a thing. Metaphysically it comes closest to the Hebrew nachash [which in Genesis is translated as serpent]. . . . It actually symbolizes a coil-springlike movement toward a center-of-being. This movement establishes a false center (non-existent spatially and superspatially). It is as if a focus of not-being. . . . This becomes the 'ego' which in a sense would be both existent and non-existent. . . . The Sufis have explained nafs in a gradient from the heaviest to the lightest breath. (1) nafs ammara — one who lives only for material satisfaction. He has no particular consideration of others, but is not necessarily opposed to those who do not interfere with him and his efforts at self-satiation. (2) nafs aluwama — one who is still subject to faults, sins and emotional disturbances. He will atone for his acts; in practice this type of person tends to be religious rather than moral. (3) *nafs mutmaina* — one who thinks, lives and acts according to moral principles or high intellectual ideals. (4) *nafs selima* — one who has attained peace, or who has surrendered to God. (5) *nafs alima* — the perfect *nafs*; one who acts as if in the manner of God. All ideas of separation and identification have been removed." (S.L.L.)

nafs alima — [See NAFS]

nafs selima — [See NAFS]

Narayana Krishna — (Sanskrit) 'Krishna, archetypal man'. In Hinduism, a divine incarnation or avatar who reached perfection through Love and is characterized by his flute playing and ecstatic behavior.

Nathan — The Jewish spokesman for religious tolerance and the brotherhood of humanity in Gotthold Lessing's play, "Nathan the Wise." Nathan is based on the character of Melchisedek the Jew in Boccaccio's *Decameron* who, "with a story of three rings, escapeth a perilous snare set for him by Saladin." [See Preface]

Nazarenes — Christians, followers of Jesus of Nazareth.

Nemesis — In Greek mythology, the goddess of retributive justice.

nescience — The state of unknowing, ignorance.

Nimaz — (Persian) 'prayer'. The ritual of prayer in Islam (*Salaat*). "Nimaz combines prayers with movements, movements which have psychic and psychological significance. When the eyes are raised, when they are lowered, when the arms or head are raised or lowered, the prayer is as if man had several bodies or vehicles, all of which are joined in prayer. The placing of the head on the ground is especially a movement of utter ego-surrender." (S.L.L.)

nirvana — (Sanskrit) 'extinguished', i.e., the flame of ego. Conscious absorption in the Unity of being. "Life beyond differences and distinctions." (S.L.L.)

Noah — (Hebrew) 'Repose'. The tenth in descent from Adam, Noah was chosen by God to survive the destruction of the Flood and to become the progenitor of a new human race. "In the flood saga Noah, the savior, rides high on the waters and is not touched thereby. The whole is emblematic of the relation of samsara to nirvana." (S.L.L.) In the Quran, Noah is said to have written books of prophetic teachings, which have been lost.

Nuri Mohammed — (Arabic) 'Light of Mohammed'. The Sufi Jili says this phrase really refers to "the light of the whole universe." "It is the same Divine Light out of which the world was created. . . . which manifests in a personality from time to time." (S.L.L.)

om — (Sanskrit) Sacred syllable of the Vedas and Upanishads, the ancient Scriptures of India. The sound of sounds.

Omar — The second Khalif in succession after Mohammed. He assumed the title of "Commander of the Faithful," and it was under his leadership that the Islamic Empire was consolidated and greatly expanded to include Syria, Palestine, Egypt, North Africa, Persia and part of Asia Minor. He himself lived very simply, in the fashion of a dervish or faqir.

oracles — In ancient Greece, the mediums by which the Divine purpose was made known; usually women priestesses who were considered pure enough to function as channels for Divine Guidance.

orthodoxy — Conformity to an official doctrine or formulation of truth.

Osiris — The ancient Egyptian god whose annual death and resurrection personified the self-renewing vitality and fertility of the universe. [See also EHYEH ASHER EHYEH]

Palestine — The Holy Land, a term which officially came into use in the second century A.D.; it was current usage at the time of the Balfour Declaration.

Paradise — The fulfillment in the kingdom of the heavens; or also on earth when man's heart becomes awakened.

Path — The path shown by the living God by which man is able to transcend his own human limitations, ascending the ladder of being to the Divine Presence. "The Way of Holiness" referred to in the Old Testament (Isa.35:8); "the narrow way" which is entered through "the strait gate" referred to in the New Testament (Matt.7:13, 14); "the straight way, the way of those upon whom [God] has bestowest [His] Grace." (Quran S. I) "There is one Path, the annihilation of the false ego in the real, which raises the mortal to Immortality and in which resides all perfection." (Hazrat Inayat Khan)

people of the Book — The name used in the Quran for the Jews and Christians as recipients of a revelation from the heavenly Book. As such, they were assigned a special status in Muslim conquered nations and allowed religious autonomy. This name was later extended by the Khalifate to include Sabeans, Zoroastrians, Hindus and the followers of all revealed religions.

philos — [See AGAPE]

phoenix — In ancient mythology, the fabulous bird of Arabia who every 500 years built itself a funeral pyre on which he was consumed by fire and then reborn from its own ashes. According to the legend, he then carried the remains of his old body to the city of Heliopolis in Egypt and deposited them there in the temple of the Sun. A symbol of immortality and resurrection.

Pillars of Islam — [See FIVE PILLARS]

pleroma — (Greek) 'fullness'. The fullness of the Divine Life.

pluriverse — The infinite accomodations of Reality.

polity — The form of government of a nation, church or organization.

prajna — (Sanskrit) 'wisdom' or 'direct insight'. "Cosmic intuition. . . . the faculty of direct insight into the nature of things called *kashf* by Sufis). . . . It means the immediate comprehension of whatever is about one of which one is conscious. . . . It may mean 'beyond intellect' or *para-jnana*. It certainly operates that way. . . . Wisdom is not something apart from man. Wisdom is a function and attribute of man. It has been divinized as a woman because man must be in the state of receptivity in order for it to function. . . . Zen in truth is not just meditative practice; it is operative *prajna* function." (S.L.L.)

Prakriti — (Sanskrit) 'Nature' or 'Matter'. In Hindu philosophy, Nature as the visible reflection and unfoldment of cosmic Spirit (*Purusha*). The living manuscript of God.

priest — "It was only when the priests began to arrogate to themselves certain rights, to proclaim that they were the intermediaries between God and man, when they collected the taxes and revenues, gave orders to the kings and warriors, and interfered with politics that the inner teachings began to degenerate and decay." (S.L.L.) Mohammed stipulated that there was to be no priestcraft in Islam.

Prophet — One whose heart is open and receives from God and speaks to man. The Prophets of the line of *Beni Israel* had a particular mission whose main feature was to fully establish the teaching of the One God. This line, which begins with Abraham

306

and includes Moses and Jesus is said to have been completed and thus sealed in the being and teachings of Mohammed.

Prophet, the — As used in the poem, it refers to Mohammed, as the prototype of prophecy, following the usage of Muslims.

psyche — (Greek) 'mind', 'soul'. Many religions teach that man has three bodies: the physical, psychic, which is also known as the subtle or astral, and the spiritual (causal). The psychic world is a world of thoughts, powers and faculties of mind-consciousness.

Pure Land — Nirvana. In Buddhism, the perfection kingdom of Amitabha, the Buddha of Infinite Bliss.

Quran — (Arabic) 'Reading', 'Recitation'. The sacred Scripture of Islam, containing the revelations uttered by the Prophet Mohammed. When Mohammed received his first revelation he was told by the Angel Gabriel "IQRA!", which means "Read!" or "Recite!." The same Arabic root letters *q*, *r*, *a* are used to form the word *quran*, the object read or recited; a book. "Because of delusion it has been presumed that one religion may teach what is contrary in principle to what another religion has taught. Quran completed the verbalization of revelation. What is beyond is not confined to written scripture. Quran also taught this." (S.L.L.) The Quran formed the basis for the religious, social, civil, commercial, military and legal regulations of Islam.

Ram, Rama — One of the Avatars of India, he was a model ascetic and, later, king, husband and warrior. The *Ramayana*, which is the principal epic poem of India, tells his life story and that of his wife, Sita.

Ramadan — In Islam, the ninth month of the lunar year, a sacred month of fasting and prayer in commemoration of the period when Mohammed received the first revelation of the Quran.

Ramayana — The spiritual epic poem of India which relates the story of Rama (the Divine Messenger) and the rescue of his wife Sita (who represents the human soul) from the hands of Ravana (the desire nature). The poem dates back to the first century B.C. and is said also to be an allegory of the Aryans' attempt to conquer South India.

Rassul — (Arabic) 'Apostle', 'Messenger'. Used often in the poem to refer to Mohammed who, "as well as Christ, Moses, Buddha and all Messengers of God . . . are men of pure essence [whose mission] is to increase the life upon earth, to bring more livingness, to bestow blessing, to radiate living magnetism. . . . The men called *Rassul*, Messiah, Avatar include all the perfect men and women who have ever appeared upon earth, who have passed through all grades of attribution to pure suchness, to *Tat*, *Tathata*, *Zat*, Pleroma, *Ain-Soph*, *Zeruan Akerene*." (S.L.L.) The prayer "Rassul" of Hazrat Inayat Khan ("Warner of coming dangers, wakener of the world from sleep, deliverer of the Message of God, thou art our Savior. The sun at the dawn of creation, the light of the whole universe, the fulfillment of God's purpose, thou the life eternal, we seek refuge in thy loving enfoldment. Spirit of Guidance, Source of all beauty and Creator of harmony, Love, Lover and beloved Lord, thou art our divine ideal."

Rassul-Lillah — (Arabic) 'Messenger of God'. A title of Mohammed.

Ravana — In the *Ramayana*, the kidnapper of Sita whom Rama pursues to Ceylon; the personification of the desire-nature.

Richard, King — King Richard I of England, Richard "the Lion-Hearted"; leader of the Third Crusade against the Sultan Saladin. [See SALADIN]

Righteous Khalifs — The immediate successors of Mohammed (Abu Bekr, Omar, Othman and Ali, respectively), known to the Muslim world as *al-khulafa al-rashidun*, 'righteous' or 'rightly-guided khalifs'. After the assassination of Ali, the office of Khalif became more political than spiritual.

rood, holy — The historical cross upon which Jesus is said to have been crucified.

Ruth — A Moabite woman who converted to Judaism; the great-grandmother of the Prophet David and ancestress of Jesus Christ. Her story is told in the Old Testament Book of Ruth, where she is portrayed as an example of loyalty and devotion.

sabbath — The observance of the seventh day of the week as a day of rest and joyful communion with God; its observance was prescribed by God to Moses and his people. In time the man-made laws and ordinances which grew up around it tended to obscure its true spirit, which is described in the poem.

Sabeans — An ancient people of Arabia who had a flourishing kingdom in southeast Arabia. Little is known of them, although their form of worship was connected with the planets and stars. In the Quran they are classed among those who possessed a divine revelation, thus "people of the Book." As such they were accorded freedom of worship in the expanding Islamic empire.

Sacred Name — YHVH, the name of God used by the early Hebrews which, according to Fabre D'Olivet signifies 'I-the-Being-who-is-was-and-who-will-be'. During the history of Judaism the invocation of this Sacred Name ceased, and since only the consonants are found in the Scriptures (the vowels being omitted as a matter of course), one cannot be sure of its proper pronunciation. As Martin Buber points out, the most likely way of pronouncing it is *Yahuvah*; and this was the principal form of pronounciation which Murshid accepted. He did not accept the reasons given for ceasing to repeat it and the customary substitution of the name *Adonoi* in its stead. "*Adonoi* is a power. It is sometimes said to mean the disc of the sun and the solar powers. It is not the universal, but an attribute. A Divine attribute, but still an attribute and not the essence. *Yah* is the essence. ... The generality could understand neither the words nor the doctrine of *Yahuva*, and instead they accepted him as *Adonoi*, the Lord or Master. In other words, they accepted the God-Ideal because they could not comprehend the God-Reality." (S.L.L.) So today, some of Murshid disciples use the above-mentioned pronunciation in their devotional practices, as, for example, in the Sufi Choir's rendition of the "*Shema*."

Saints — Perfected men who, through renunciation and self-sacrifice have become tuned to the whole universe and thus serve as channels of blessing for all of life. In the Quran, "they are those who among men are the nearest united to God, and who consequently enjoy His most intimate Presence."

salaam aleikhum — [See AS-SALAAM ALEIKHUM]

Salaat — (Arabic) 'prayer'. "The Islamic prayer, *salaat*, is essentially one of surrender to God." (S.L.L.) [See also FIVE PILLARS and NIMAZ]

Saladin — Salah-ud-Din Yusuf ibn Ayyub (1138-1193). The meaning of Saladin's name, Salah-ud-Din, is 'Rectitude of the Faith', or in the terminology of this poem, 'Sword of the Faith'; the aptness of this title is seen throughout his life.

Little is known of the early years of Saladin except that he exhibited an intense interest in religious studies. The beginning of what is known as the First Crusade and the bloody capture of

Jerusalem had taken place before Saladin's birth; during the first half of the twelfth century the Mid East had become a patchwork of Christian and Muslim states. Saladin's first battle with the Crusaders occurred during a campaign led by his uncle, Shirkuh. Some Muslim historians say that he was reluctant to accompany his uncle because he had set his heart on becoming a religious devotee and not a soldier. Whatever be the case, Saladin came to feel that driving the invaders out of the Holy Land was his mission. After assuming power in Egypt, Saladin, in his preamble to a decree abolishing exorbitant taxes states: "We praise God that He has established us firmly in the land, and has made agreeable to us the performance of every duty, whether supererogatory or obligatory, and has raised us up to remove from amongst His creatures whatsoever intrudes upon the worship of Him, and has chosen us to engage in the Holy War on behalf of God in the true sense of the term . . . " (Gibb, *Life of Saladin*, p. 15)

Before he could launch an effective jihad, he had first to unite the various Arab states, whose disunity had prevented any effective reprisal after the Crusaders had first taken Jerusalem. He would not permit mutual warfare between Muslim princes to prevent a unified Muslim jihad, and stated that his own friendship or hostility to other rulers depended upon their attitude toward the cause of God. He is quoted as saying: "In the interests of Islam and its people we put first and foremost whatever will combine their forces and unite them in one purpose . . ." (*ibid*, p. 12) In the circumstances of his time the only way this objective could be realised was by concentrating power in his own hands, and establishing in all key positions persons on whose loyalty he could depend upon with absolute certainty. Saladin's concept of government differed radically from other rulers of the time however: if the purpose of unity was a true jihad, a true holy war, he felt that the governing of the nations must be conducted with a scrupulous observance of the revealed Law of Islam. "A government which sought to serve the cause of God in battle must be not only a lawful government, duly authorized by the supreme representative of the Divine Law, but must serve God with equal zeal in its administration and in its treatment of its subjects. In brief, Saladin's object was to restore to Islamic politics the reign of law, a concept that had become for the contemporary princes not only an empty phrase but an absurdity." His general practice was to confer full authority to his viceroys, "only requiring them to promise just and equitable treatment of their subjects in the spirit of the *Shari'a*, a contribution to the warchest of the jihad, and the maintenance of their regiments in good order and discipline, in readiness to set out when they were called for." (*ibid*, p. 14)

When conditions were right, Saladin quickly captured Jerusalem and most of the other cities held by the Crusaders. Whereas the First Crusade celebrated its conquest of Jerusalem by butchering every inhabitant, men, women and children, Muslims and Jews (some 65-70,000 people) in the name of the Prince of Peace, Saladin seems to have had a different understanding of the teachings of Jesus. "Rarely has a general who has won an overwhelming victory on all fronts been found to show such consideration, courtesy, and even sympathy for his adversaries of the previous day, especially when those adversaries were the enemies of his religion. The Sultan not only distinguished himself by his chivalrous treatment of the great Frankish ladies, he not only behaved with great clemency to all who came to him as suppliants, readily granting their freedom to captive fathers and husbands; he even took a personal interest in escorting the emigrants to Christian lands, giving them protection and supplying them with food at his own expense, and instructing the officials at the gates to see their transport in good condition, and seems to have tried, as far as possible, to limit the damage and avoid causing needless suffering . . . " (Oldenbourg, *The Crusades*, pp. 108-109)

A Third Crusade was mounted against Saladin, led by Richard of England. Unable to reach Jerusalem, a treaty was concluded with Saladin. The coast would belong to the Latins, and the interior to the Muslims, and Christian pilgrims would be allowed to visit Jerusalem unmolested.

"Although Saladin possessed personal military virtues of a high order, his victories were due to his possession of moral qualities which have little in common with those of a great general. He was a man inspired by an intense and unwavering ideal, the achievement of which involved him necessarily in a long series of military activities. . . . It was by the sheer force of personality, by the undying flame of faith within him, and by his example of steadfast endurance that he inspired the dogged resistance which finally wore down the invaders." (Gibb, *Life of Saladin*, pp. 57,59)

sarcophagus — A sepulchre or coffin.

schismatic — Pertaining to divisions within a religion based on theological disputes.

scimitar — A sword having a curved blade with the sharp edge on the convex side.

Scribes — In a broad sense, scribes refers to those involved more with the letter of the Law than its spirit. On the return of the Jews from their exile in Babylonia, the Scribes were organized by Ezra into a distinct body whose function was to record and interpret the Scriptures to the people. As the keepers of the oral traditionary comments and additions to the Law, they revised the scriptural text amending it and integrating commentary into it. By the time of Jesus their power and influence had grown to the point where they were, next to the High Priest, leaders of the community. The people were increasingly dependent on them for a knowledge of their own Scriptures which they were unable to understand due to the changing language. The Scribes adopted forced interpretations of the Law, endeavoring to find a special meaning in every word, syllable and letter. This literature became so vast that it was regarded by many as of equal value with the Law itself. Jesus denounced them as hypocrites who took away "the key of knowledge: ye entered not in yourselves; and them that were entering in ye hindered." (Luke 11:52 A.V.)

Seal, Seal of the Prophets — Mohammed as the culmination of the prophetic line of the *Beni Israel*. He confirms all who have gone before him. Their missions are fulfilled through him. "We can see the perfect souls who have come from time to time have maintained a complete universal consciousness, but they did not always manifest or operate on all planes. Often they functioned on the higher or highest planes but did not function as ordinary men in the midst of the world. This was the work of Mohammed who carried this perfection and perfectability down to the lowest level. . . . He was successful in maintaining the presence of God in all his affairs of everyday life and thus opened the door for all humanity to keep consciousness of God along with everything else and thus surmount dualism." (S.L.L.)

sempiternal — Everlasting.

sheikh — (Arabic) 'elder'. As used in the poem, a spiritual guide.

shekels — The coin of the Hebrew people in Biblical times. According to Mosaic law, a certain portion of shekels were to be given by every individual as an offering to God, "a ransom for his soul." (Ex.30) This money was to be used for the appointment of the Tabernacle.

shechinah — (Hebrew) 'dwelling'. The Divine Presence or Radiance abiding on earth, "so narrow it can be set in a coffer and so great that it contains the Universe." (S.L.L.) Its mystical meaning is that God resides in the smallest of the small as well as the greatest of the great.

Shem, Japheth and Ham — The three sons of Noah.

shirk — (Arabic) 'polytheism'. Ascribing partners to God.

Shiva — One of the Avatars of India, Lord of the Yogis and the perfection of Dance.

shalom aleichem — (Hebrew) 'peace be with you'. This is the Hebrew counterpart to the Arabic *as-salaam aleikhum.*

shuvo — (Hebrew) 'return', commonly translated as 'repentance'; "It is the most important element in the Jewish spiritual life, and is climaxed on *Yom Kippur,* the 'Day of Atonement' " (S.L.L.)

Siddiq — (Arabic) 'Sincere'. A title given to Abu Bekr, Mohammed's close Companion and advisor. He was the first male convert to Islam, and after Mohammed's death he was elected to be his successor as leader of the Muslim community. Following the example of the Prophet, the great victories and rapidly increasing wealth of the Muslims made no difference to his way of life. He dressed simply, lived in an adobe hut with his family and retained no worldly wealth for his own use. All was scrupulously distributed to the needy and the widows of those killed in the wars.

sindu — (Sanskirt) 'ocean'. [See BINDU]

Sita — [See RAM]

Sohrawardi Maktul — Shahab-ud-din Sohrawardi. He was executed at the age of 36 at the order of Sultan Saladin who gave in to political-religious pressure against the mystic for his open and extravagant espousals of his inner spiritual states. The appelation *al-maktul* ('killed one') was given to him to avoid his being considered a *shahid* (a martyr in the pursuit of the Faith). Sohrawardi's major work, *Hikmat al-Ishraq* ('Wisdom of Illumination'), concerns the different spheres of light and the hierarchies of the effulgent beings. It has been translated by Professor Henri Corbin. Sohrawardi attempted to reconcile traditional philosophy and mysticism, linking the diverse traditions of Aristotelian philosophy with the Persian Zoroastrian doctrines and Egyptian Hermetic traditions, and showing their similarity with the mystical traditions of Islam. It is an interesting feature of the poem that it is Sohrawardi Maktul who acts as the spiritual guide for Saladin during the first phase of his journey in the heavenly spheres.

Subhan Allah — (Arabic) 'Glory be to God'.

sukhavati — (Sanskrit) 'happy land'. In Buddhism, a joyous Paradise where the pure in heart reside; here the devotees are taught how to achieve Buddhahood.

sultan — (Arabic) 'authority'. Originally used in the Quran in the sense of moral or spiritual authority, it later came to designate a powerful political ruler, an independent sovereign of a certain territory within the Islamic empire. As sultan, Saladin set the example of honoring the Khalif as the central leader of the entire Muslim community.

Sunna — (Arabic) 'well-trodden path'. In Islam, a body of rules based on the precedents established by the Prophet Mohammed in his everyday life. As such, they serve as a model for the faithful and became the basis of law and government as well as religion.

super-logical — Beyond ordinary logic.

supernal — Celestial, heavenly.

Sura — (Arabic) 'step'. A chapter in the Quran.

Sword-ark — The haven or refuge on earth given by the Divine Sovereignty. [See also THEBES]

tabernacle — The physical accommodation for the indwelling Presence of the Infinite Living God (the *shechinah*). Historically, the tabernacle was a portable sanctuary constructed by the Israelites during their 40 year trek through the desert: "And let them make Me a sanctuary, that I may dwell among them." (Ex. 25:8 M.T.) "It shall be . . . throughout your generations . . .

314

where I will meet with you, to speak there unto thee. And there I will meet the children of Israel; and the tent shall be sanctified by My glory. . . . And I will dwell among the children of Israel, and will be their God. And they shall know that I am the Lord their God, that brought them forth out of the land of Egypt, that I may dwell among them." (Ex.29:42-46 M.T.)

Tannhauser — A German lyric poet who took part in a Crusade to the Holy Land in the time of Saladin. According to legend, he visits the Pope to seek absolution for past sins. The Pope tells him that it is as impossible for him to be forgiven as it is for the papal staff to sprout to life. Three days later, to the Pope's amazement, the staff bursts into bloom. The Pope sends out after him, but Tannhauser has gone home and retired from life as a hermit, where he eventually attains realization.

Tao — (Chinese) 'Way'. In Chinese philosophy, the way of serenity in accord with nature, of oneness with the flow of life.

Tarikat — (Arabic) 'Way'. The esoteric path in Islam, based on the inner understanding of the outer religious law of Islam (*Shari'a*); the path of the dervishes.

tauba — (Arabic) 'return'. "*Tauba*, or repentance, does not mean the dualistic contriteness; it means turning from self-hood to Godhood. . . . It is the door to life-in-the-heart. *Tauba* corresponds exactly to the Hebrew *shuvo* and the Greek *metanoia*. Here we come to the junction of the Hebrew, Christian and Islamic religions." (S.L.L.)

Taurat — (Arabic) 'Torah'. The 'Law' revealed by God to the Prophet Moses.

Thebes — (from the Hebrew *thebah*, 'sanctuary' or 'place of refuge') The traditional English rendering of the Hebrew word *thebah* is 'ark', i.e., the "ark" in which Noah and his family escaped the Flood (Gen.6:14ff) and the "ark" in which the tablets of the Ten Commandments were housed. "It appears to be the Samaritan translator who, rendering this word . . . a 'vessel', was the first to give rise to the absurd ideas that this error brought forth. Never has the Hebrew word [*thebah*] signified a vessel, in the sense of a ship, as it has been understood; but a vessel in the sense of a thing destined to contain and to preserve another. . . . It is a place of refuge, an innaccessible retreat. . . . It is also the symbolic name given by the Egyptians to their sacred city, Theba [or Thebes] considered as the shelter, the refuge, the abode of the gods." (Fabre D'Olivet, *The Hebraic Tongue Restored*)

tone, pitch, amplitude — Tone refers to any sound, pitch to the frequency of vibrations and amplitude to the fullness of vibrations.

Torah — (Hebrew) 'Teaching', 'Law'. The substance of Divine revelation to Israel. Specifically, the Pentateuch, or first five books of the Old Testament: Genesis, Exodus, Leviticus, Numbers and Deuteronomy.

Tribes — The Twelve Tribes of Israel, formed by the twelve sons of Jacob and their descendants.

Trimurti — (Sanskrit) 'Three forms'. The three aspects of God in the Hindu teachings — Brahman, the Creator; Vishnu, the Preserver; and Shiva, the Destroyer or Assimilator.

Trinity — The Christian doctrine that: "God is one in nature, but in that one God there are three distinct persons, the Father, the Son who proceeds from the Father by generation, and the Holy Ghost who proceeds from the Father and the Son, as from one principle, by spiration." (*A Catholic Dictionary*, ed. By Donald Attwater) The doctrine of the Trinity is not explicitly or formally a scriptural teaching; it was first formalized in the 4th century A.D. "Such a concept assumes a three-in-one as if equals, but the idea of equality and inequality can be applied only to finite matters. God is beyond conception, and attempts to explain the inexplicable only lead to confusion." (S.L.L.)

Ulysses — The central character of Homer's *Odyssey*, which recounts the wanderings and adventures of Ulysses after the fall of Troy and his eventual return home.

Unity-Doctrine — The affirmation of the Unity of God, the teaching which the Prophet Moses brought to the Children of Israel. It was taken to simply affirm the formless Absolute, but should be understood to include the Presence of God in all manifestation.

usury — Money-lending at interest, forbidden by God to the Children of Israel: "If thou lend money to any of My people, even to the poor with thee, thou shalt not be to him as a creditor; neither shall ye lay upon him interest." (Ex.22:24 M.T.)

Vedic — Referring to the *Vedas*, the oldest of the Hindu sacred writings.

vice-gerent — Representative.

316

Vishnu Purana — A Hindu Scripture which has in common with the Old Testament certain myths, including the story of the Flood.

Voice of the Dove — "In ancient times the Dove was regarded as specially holy. For the Dove gave forth the sound *hu*, which is the sound of the Holy Spirit." (S.L.L.) It is an actual sound which can be heard with the inner ear.

Voice of the Turtle — Same as the Voice of the Dove ('turtle' refers to the turtle-dove). "In the Jewish writings it represents the principle that the Divine Presence was manifest." (S.L.L.)

"Waste Land" — The poem by T. S. Eliot which expresses the disenchantment and disillusion of the post-World War I period. It portrays man in a landscape of despair, eternally awaiting salvation.

women of Samaria — This refers to the story of how Jesus spoke openly to an unknown woman at a well in Samaria (John 4:7-42). Although she refused to draw a drink for him as he asked, he did not refuse her his guidance. Furthermore, this meeting was an abandonment of the convention of the Jews of his time, as the Samaritans had been a hostile neighbor for centuries. And, according to the custom of his time, as a rabbi he was not to be seen speaking to women in public.

Ya Allah — (Arabic) 'O God!'

Yoga — (Sanskrit) 'Union'. Union with God, often associated with certain techniques for its attainment.

Zakat — (Arabic) 'Purifying'. Charity. In Islam it has been instituted as a regular religious tax, a way of paying 'God's due' for whatever one receives.

Zakir — (Arabic) One who practices *Zikar*.

Zem-Zem — The well in the courtyard of the Kaaba in Mecca, whose waters are considered sacred by Muslims.

Zikar — (Arabic) 'Remembrance'. In general, *Zikar* refers to any practice of invoking God *aloud* through the sacred phrases. It also has a very specific reference: "The *Tarikat* or esoteric path in Islam has disciplines with the generic name of *ryazat*. Best known of these is *Zikar*, the repetition in some form of the phrase LA ILLAHA EL IL ALLAH. *Zikar* may be divided into two portions:

(a) LA ILLAHA, there is no God, *or* there is no Being. Negative. Leads to self-effacement, *fana*.

(b) EL IL ALLAH, but God. Positive. Leads to eternal life or *baka*.

Self-control or ego-subversion is offered first. But there is no actual separation betwen ego-restraint and divine expression. The more the ego-self is put under subjection, the more the divine light WHICH IS ALWAYS PRESENT is made manifest." (S.L.L.) "Then do ye remember Me; I will remember you." (Quran S.II:152)

Appendixes

MYSTICAL PRACTICES IN *THE JERUSALEM TRILOGY*

"Sufism is based on experience, and not on premises." This quote from the 11th century Sufi Al-Ghazali is one which Murshid Samuel L. Lewis repeated to his audiences of disciples and non-disciples. In keeping with this fact, we have decided to include a brief selection of spiritual practices taken from "The Day of the Lord Cometh", "What Christ? What Peace?" and "Saladin." Since these practices appear within the flow of these poems, they might easily be overlooked; hopefully by listing a few, they will all become more readily available.

"Words are never truths . . . learn to praise God for in that is fullness of being." This is what Saladin tells us, before giving the following series of practices.

> Consider the morning brightness and the dawn,
> The scented blossoms of fruit trees in the Spring,
> The babbling music of happy rivulets,
> The symphony of birds upon awakening,
> And become aware of the blessings of Allah,
> The bliss which is no dream but The reality.

This can be done, instead of merely reading the words. The poem continues:

> *Allahu! Allahu! Allahu!*
> In the morning before my prayers: *Allahu!*
> In the hours between my prayers: *Allahu!*
> Between prayer and sleep at night: *Allahu!*

The phrase *Allahu!*, which literally means "God, He!" is repeated aloud and silently by Sufis as a means of remembering constantly the Divine Presence.

> The *Zakir* keeps remembering his Deity,
> The *Zakir* is not concerned with self,
> The *Zakir* needs Allah and nothing else,
> We Muslims are aware to Whom we pray,
> We feel the nearness of the One adored,
> There is no power or life save in Allah,
> There is no emptiness or fullness save He
> Learn to appreciate my feelings when I say:
> *Allahu! Allahu! Allahu!*

In this trilogy one comes to see the richness of the Murshid's poetry;

not only is there a wealth of historical information and religious philosophy, but also a wealth of spiritual practices. And these practices become accessible and clear to us when we approach the reading with an eye toward toward experiences which bring us closer to God.

Many of the practices in *The Jerusalem Trilogy*, if performed, give us an experience of certain terms used in these writings, terms which are here restored to their proper place after long disuse and misuse by orthodox religionists who have coveted for their own purposes the sacred words of Divine Scripture. The word *Zion* (see Glossary) is an example to which we will return.

Now, Saladin's description of his journey in the Heaven of Noah, beginning on page 186, can be seen as a full meditation in itself. Saladin says that he and Sheikh Sohrawardi reposed in profound meditation upon the Ararat of the Bible, the Meru of the Vedic texts. By looking at the Glossary one finds that, esoterically, Mount Meru represents the spinal column of the human organism and that "its summit is the Thousand Petalled Lotus of the brain nerve-center, the *Sahasrara-Padma*." One climbs this mountain by first refining the breath, then by breathing from the base of the spine to the top of the head, then exhaling naturally. We also can find repose along with Saladin by pausing a moment at the summit, in the space between inhalation and exhalation, and *experiencing*. Notice the feeling of equilibrium that results from this method of breathing, this refined breath moving up the mountain of the spine, resting at the crown center and then out, to begin the journey once again with the next inhalation.

> Through experience one reaches the Heaven of Repose,
> Or else it comes by a special Grace of Allah;
> In mastery one stills the storms within himself
> And the sabbatized sabbath takes on full meaning:
> To calm all thoughts and watch the flow of life,
> To focus the consciousness within the heart-of-hearts,
> To find one is engulfed in this universal peace,
> This superlove, this source of all activity,
> This potentissimility of every energy
> Whence everything outlets, whither all return.

This section of "Saladin" goes on to help us experience the meaning of Zion, rather than merely reading another word. We are invited to know the meaning of words through our own experience and not limit ourselves to intellectual understanding. This invitation is extended many times in the course of *The Jerusalem Trilogy*; the next theme, suggested by the poem "The Day of the Lord Cometh" is one more example of this expansion of our "vocabulary" through meditation.

One may follow the instruction given to the Prophet Jeremiah by God, in order to attract *ruach hakodesh*, the Divine Spirit or Breath, to earth: to feel the heart illuminated by that Light which interpenetrates all, which casts no shadow. One breathes in a refined peaceful manner with the eye of the heart open to the whole of humanity, radiating this peace to all. Thus Jerusalem, which literally means 'the abode of peace', becomes located in one's own heart and becomes the seed for universal peace.

Not all of the practices are given in complete form — some sections intimate or indicate that a path exists to be further pursued with a living teacher or guide. Saladin's journey through the heavens shows how he was led through the first stages by his Sheikh, later by the Prophets Moses and Jesus, and then Mohammed. So if a reader gets an intimation of a path or method to which his heart responds, we suggest that he note the example of Saladin. As Saladin learned, there may be many teachers but there is only one Spirit of Guidance. And this Spirit of Guidance is everywhere present. That this guidance is present within our very bodies is shown by the following yoga practice suggested in "What Christ? What Peace?"

One becomes aware of the circulation of the blood in one's body. Especially one notices the outward pulse of the blood from the heart, and the inward pulse into the heart where the blood is rejuvenated by the breath. So, with each round of the blood one notices the ongoing processes of pollution and purification.

> The outward psychic function revealing Adam,
> The inner spiritual functions evidencing Christ,
> The resurrected Adam through purification.

Thus one may find the being of Christ within the functions of one's own body, which He called the Temple of God.

> Whenever man attains this blessed communion,
> He never will grow old, though long in the flesh,
> He will attain to the proclaimed Kingdom of Heaven,
> Becoming perfect, even as God is perfect.

In this meditation one equates the flow of blood within the body as the course of love throughout the world. And just as the blood can be purified by the Divine Breath, so the Holy Spirit — the Divine Breath by another name — permeates the world as

> ... the common breath for all mankind
> The nexus of the union of God and man,
> Obtained through Christ, the universal Savior.

We have mentioned only a fraction of the practices presented through Murshid Samuel L. Lewis, Sufi Ahmed Murad Chisti; practices which include the use of breath, mantras or *wazifas*, concentrations, meditations and many of the principles involved in doing the Sufi Dances which have come through the Murshid. The purpose of this Appendix is, once again, not to list every practice which appears, rather it is to help the reader realize that if he approaches the reading of these poems seeking after guidance, he will find not only *words* of wisdom, but many actual paths to Wisdom. As with meeting Murshid in the flesh one had to be "on one's toes", so it is with meeting him through his poetry. Be aware and make use of opportunities to *do* when they are presented, read and keep one's heart and inner ears open, and *The Jerusalem Trilogy: Song of the Prophets* will provide a rewarding experience.

> Sing, Ya Allah, and let Your song be one of triumph for the
>   world!
> Sing, O man, and let your song be one of rejoicing in your God!
> Sing, O heart, and let your ebullient harp-strings resound!
> Sing, O breath, and let your flute-notes penetrate the air!

APPENDIX B:
RECONCILIATION BETWEEN JUDAISM AND ISLAM

Contentions and disputations about religion have been legion. And what has been decided? Has a single question been settled? Or if settled has it not been to bring a myriad more in its wake? The Catholic Church, deciding upon the Infallibility of the Pope in theological affairs took perhaps the only possible course to end centuries of argumentation and still hold its ground. In our arguments and bickerings the spirit of every founder of every religion has been forgotten, calumnies and anathemas have been hurled, wars and persecutions have taken place, and in the end what has been accomplished?

Religion is that which binds the finite with the Infinite, the many with the One, the one with the All. As there can be an infinite number of relations between the finite and the Infinite, so can there be an infinite number of religions. The mathematical truth is a universal one and indeed every man's religion is peculiar to himself. There can no more be a false religion that to say that a triangle is a false polygon because when you conceived of a polygon you had a hexagon in mind. As no two people are alike, as no two trees are alike, as no two leaves are exactly alike, so no two religions can be exactly alike.

Yet mankind, being gregarious must form groups. There are effects of environment and effects of heredity upon our thinking, upon our customs, habits, manners. The morals of one race are different from another, those of one age different from those of another and clime and stage of civilization or culture determine in different manners what is right and what is wrong.

The founders of every religion came to meet the need of their time. Their messages have differed according to the degree of evolution of the people to whom they were sent, according to the problems they faced, upon their experiences in life. All this is truism.

But the time has now come to consider whether it is possible for men to step beyond the differences of religion as they are stepping beyond the differences of class and race. The printing press resulting in the book and newspaper, the expansion of commerce, the telegraph and radio, the world war and the growth of internationalism have drawn men closer together, closer perhaps than they realize it. They see that their 'right' is not the other man's 'right' and their 'wrong' may be 'right' in another place, and but two courses seem open — either to force the other man to adopt your standards or to reconcile them in some way.

The reconciliation of religions is most difficult. Prejudices and traditions thousands of years old sometimes stand in the way. Principles are forgotten. It is always the other man who is a fanatic, his religion is full of superstitions, his customs and ceremonials belonged to another day, the sacredness of his Book may be questioned or despised, his cult stands in the way of progress, it has a history of iniquities, its followers persecuted ours, ours is a God-given religion like no other one, and so on in endless fashion. Yet the one who has read the literature of every race and every religion concerning the cults of other races and countries finds ever the same arguments, ever the same appeal, ever the same paeons to their own Founder and the inhabitants of Mars could scarce tell whether a work was written by a 13th century Hindu, an 11th century Moslem, or a 19th century Christian if it dealt with a discussion of all religions, so far as the criticisms of other religions were concerned. For instance all three would agree in their criticism of Budddhism, Judaism and the Mazdaznian cult; the Hindu and Moslem would agree as regards the Christians, and the Christian and Moslem as regards the Hindu.

The Prince of India and Nathan the Wise would recognise a religion based on the Unity of God alone. Even during the war Cardinal Mercier wrote to the Archbishop of Canterbury, "we are one in our belief in the Fatherhood of God". . . . not one in our belief of the sacredness of the Bible, or the Virgin Birth, or the Trinity or the Creed, or in Apostolic Succession, or in Transubstantiation, or in the descent of the Holy Spirit or any of those doctrines which have long vexed divines. If the reverend Cardinal could step so far, indeed it might seem an easy matter to reconcile in some degree those whose very religion is supposed to be founded on this principle and this principle alone.

But here we are faced with a great difficulty. Ishmael teased Isaac. For this the Arbi went one way and the Abri another. For this one race has followed a religion which it claims came from their common ancestor and which belongs to it alone and the other claims that it only has the true faith of the common ancestor. The one reserves to it the right of prophecy alone and the other puts it to scorn by asking why none of them have ever come face to face with God, that even their Law Giver was forced to see its Prophet rise higher. Each throws at the other the common stock words too readily called into use when matters of religion, theology, and customs are discussed and each has scorned the other as vastly inferior. Yet both are of the same blood, both possessed with the same pride, the same racial and physical characteristics and only in common attack upon others have they stood together.

What is the doctrine of Judaism. "Hear O Israel, the Lord our God, the Lord is one." "And besides Me, there is none else." And what is the doctrine of Islam, "There is no god but Allah," even to the interpretation, "Naught is but He." Why then the differences? Why the hated and persecuting?

Both alike are to blame and maybe neither is to blame. To blame is the easiest thing in the world. Despite "Judge not that ye be judged," not a handful in a million follow this precept. We only see the evil which is in ourselves when it is reflected in another. Man was born with limitations and one of these limitations has been that he cannot readily see another's view point. It is almost as difficult as physically standing where the other one is, but it is not impossible.

The prophets of Israel and the Prophet of Islam are singularly alike. Their hand and tongue were against idolatry and immorality which seemed everywhere associated. Criticism has been made that Mohammed in writing about the earlier messengers and prophets made them but shadows of himself, but this is far more true than many of the conclusions that have been made. Born of the Semitic race, living in similar climes, engaged in like occupations, seeking the silence of the great open spaces, filled with a mighty Spirit that led them to the city, to face the hostility of the authorities and the mob, bearing the same universal message, except that he was an Arab and not an Israelite, Mohammed was in every sense a prophet. He never disparaged those who proceeded him and it has only been his followers, in their eagerness and zeal to prove his greatness have endeavored to do this by belittling the others. Can not there be two high mountains in different lands? Can not one be a great poet in one age and another in another? The Mussalmen have greatly weakened themselves by contrasting one to another. Mohammed said he was a man like other people. His followers use this as an argument for their religion and its greatness and then follow by insisting he was the greatest one that ever lived, and even the mediator between God and man and besides him there was no mediator nor can there be.

Much stands against the Prophet from the standpoint of the Jew. He did not accept the Mosaic laws. He did not accept the ritual. He made another city the holy city. He persecuted the *Beni Israel* violently committing or allowing to be committed deeds of great violence against them, even using deceit and teachery. He was apparently inconsistent in many respects and what he stated one time, he denied another. His followers have gone to such extremes to justify him that they have invented lies or made numerous insinuations. Yet if we could protect Mohammed from his friends, it would not be difficult to determine that he was not entirely unjustified in his actions.

The prophets reiterate over and over that the message of the Unity of God would be spread upon the earth. How was this to be done? The Hebrews did little or no proselytizing. They themselves admitted that prophets came from God to other races. Was there any manner in which this could be accomplished except by a prophet coming to another race? Yet they rejected him — in fact it was not necessary for them to accept him. He did not come to them, he came to some other race. In fact every argument that the Hebrews used against Mohammed has been dropped by them since that time. They no longer hold to the Mosaic Code, they are dropping the Orthodox rituals and ceremonies which Mohammed rightly regarded as innovations and extraneous to the pure spirit of what he considered Islam, the religion of Abraham. They are lopping off the dead branches of theology, keeping alive the vital trunk that it may bring forth finer blossoms and more beautiful flowers.

Furthermore the Mosaic Code was for a people and for a particular country. The Israelites themselves admit this. Why then should they so violently oppose as they did, one bringing the Message of Unity to another people? Why did they not look with at least the tolerance or indifference they held toward the Mazdaznians?

Back of it all lay those political and economic factors which have played so great and so nefarious a part in the history of religions, forcing them in time to drop the beautiful ethical codes of their founders and adopting as the cornerstones some theological dogmas vaguely related to the mission or the personality of the teacher. The *Beni Israel* occupied an important place in Arabian life. They were merchants and artisans. They prided themselves upon not being idolators, yet their hand was turned against others who were opposed to idolatry, most against the Samaritans and much against the Christians and their own Karaites. Furthermore they had only a generation previously persecuted the Christians in the Yemen which led to an invasion of that country by the Abyssinians. Again, worst of all, their hand was turned against each other, even as it was when Rome was fighting Judaea to conquer it. As Rome succeeded, so Mohammed succeeded. When he fought one tribe in Medina, the other silently watched, and when he drove the second from Medina, the *Beni Koreiza* of the neighboring area did nothing to help their brethren. All would join the idolators in intrigue but none would help the other. They were the great merchants and landowners and during the early stages of Islam, the leaders strove everywhere to give the pure land and opportunity. This, next to their great faith in their founder was the greatest cause for success, standing above the assistance received due to schisms in the Christian church. Furthermore, the Jews who lived further north actually helped the Mohammedans and for a long time afterward there was no trouble between them.

Yet too often the period of good will has been forgotten. At his worst, Mohammed, justified to a certain degree, dealt far more kindly than Justinian or Charlemagne between who he stands in time. Then the degree of tolerance that was granted, was granted. It was never one thing on paper and another in fact. The Prophet is not to be attacked because of the later persecutions by Mameluke and Abbaside and Shiah and Berber. These are all due to economic factors in great degree.

On the other hand, Mohammed was forced to give a code to his people, one which was admirable for the Arab of the desert at that time, eliminating forever many evils, instituting many good customs which, although they may stand in inferior place to the customs or principles of other religions, have been practiced, which is most important. Today the Arabs themselves are turning their hands against those who adopted a legalistic program and an intricate theology on the basis of pure Islam. The Wahabi may be a fanatic, but one wonders if he is not at the base much the same as the early Syrian Christians who, appalled at the wickedness of the cities, fled to the desert. Today we are all linked together by modern machinery and the Wahabi must go forward or die. Perhaps he is not entirely right, but the main principle, the restoration of the Unity of God as the guiding spirit of Islam, opens up the way for a universal reformation as Ameer Ali clearly sees it.

So we have these two forces, yet far apart slowly working in the same direction, clearing the debris of dogma and legalism and questionable tradition and ritual and standing as firm as possible on the one Universal Principle upon which their respective cults were found. The Arab and the Hebrew must again mingle in Palestine as their ancient forefathers did. To dwell at enmity with one another would serve neither. To understand, to tolerate, to reconcile as far as possible and to cooperate is their only solution and salvation, or must they leave it to others to practice that which each alone claims is the cornerstone of their religion, "We are one in our belief in the Fatherhood of God."

Samuel L. Lewis

APPENDIX C:
RECONCILIATION BETWEEN ISLAM AND CHRISTIANITY

After thirteen centuries of rivalry and hostility one wonders if it is possible to bring the forces of Christianity and Mohammedanism to a place where they will mutually regard one another as divine religions. Certainly it is not unthinkable and we see in the conversion of certain noted Englishmen to Islam that the gap is not too great to be crossed. Mohammed himself bore no hostility to Christianity in its broadest sense. In fact he believed as Moslems believe that most of so-called Christianity is not the religion of Christ; they accept the Gospels but question the Pauline and later interpretations of the mission and personality of Jesus.

The learned Khwaja Kamel-ud-Din, Imam of the Mosque at Woking, England, has shown that the Moslems rejected just such points in Christian Orthodoxy as the Modernists are now questioning, and if anything, they are more conservative than some of the Modernists. Montcure Conway was surprised and dismayed when visiting India to find the Moslems good orthodox Christians on several points of doctrine.

The Mohammedans accept Jesus as a prophet, if not the Messiah of the Hebrews; they regard the Gospels as divine revelations in their origin; they consider the words of Jesus sacred and it can easily be shown have taken them far more seriously than their Christian brethren. The Mohammedans differ from accepted forms of Christianity less than Gnostics, Manicheans and other cults which are often regarded as offsprings of Christian doctrine. Mohammed did not regard himself as the founder of a religion so much as a restorer and he always had the greatest admiration and respect for Jesus; indeed he made him into his personal ideal in many ways.

What then had led one to reject the Mohammedans from the ranks of Christianity? Its success. The Nestorians at first took Islam for another outgrowth of Christianity. If the Mohammedans rejected Paul, other 'heretical' movements had rejected much of the rest of the New Testament, or even all the Old Testament. If they have their Koran, the Mormons and the Christian Scientists have their other sacred scriptures. Political and economic factors, and its great growth have led us to consider the cult of Islam as an extra-Christian movement.

Indeed it may be questioned if Mohammed differed in a single point from the Ebionites who seem to have been the earliest Christians. Many of the Dervishes scattered throughout the Moslem world not only have the same doctrines but live the life that Jesus commanded most literally, or far more literally than any of the groups called "Christians" have since the early centuries. The word "Fakir" held up so much as the object of ridicule by the western world, instead of having anything to do with 'faking', or phenomena producing or charlatanism, was applied originally to just such a one who would give up his property, his attachments and his place in the world, take up his cross, travel from place to place if necessary and live the most spiritual life.

Christian and Mohammedan alike have been blinded in regarding the other. The Christian condemns the Mussalman for failing to live the life that the Prophet commanded and pointed to the evils of his cult and society; the Mussalman condemns the Christian for failing to live the life that the Prophet commanded and points to the evils of his cult and society. The one sees the evils of polygamy and divorce; the other of prostitution, extra-marital sexual relations and other forms of corruption and vice. The beauty of the New Testament is contrasted with the viciousness in the lives of Mohammedans; the beauty of the Koran is placed alongside the corruption in countries which claim to be Christian. The one proves that his Scripture is more beautiful than the other and the other proves that his Scripture is practical and livable and the other is not.

Jesus came to teach men to love each other; Mohammed came to teach men to live in concord with each other. History shows the various success and failure of their missions. But whatever the verdict of history, the question arise, can there be peace? can there be understanding? can there be tolerance?

We must cease to hurl words for arguments. Ceremonies and customs have their place and their purpose. The vast majority of Christians insist on baptism, but baptism was no more important than healing in the Message of Jesus. A few insist on healing and reject baptism. Within the worlds of Islam and Christianity we see every form of doctrine and dogma and belief. Tolerance has come through the inability of any one group to force its dictates upon the others and through the modern means of communication both of material goods and ideas. The anthropologist does not condemn, he examines.

Possibly after making thousands of examinations he makes a conclusion, possibly he does not. He cannot call any ceremonial or custom or habit a "superstition." It has had a history and it is his duty to unravel that history.

Those who believe in brotherhood must adopt a like policy. There is no use in considering oneself superior to the often agnostic scientist; he at least looks upon all alike and is necessarily tolerant. Hatreds and rivalries foment, ending in wars. The recent war has at least forced the many Islamic groups to realise there is some possibility that they must recognise each other or be destroyed. The Christians have not yet done this, the Jews are now doing it, but the Buddhists did it long ago, through the cooperation of Colonel Olcott of the Theosophical Society.

The work of Colonel Olcott should be held as an example. We do not have to believe in a single doctrine of theosophy and we may hold any view we wish of Madame Blavatsky and Colonel Olcott but this gentleman succeeded in making the Mahayanist and Hinayanist schools of Buddhism recognise each other.

This task was far from simple. These schools, both calling themselves Buddhists, both with a form of priesthood and having the hope of attaining Nirvana, differ on almost every other doctrine: On the personality of Buddha, on the relative importance of the historic Gotama and the 'resurrected' Sakya Muni, on the existence of other Buddhas, on the existence and place of gods, or even of a God, on the importance of meditation and other practices, on the silent life, on the use of mantric and tantric practices, on the importance of the Scripture, on the question of what Scriptures are to be considered, each ignoring those of the other, in the putting into practice of the moral principles, etc., etc.

A thorough examination will show that there are sects calling themselves Buddhists who differ more from each other than Catholic from Unitarian, Nestorian from Christian Scientist, Swedenborgian from Armenain or Wahabi from extreme Shia, or even from any extreme sect of the Islamic cult from the furthest extreme of the Christian sects.

We fail to realise, and it often is not realised by the very men who have made deep researches into the life of the Prophet and the studies of Oriental history that the problems which vex one age are not even considered by those of another. There was a time when men killed each other on the question of the validity of certain books of the Bible, on the question of the nature of Christ, on the problem of what constituted a church.

A later age brought entirely different problems to the fore and our modern disputes or disagreements in religious views differ greatly from those of our ancestors. Questions we argue about they did not consider and questions they argued about, we never think of. Haeckel has hurled at Protestantism a defy to explain the procession of the Holy Spirit.

No one, studying the prophets of all races, can, with an open mind, reject Mohammed. The Christians are today pointing with pride that there are Jews and Hindus who are willing to admit Jesus into the ranks of prophethood. Rather it is the Jews and Hindus who should be considered worthy of being tolerant and broad-minded. The acceptance of Mohammed as a prophet does not destroy Christianity. A Lord Headley can well consider himself a better Christian after making this step. But acceptance or not, the broadest view must be necessary.

History has shown that the Turk will all his faults dwelt on better terms with Serb and Bulgarian than they with each other; it was the Nestorian and the Jew who sided with the soldiers of the early Caliphate in the east and west and the Monophysite who did not oppose them in Egypt. Saladin even in the midst of the Crusades did not harm the Christians in his realm.

The growth of maritime empire and of imperialistic power has made nations tolerant toward the religions of the subjects. Governments which are not founded upon Christian but upon human principles, governments often corrupt or selfish, have granted a greater degree of liberty and good will to people than the very sects that claim to be most zealous in following the dictates to their founders. There is nothing in the Christian Scriptures to countenance hatred and the very meaning of Islam is peace and good will and resignation.

We are then forced to fall back on that greatest of sophistries: We love 'our' enemies but we hate 'God's' enemies. How can God have an enemy? The very enemy who is called God's enemy claims it loves God and you may be God's enemy. The day of seeing the devil behind every antagonist's movement is gone. No human is perfect, at least to the extent of being regarded as perfect by everyone. The message of Christ was that each should purge himself, each should make clean his own heart, should remove the beam from his own eye. Paul and Jesus both urged reconciliation as quickly as possible in case of dispute. Cleansing and purifying oneself inwardly was one of the most important objects of Christianity, as well as of other religions.

If we cannot rise to the point of seeing the world from another's point of view, we should at least recognise our own shortcomings. The sun shines on saint and sinner, believer and infidel alike. If we are not universalists then how can we see the world as God sees it or as God would have us see it. There can only be One Infinite. Philosophy, science and mathematics point the way, Nature proves it and man must either learn to see from a larger point of view or else admit that he cannot see. In either case the result is tolerance and accepting the right hand of fellowship from his human brethren.

Samuel L. Lewis

PUBLISHED WORKS OF MURSHID SAMUEL L. LEWIS

Murshid S.A.M.: In the Garden
The Jerusalem Trilogy: Song of the Prophets
This is the New Age, In Person
Crescent and Heart
Introduction to Spiritual Dance & Walk, Vols. 1 and 2
Suras of the New Age
Ten Lessons on Walk
The Rejected Avatar
"Excerpts from the Diaries and Letters"
as part of Lama Foundation Sufi/Hassidic package
"Six Interviews with Hazrat Inayat Khan" in "Inshallah"

see also: *The Sufi Song and Dance Record*

For further information contact:
Sufi Islamia Ruhaniat Society
410 Precita Avenue
San Francisco, California 94110